ELECTING PEACE

ELECTING PEACE

VIOLENCE PREVENTION AND IMPACT AT THE POLLS

JONAS CLAES, editor

**UNITED STATES
INSTITUTE OF PEACE PRESS**
WASHINGTON, DC

United States Institute of Peace
2301 Constitution Avenue, NW
Washington, DC 20037
www.usip.org

First published 2016

Printed in the United States of America

The paper used in this publication meets the minimum requirements of American National Standards for Information Science—Permanence of Paper for Printed Library Materials, ANSI Z39.48-1984.

Library of Congress Cataloging-in-Publication Data

Names: Claes, Jonas, editor.
Title: Electing peace : violence prevention and impact at the polls / edited
   by Jonas Claes.
Description: Washington, DC : United States Institute of Peace Press, [2016] |
   Includes bibliographical references and index.
Identifiers: LCCN 2016018230 | ISBN 9781601275226 (alk. paper)
Subjects: LCSH: Political violence—Prevention—Case studies. |
   Elections—Corrupt practices—Case studies. | Election monitoring—Case studies.
Classification: LCC JC328.6 .E428 2016 | DDC 324.9--dc23
LC record available at https://lccn.loc.gov/2016018230

CONTENTS

Introduction

The Impact of Prevention

JONAS CLAES

Elections create anxiety around the world, and with good reason. In the first round of Afghanistan's 2014 presidential elections, for example, Taliban gunmen and bombers orchestrated some four hundred attacks on voting day alone. The entire world held its breath as the 2015 general elections in Nigeria approached: widespread violence was deemed almost unavoidable. However, because of sound leadership, the use of biometric voter cards, and the gradual strengthening of democratic institutions, no mass killings were reported and Africa's most populous country transitioned power in a relatively stable election process. Explaining this variation in outcome and identifying the most effective ways to prevent violent elections, though, are still enormous challenges. More and more funding is directed at electoral support; countries are generally becoming more democratic worldwide; yet violence around elections remains a common thread in many parts of the world. At any given moment, more than a dozen countries face the risk of election violence. Elections are on the horizon—at the time of writing—in the Philippines, Liberia, the Democratic Republic of Congo, and Nicaragua. Time is running out in which to identify and implement the evidence-based prevention strategies most likely to work.

"Election violence is not inevitable."[1] Targeted peacebuilding efforts focus on keeping instigators or perpetrators of election violence in check. One way is to limit their capacity to use violence to manipulate the electoral process. Another is to remove their incentives to do so. At the same time, prevention efforts aim to empower and protect vulnerable members of society and to provide peaceful ways to express disagreement or frustration about the election process and outcome.

Still, the ability of preventive practice to achieve its intended outcome merits further investigation. Thanks to research and practitioner observation, the risk of violence that elections pose is increasingly appreciated and understood. This knowledge has facilitated the creation of institutions, policy tools, and funding streams dedicated to preventing election violence. Related efforts also benefit from an extensive body of international law and jurisprudence.[2] The struggle continues, though, to identify the strategies that most effectively mitigate the risk of violence. Programming options include peace-messaging campaigns to build inclusive trust and positive engagement, and support for a professional and visible police presence in potential hotspots. One election may see widespread violence despite local observers and a well-trained electoral management body (EMB), whereas another may fare much better even without extensive international support.

Tom Carothers of the Carnegie Endowment for International Peace finds that "accumulating and acting on knowledge drawn from experience is a chronic problem for international assistance generally."[3] Although election support teams routinely conduct project evaluations, "they are deeply wary of outside critical scrutiny and too rarely fund the sort of in-depth, independent studies that examine the underlying assumptions, methods, and outcomes in a sector of democracy aid."[4] Too often the choice among preventive measures is made intuitively or impulsively rather than based on empirical evidence and risk assessments.

This volume aims to provide such an assessment. What works, what does not, and under which conditions? Through a comparative cross-national evaluation, this book gauges the individual and combined impact of eight prevalently applied peacebuilding practices or tools commonly thought to reduce the risk of election violence as intended or indirect outcome:

- security-sector engagement,
- election management and administration,
- preventive diplomacy,
- peace messaging,
- civic and voter education,
- monitoring and mapping,
- voter consultations, and
- youth programming.

Preventive measures are continuously expanding in terms of funding and scope. Between 1999 and 2011, the United Nations Development Program (UNDP) completed 394 electoral support projects through eighty-three country offices at a total cost of $3 billion.[5] But the impact of prevention remains questionable. Across sub-Saharan Africa, for example, though states are becoming more democratic overall, average levels of election violence have not declined since the early 1990s.[6]

Even if promoting democracy seems worthwhile, it is not clear that current strategies are effective.[7] Further research is needed to evaluate prevalent models of practice to help prioritize the most cost-effective and appropriate prevention tool in a given context, and to identify the required conditions for effective engagement by state or international actors. The need for cross-national research about the effectiveness of violence-prevention measures, beyond localized or anecdotal best practices, is pressing.[8] This volume aims to improve practice by identifying those measures with demonstrated impact, based on a comparative evaluation of five recent general elections with relatively equal levels of risk but vastly different violence levels: Honduras (November 2013), Bangladesh (January 2014), Thailand (February 2014), Malawi (May 2014), and Moldova (November 2014).

By generating insight on how prevention is and is not effective, this study facilitates a transition from intuitive or habitual programming toward sustained election support grounded in empirical research and rigorously evaluated for impact. The findings will help identify whether prevention efforts made a difference and present new thinking on the required conditions for effective programming. Equally important are the cautionary insights discouraging the use of certain prevention tools that would not produce meaningful impact, or would risk worsening conflict dynamics. The research here paves the way toward an evaluative framework for the prevention of election violence (PEV). The limited case data cannot by definition yield fully generalizable results, but the findings can guide future programming in similar risk environments.

Identifying the Problem

Elections are inherently competitive. Bellicose language abounds as candidates and parties clash for office, stirring up the groups, ideologies, or values they represent. Above all, elections feature a struggle for personal power and glory; victory offers influence over the direction both nation and society will take. When properly managed, electoral processes are the epitome of peaceful conflict management, allowing groups to contest their views and compete for influence without resorting to violence. In societies previously marred by conflict, elections may channel social or political conflict, sow the seeds of stability, and facilitate peaceful political transition. The voting process triggers hope, expectations, and an opportunity for change, but also uncertainty, anxiety, and fear of defeat. In poorly governed states, elections commonly trigger violence in the form of intimidation, targeted assassinations, and occasionally widespread killings. About one in five elections are violent, according to UN reporting and academic research.[9]

Election violence is a long-standing challenge, dating certainly to the city-states of the Renaissance and the Holy Roman Empire, and may be as old as politics itself. During the Holy Roman Empire, the uncertainty surrounding elections, as an alternative to hereditary systems, would commonly trigger a civil war.[10] Even today the human cost of election violence remains significant, despite an estimated $6 to $8 billion spent on democracy assistance each year.[11] In the run-up to the 2013 Bangladesh elections, political clashes claimed around five hundred lives, the heaviest toll since the country's independence. In the April 2014 Afghan presidential elections, as mentioned, Taliban gunmen and bombers orchestrated some four hundred violent attacks on election day alone, targeting voters, election personnel, and security forces guarding the polling centers.[12] The election violence in Honduras was more targeted: various sources reported up to forty-eight political assassinations in 2013.[13] In addition, candidates, voters, and other election stakeholders face violent intimidation, vandalism, arbitrary arrests, and other physical or psychological abuse.

Elections at risk, though, do not consistently turn violent. In Tunisia, the run-up to the 2014 parliamentary and presidential elections was mired with tension, and election observers nervously awaited the outcome. Fortunately, the elections proceeded without major incident, instead presenting a potential "model of democracy" or "beacon of hope" for the region.[14] Ukraine's presidential and parliamentary elections in May and October of 2014 were similarly high risk, given the escalation of protests into an armed separatist insurgency and proxy war between Western powers and Russia earlier that year. But, apart from minor sporadic incidents, violence was minimal across the country.[15]

The objective of this book is to evaluate and improve existing methods to prevent this type of political violence. The evaluation starts with a brief overview of the conceptual and theoretical foundations of election violence, which includes relevant definitions and key findings about the structural risk and triggers behind this complex phenomenon.

Forms of Violence

Researchers and institutions have applied various angles in their attempt to define *election violence*.[16] The term remains poorly conceptualized and refers to wildly different phenomena, creating an "empirical muddle" that undermines the ability to design effective prevention strategies.[17] A UNDP guide, *Elections and Conflict Prevention*, indicates the motivation of the perpetrator as a characterizing feature. The authors, Timothy Sisk and Chris Spies, describe election-related violence as "acts or threats of coercion, intimidation, or physical harm perpetrated to affect an electoral process or influence the outcome."[18] In this volume's chapter on Honduras, Elizabeth Murray demonstrates how motivation-based definitions are problematic. Where violence is commonplace and investigations are scant, it is not realistic to use the perpetrator's motivation as the sole qualifying characteristic. The Honduras study demonstrates the difficulty of determining what makes violence electoral. Even the best datasets are often burdened by ambiguous coding rules.[19]

Scholars such as Jeff Fischer emphasize the different modalities of the violence more comprehensively, to include "any random or organized act or threat to intimidate, physically harm, blackmail, or abuse a political stakeholder in seeking to determine, delay, or otherwise influence an electoral process."[20] In his role as UN special rapporteur on extrajudicial, summary, or arbitrary executions, Philip Alston demonstrates how popular definitions commonly omit the use of excessive violence by state actors to quell election protests or punish political expression. Killings by security forces in response to riots may lack a political intent, but present a relevant form of election violence nevertheless given its direct link with the electoral process.[21] This study thus uses a definition by Sead Alihodzic, who emphasizes both the target and context of the violence: "Election-related violence can be defined as acts of violence directed against electoral actors, events, and materials in the context of electoral processes or its outcomes."[22]

In most cases, election violence is *nonlethal*, taking the form of voter intimidation, harassment, or the destruction of infrastructure, ballots, and information systems. In extreme cases, the violence can take a *lethal* form: candidates are assassinated, violent protests or boycotts claim casualties, or insurgents target voting stations. Women are particularly vulnerable to election violence, both in public and private settings. The different gradations of violence intensity are relevant to assess the impact of preventive measures (see box 1). Vote-buying, corruption, and bribery are not considered forms of election violence.

Box 1 Measuring Election Violence

The intensity of election violence is the dependent variable in this study, and is coded in each of the selected cases using a variant of the rubric introduced by Scott Straus and Charlie Taylor:

- CODE 0—No reported electoral violence
- CODE 0.25—Violent harassment: No or few deaths reported but elections still feature nonlethal forms of violence, including police or security forces breaking up rallies, party supporters brawling in the streets, confiscation of opposition newspapers, candidate disqualifications, or limited short-term arrests of political opponents (no or few deaths)
- CODE 0.50—Violent repression: high-level assassinations and targeted murder combined with long-term high-level arrests of party leaders, consistent violent intimidation and harassment (approximately one to nineteen deaths)
- CODE 0.75—Highly violent campaign: repeated, widespread physical attacks leading to a substantial number of deaths over time (approximately twenty to one hundred deaths)
- CODE 1—Extremely violent campaign: repeated, widespread physical attacks leading to mass violence and many deaths (more than one hundred deaths)

Unfortunately, no unified dataset exists past 2012 that tracks the intensity of election violence for all the selected countries, nor does one include the most recent election for the selected cases. The data on election violence has been collected from piecemeal state, media, or NGO reports. Most of their accounts include nonlethal actions taken by various parties, including regime crackdowns on protests, partisan attacks and intimidation, and other forms of harassment.

Source: Scott Straus and Charlie Taylor, *Democratization and Electoral Violence in Sub-Saharan Africa, 1990–2007*, paper presented at the APSA annual meeting, Toronto, September 3–6, 2009.

The existing literature on election violence draws heavily on the African experience.[23] But election violence is not unique to any continent, regime type, human development level or electoral system, and may erupt before, during, or after election day. When the electoral process turns violent, it does so almost without exception before voters head to the polls.[24] If the violence erupts after voting day, however, it is more likely to be more intense.[25] Large-scale political violence rarely erupts spontaneously and requires elite planning and organization. Violence before elections and after is usually driven by different motivations. In the face of an impending defeat or uncertain outcome, political incumbents or challengers may regard violence as a viable strategic alternative or complement to patronage and other types of persuasion.[26] Under such circumstances, political leaders may opt for violence, mobilizing their support base to delegitimize or boycott the electoral process, and intimidate or neutralize opponents. The perpetrators may be outraged voters, security forces, insurgents, and party activists, including youth or student wings of political parties. Incumbent officials are the most common perpetrators, often operating through militias, security forces, youth wings, or other affiliated groups.[27]

Historically, elections have been associated with outbursts of violence, but the scope of the challenge should not be dramatized.[28] On average, election years are no more violent than any other.[29] The importance of effective prevention during elections cannot be overstated, however: its failure may lead to more costly reactive interventions, reverse years of development, and generate a deep distrust in democratic governance and the rule of law.[30] When peaceful, fair, and orderly, elections further the democratic consolidation of a country. Even more than other types of political violence that may claim more human lives, election violence undermines the legitimacy of political leaders and institutions and negatively affects a country's regard for democratization.

Risk Factors

A growing body of scholarly work has helped conceptualize the challenge presented by election violence, identifying patterns of motivations, common perpetrators, and discernable warning signs.[31] Published research and practitioner manuals offer useful insight into the contextual vulnerabilities that enhance the risk of election-related violence. The relationship between the drivers of election violence and the underlying causes of violent conflict more broadly remains unclear and presents an important challenge to further defining the boundaries of this field. Identifying where election violence differs or overlaps with other forms of violence is difficult. It is critical, however, to ensure that the prescribed preventive measures address the specific incentive structure of perpetrators and the unique windows of vulnerability elections present.

 UNDP's *Elections and Conflict Prevention* identifies fifty-one risk indicators and causes.[32] Some are internal to the electoral process, such as premature victory claims; others are external, such as the availability of small arms. Indicators also differ in the proximity of their impact. Structural causes are underlying attributes of a country or region that build up increased risk of violence over time; examples include a country's history of violence, its ethnic make-up or electoral system. Others are described as triggers or single acts and events that may exacerbate an already tense political climate beyond the threshold of violence, such as the exclusion of a party or fraud allegations.[33] The reference to a discrete set of causes or drivers is problematic because it implies the existence of discrete variables that may independently explain the presence of violence. Because election violence is a complex phenomenon that materializes in many forms, and has multiple, often overlapping motivations and various combinations of causal pathways and triggers, it is opportune to speak in terms of risk factors or contextual vulnerabilities instead.

Several contextual vulnerabilities, with various levels of empirical support, are considered throughout the case studies.[34] The comparative analysis presented in the final chapter evaluates this by no means exhaustive list of vulnerabilities and triggers. Each presents a plausible and common explanation for the intensity of election violence and may further complicate the environment in which prevention operates:

- **Centralized power structures.** In countries characterized by an unequal distribution of power and resources, elections are a high-stakes endeavor that increase the risk of violence.[35] The centralization of power speaks not only

to the structure of the national government—whether the government is
organized around a powerful executive or a preeminent legislature—but
also to the devolution of decision-making, from the central government
to federal divisions, districts, or municipalities. Unitary states, as opposed
to federal states, raise the stakes of elections by providing the winning
party control over substantial state powers.[36] The political science literature
presents institutional engineering as a risk-mitigating measure by reducing
the powers that constitutions attach to presidential rule through decentralization, or by altering the balance between the executive and legislative
branches of power.[37]

- **Horizontal inequality and societal diversity.** In international development
and peacebuilding, horizontal inequality refers to imbalances in the distribution of assets, income, and opportunity across identity-based groups.[38]
The close and reinforcing link of centralized state control, economic opportunity, and identity politics is arguably a dominant cluster of risk.[39] The
systematic exclusion of political parties and ethnic, religious, linguistic, or
regional communities from the nomination, voting, or registration process
exemplifies this pattern of exclusion or discrimination. Actual and perceived horizontal inequalities heighten not just the risk of election violence,
but also that of violent conflict more broadly. Social cleavages and diversity
can enhance the risk of conflict as well, but mainly through manipulative
identity politics.[40] In their classic work on ethnic politics, political scientists
Alvin Rabushka and Kenneth Shepsle argue that "plural societies" are
prone to violence and instability.[41] The identified challenge is not diversity
itself, however, but politically salient diversity. Elite politicians may play the
identity card, exploiting societal diversity and elevating a fear of the Other
to fulfill political ambitions.[42] Dominant majority demographic structures
may arguably generate anxiety among the minority, particularly when
political parties run on identity platforms. Politicized ethnic identities
raise the stakes of elections because group security is linked to its election
performance, raising fear of political exclusion or violent repression after
the election. The Minorities at Risk project at the University of Maryland
monitors ethno-political groups that often face repression, persecution, or
other types of violence in the context of elections and beyond.[43]

- **Unfit electoral systems.** A third structural factor increasing the stakes
in electoral contests, and the consequent distribution of political power,
is the choice of electoral system. Electoral systems define the rules and
procedures through which votes are translated into seats in parliament
or other legislative or executive offices, such as the presidency.[44] Political
scientists have written much about the conduciveness of both majoritarian and proportional systems of government to violence. By giving the
winner of a certain threshold of votes full power to make decisions for the
entire community, majoritarian or plurality systems would raise the stakes
significantly, promoting fear, frustration, and exclusion.[45] Systems with

proportional representation (PR) offer parties a number of seats tied to the number of votes cast in their favor, that is, a more equitable share of power. In some jurisdictions, proportional systems arguably mitigate conflict by incentivizing cooperative behavior, inclusion, and consensus-based decision-making.[46] PR systems, though, may also yield indecisiveness or induce ethnic politics by lowering the threshold for access to power. Transitions between electoral systems may present risk of conflict as well because the state of flux creates new winners and losers among elites and throughout society. Although first-past-the-post systems are generally considered more violence-prone within divided societies, no electoral system is considered "best" for ameliorating conflict.[47] The incentives of different electoral systems will play out differently depending on the societal cleavages or voting blocs based on identity or ideology.[48]

- **Uncertainty about the election outcome.** The potential for election violence does not depend solely on the structure of institutions or the electoral system; the trajectory of the race may enhance the risk as well. When the outcome of an election is highly uncertain, anxiety levels will rise among key competitors. Uncertainty may create fear of defeat and exclusion, raising the appeal of coercive measures to tip the balance. Close elections enhance the risk of pre- and postelection violence.[49] Parties facing close preelection polling are more suspicious and desperate to shape the turnout in their favor; a close final poll increases the likelihood that the losing party will violently contest the results. If reliable polls indicate that the incumbent is popular, violent preelectoral tactics are unnecessary.[50] Even in an uneven race, however, high levels of uncertainty may persist in the absence of credible polling. The conclusion of power-sharing arrangements or other electoral agreements may dampen anxiety among the elite.

- **Consolidating democracies.** Representative democracies are commonly presented as the best guarantee against political instability.[51] However, research findings by Edward Mansfield and Jack Snyder demonstrate how political transitions present real and immediate dangers. Countries moving from authoritarianism to multiparty politics—the gray zone of partial, unconsolidated democracy—are deemed the most vulnerable to violence, more so than autocratic or democratic regimes without change, or "autocratizing" states.[52] These anocracies, or recent democracies, are easy to exploit, have a weak central authority, and are commonly characterized by unstable coalitions.

- **History of violence.** A pattern of election or political violence is a reliable indicator of future violence. The African Electoral Violence Database shows that half of all countries in sub-Saharan Africa experience persistent electoral violence, indicating the recurrent nature of this type of conflict.[53] Holding elections during a violent conflict, or soon after the conclusion of a peace agreement or cease-fire, also presents significant security risks. Elections are a fundamental element of postconflict peacebuilding efforts, but might increase rather than decrease the risk of renewed fighting.[54] Recent violent conflict leaves behind it a fragile climate, in that the memory of violence lingers and disarmament or demobilization processes may be incomplete. The violence deepens societal and political divides, nurtures the desire for retaliation, and creates the acceptance of brutal aggression as a legitimate strategy. The memory of violence increases the acceptance of coercion and intimidation, creating a "culture of violence," according to Kristine Höglund.[55] However, vivid memories of the human or financial costs of violence may also have mitigating effects. Field research demonstrates that during the 2013 presidential election in Kenya, collective memory of the devastating impact of previous violence encouraged restraint, triggering fear of a repeat of violence and keeping a tight lid on boiling tensions.[56]

These risk factors offer theoretical and empirical insight on the importance of context in driving election violence. Each represents a prominent theory about what drives election violence but has mixed support in the literature. The election outcome and electoral system are internal to the electoral process; the history of violence, existing power structures, the status of democracy, and societal inequality relate to the social context in which elections take place.[57] Both structural attributes of the political society, such as the inclusiveness of an electoral system, as well as unanticipated triggers, such as a postponed announcement of the election result, may create the fears, incentives, or frustrations necessary for violence to erupt. The question remains whether dedicated peacebuilding efforts can counter or absorb these risk factors and effectively prevent violence related to electoral processes.

Designing Solutions, an Emerging Practice

International organizations have recognized the risk that elections pose to peace and security since World War II, which is reflected in their historically strong engagement in democratic support.[58] The United Nations set the tone, administering elections as former colonies transitioned to independent status or as civil wars came to an end. Following the Cold War, UN resolutions or peace agreements typically prescribed internationally supervised or verified elections as the formal closure of a violent conflict. Within countries previously marred by war, free and fair elections would present a common exit point to international donors or peace operations, indicating a level of democratic maturity that justified a reduction in funds or staff. International nongovernmental organizations (NGOs)—such as the National Democratic Institute, the International Foundation for Electoral Systems (IFES), and the Carter Center— and development agencies—such as the U.S. Agency for International Development (USAID), DFID, and UNDP—adopted a growing role in the 1990s. Over time they transformed the practice of election support. From directly overseeing election administration and security, international players would increasingly operate in support of domestic bureaucrats, political parties, and NGOs.

The scene on the ground during elections became increasingly crowded after the creation of specialized election units within regional organizations and development agencies. This combination of support—"a patchwork," according to Bekoe—"attempting to affect a panoply of variables simultaneously, often fails to have an effective impact on the drivers of electoral violence."[59] Many engage in elections as a form of democratic support or development assistance. However, as an established peacebuilding domain, prevention of electoral violence differs in its objectives and indicators of success. The explicit aim of PEV is to keep demagogues, instigators, and perpetrators in check by addressing their capacity and incentives to violently manipulate the electoral process. At the same time, efforts to prevent violence aim to protect communities at risk and to provide peaceful ways to express disagreement, frustration, or concern about the election process and outcome. Peacebuilding tools are rarely implemented with the sole purpose of preventing election violence, and may serve different wider goals in line with the overall mandate of the implementing organization. Some of the instruments selected for this volume—preventive diplomacy, peace messaging, and security-sector engagement, for example—explicitly target the instigators or victims of election violence. Others, such as election administration, are more technical but could plausibly reduce the risk of election violence either indirectly or as part of a holistic prevention strategy.

Development actors like UNDP and USAID gradually realize their commitment to prevention. Their electoral cycle approach demonstrates strategic vision and enables longer-term impact after years of inconsistent programming. Prevention in accordance with the electoral cycle approach usually starts up to eighteen months before election day, at the time of the voter registration or candidate nomination. The election cycle concludes on inauguration day, following the adjudication of electoral disputes, or after addressing legal or institutional gaps revealed in the electoral process.[60] However, democracy promoters often remain preoccupied with technicalities, such as observer accreditation or tabulating the results, and pursue democratic governance goals that may leave the underlying drivers of election violence unaddressed.[61] As a strategic objective, preventing election violence goes beyond organizing free and fair elections as measured by level of transparency, inclusiveness, or popular engagement.[62] Peaceful elections are no guarantee for democratic quality, and free and fair elections are no guarantee for election security.[63] Although the aim of democratic governance overlaps considerably with the goal of peaceful elections, the two present distinct objectives that require careful and constant balancing.

At the same time, prevention initiatives commonly fail to address underlying motivations of conflict, given the focus on neutralizing short-term triggers of anticipated violence. PEV practice remains driven by short-term aspirations and rarely incorporates enough attention to structural conflict drivers such as unresolved land disputes, group-based inequalities, or historical injustices, which may be exacerbated in periods of electoral competition. In an effort to mobilize an exclusive support base, political candidates and parties are tempted to position themselves along one side of the cleavage societal conflict provides, further exacerbating the fault lines. Unless structural conflict dynamics are addressed, elections will remain a flashpoint for violence and tension.

The prevalent models of preventive practice selected for evaluation are a sample of the activities PEV actors undertake, and thus the case studies permit comparative practice-level evaluation. Each instrument is commonly applied with election violence prevention as a stated objective on the basis of its potential to affect the behavior, attitudes, or capacities of potential perpetrators. But the practices vary in terms of the population segment they target, the ideal timing of implementation within the election cycle, and the underlying theory of change.[64] The instruments may be implemented by a mix of state actors, local or international NGOs, or external state and intergovernmental entities. Throughout, each of these tools is assessed (and coded) based on the geographic extent of use and the quality and duration of implementation. Increased investment in PEV does not necessarily reduce violence; in the absence of a clear understanding of the motivations behind election violence in a given context, even perfectly executed strategies can have negligible or even detrimental effects. Incomplete or ill-designed prevention instruments may do more harm than good in the face of popular expectations.

Practice 1: Security-sector engagement. A well-trained and equipped police and military force provides an important domestic guarantee for election security as long as the actors prioritize the protection of the electorate over elite interests, are held accountable for abuse, and display professional conduct. By operating in a nonpartisan, integrated, and visible manner, according to clear rules of engagement, state security actors can deter election violence or mitigate its spread. When poorly trained, biased, or ill-equipped, they may serve as active perpetrators, provocateurs, or passive bystanders, neglecting their role in managing public order, apprehending culprits, or investigating incidents. Particularly within authoritarian regimes, military and intelligence agencies may not promote democratic consolidation but instead disrupt the electoral process as an independent force or the vehicle of a political contender or faction.[65] The security-sector role in providing election security may differ from the sector's day-to-day capacity or performance. Because a heavy-handed security-sector presence might be seen as a provocation, given previous instances of abuse during crowd control, a low-profile presence may be advisable to mitigate tensions. Security forces are suitable for crisis prevention and management but are unlikely to resolve underlying conflict dynamics. When security forces are part of the problem, thorough reform and training may contribute to a sustainable solution. Programs that focus on reforming or capacity-building are the most relevant long before the electoral race heats up, and in weak or fragile contexts when nonstate actors are most likely to perpetrate the violence.[66]

Police or military personnel are often responsible for protecting election materials and stakeholders, including candidates, voters, and poll workers. Special consideration should be given to key milestones within the electoral cycle that traditionally create tension, including the candidate nomination process, focal campaign points like debates or rallies, the announcement of results, and the adjudication of disputes. Rapid response plans and clear coordination mechanisms should be in place well before these periods of heightened risk. Hotspot analyses involving intelligence officials help prioritize areas where violence is anticipated; a Joint Election Operations Center may facilitate security planning and coordination between election officials, security agencies, and local or national officials. Security-sector engagement concerns both the regulatory framework shaping the mandate of security agencies, as well as their ability to protect voters, candidates, electoral events, facilities, and voting materials during the elections. More than training determines tension and security-force behavior, such as community trust in police.

Election security is a multistakeholder effort and generally falls under the final responsibility of police authorities or the electoral management body.[67] If involved, the military ideally serves under civilian control. Although primarily a state function, local security may benefit from customized international training or support upon request.[68] When elections take place amid ongoing violent conflict or following a recent cease-fire, election security may be provided by international forces (UN peacekeeping troops, for example). International organizations and foreign states may provide support should the host country formally request it.

Practice 2: Election management and administration. The quality of election management and administration throughout the electoral cycle is a second responsibility of state authorities that can have a strong bearing on the level of election violence.[69] Election management involves regulating how campaigns are financed, determining the eligibility of candidates and voters, locating and staffing polling stations, and counting the ballots—technical tasks that offer multiple opportunities for error or malfeasance. Mistakes, delays, and real or perceived fraud can trigger violent conflict, especially in the absence of credible dispute resolution mechanisms. Political processes that are perceived as inclusive and fair remove important motives for violence.[70] Election management also requires a sound legal framework. Electoral, institutional, or even constitutional reform may be necessary to mitigate tensions and prevent violence by enhancing the transparency of the electoral process and ensuring a fair distribution of political power. Less formal reform efforts include establishing political party codes of conduct. Well-executed reform may bolster confidence in the authority of national institutions. Unfulfilled promises or partisan reforms may trigger frustration and violence. Efforts to extend or abolish term limits for the executive office illustrate the risks reform may present to election security. More important than institutional form or legal design is the quality of management and administration. Even the best rules and processes can be abused, manipulated, or ignored.

Electoral administration involves a complex set of actors that includes politicians, police, judges, and other civil servants.[71] Typically, the electoral management body holds primary responsibility for election oversight. EMBs can take different shapes, with various levels of independence or government control, and in the form of an ad hoc body or permanent commission. Regardless of their form, EMBs are responsible for managing and overseeing the conduct of elections—from the voter registration to vote counting and result verification.[72] In the rare case of extreme state fragility or postconflict instability, international actors engage in electoral supervision by formulating the rules, certifying the results, or assuming full operational responsibility over the elections.[73] The independence of an EMB depends on the diversity of appointment and confirmation, the relationship to government authorities, and the willingness of individual members to withstand political pressure.[74] The bodies should be "fearlessly independent" in this regard.[75] A capable, professional, and impartial EMB provides clear nonpartisan guidelines that can be consistently applied. Politicized, fraudulent, or toothless EMBs are a recipe for conflict. Although primarily concerned with the technical quality of elections, a well-functioning EMB will help reduce the risk of violence by conferring legitimacy and alleviating frustrations and suspicion. The body deters or mitigates election violence by providing incentives for codes of conduct and legitimate ways—formal or informal—to settle disputes, and by sanctioning parties and candidates who use violence.[76] An independent EMB is the ideal administrator of elections, responsible for keeping political parties and their leaders in check. It is therefore no surprise that EMBs are prioritized as a domestic target for capacity-building and democracy assistance funded and implemented by international actors.[77]

Practice 3: Preventive diplomacy. The diplomatic involvement of international organizations, world leaders, neighboring countries, or other external actors may help deter or mitigate election violence. Diplomacy can work through persuasion or coercion, such as when senior leaders apply their stature and charisma to resolve disputes, or alert potential instigators about the punishment that may follow violent strategies. Preventive diplomacy, in UN terms, refers to diplomatic action taken "to prevent disputes from arising between parties, to prevent existing disputes from escalating into conflict and to limit the spread of the latter when they occur."[78] Within the context of elections, preventive diplomacy is commonly applied as a short-term crisis-management instrument in the face of imminent risk or ongoing violence. Incumbents unwilling to accept defeat may be persuaded or coerced through targeted economic sanctions, incentive-based foreign assistance, and suspension from regional organizations.[79] International organizations routinely authorize mediation teams or senior envoys, in addition to more permanent political missions, to mitigate election-related tensions. Influential diplomats can bridge the interests of political contenders through private mediation or formalized political party councils. Local civil society or traditional community leaders can be engaged as ambassadors for peaceful elections and to ensure local disputes are resolved peacefully.

The access or leverage of international players depends on the weight of existing diplomatic relations, the acceptance of a foreign presence by state authorities, and the acknowledgment of the risk for violent conflict by local actors. As with any external intervention, diplomatic action requires respect for national sovereignty.[80] In the end, local authorities carry a primary responsibility for the peaceful management of elections. Diplomats do not engage solely for the sake of peace or stability, unfortunately, and merely interfere, at times, to affect election outcomes in their favor.[81]

Practice 4: Peace messaging. Community events or popular media are commonly used as a relatively low-cost platform to engage voters peacefully in the electoral process. Sports events, cultural activities, social media, or public communications, such as radio broadcasts or SMS blasts, have served as vehicles to persuade potential perpetrators as well as average voters to reject violence or counter hate speech.[82] International campaigns in Afghanistan and Pakistan have featured peace banners on trains or rickshaws, as well as street theater or cricket games with a central message of tolerance. Common organizers include religious, youth or women's organizations, local media, or even political parties. An effective peace campaign that targets communities vulnerable to violence or recruitment will change the attitudes of individuals while exerting social pressure against the use of violence. Ideally the messages are crafted by locals, extend beyond urban centers (depending on the areas deemed at risk), and initiate before the election campaigns are in full swing. Persuasive messages aimed at community leaders may exert social pressure, and indirectly persuade potential perpetrators to reject violence.

Peace-messaging campaigns aim to affect attitudes and behavior of the broader electorate, and are deemed more effective when informal groups, including gangs and militias, are the likely perpetrators.[83]

Practice 5: Civic and voter education. The UN describes voter education as "the dissemination of information, materials, and programming designed to inform voters about the specifics and mechanics of the voting process for a specific election."[84] Voter education campaigns may introduce newly applied technology, encourage participation, and explain where to vote and how to file a complaint. Civic education campaigns have broader objectives beyond the immediate election as they inform citizens about their democratic rights and responsibilities, the political system or candidate platforms, and aim to overcome voter apathy. Campaigns commonly include neighborhood problem-solving or cultivating tolerance, and foster a positive, collective civic identity as an objective. Education campaigns are primarily the responsibility of the government administration and election management body. In practice, local media and civil society commonly take the lead, filling the vacuum of government authorities in providing information services.

Alleviating the risk of violence is an anticipated if indirect outcome of both educational approaches, in that transparent elections with a high voter turnout are considered to legitimize political processes and promote social cohesion. Voters in conflict-ridden elections that receive civic education would be more likely to vote, sanction poor-performing politicians, and feel more empowered to voice their thoughts on the electoral process through ways other than violence. In practice, peace messaging and civic education often overlap, using similar outreach techniques that target the broader electorate. Campaigns involve elements of advocacy; messages can be informational and motivational, or can admonish particular behaviors.[85] To ensure effectiveness, education efforts should start early, before the registration process, and continue throughout the electoral process until after the results are announced.[86] Civic and voter education is a common instrument in preventing violence, particularly in the aftermath of major constitutional or electoral reforms. Minorities, youth, women, or other underrepresented groups are frequently targeted through the campaigns.

However, educating and empowering the electorate in a weak democratic system implies certain risks: informing citizens could trigger unrealistic expectations. A passionate electorate may be mobilized for violence more easily. Enhanced voter turnouts could expose citizens to election violence in hazardous environments.[87]

Practice 6: Election monitoring and mapping. Monitoring and mapping efforts mitigate election violence by identifying areas at risk and deterring or exposing perpetrators of violence. Although encompassing vastly different activities, monitoring and mapping may both reduce the risk of violence in a similar way: they enhance transparency while offering a means to track or analyze violent incidents or threats. If accurate, timely, and actionable, the accumulated data will inform risk assessments or crisis centers, and enable an effective response.

Election monitoring refers to the observation and evaluation of the electoral process against universal standards for democratic elections by an independent actor.[88] If access is granted by the host country, international missions composed of neutral short-term observers will often arrive close to election day, accompanied by political party observers or accredited NGOs. In some instances, organizations will deploy fewer long-term observers to complement the core observation team for up to two or three months.[89] Local civil society or political representatives will staff the polling stations in countries that fail to appear on the international radar. Election observers can confer legitimacy and transparency by evaluating the quality of the electoral process, confirming victory or defeat, and backing the election management body in event of fraud allegations. In the experience of citizens at risk, international monitors effectively deter violent actors or instigators. Determined perpetrators of violence may feel intimidated by a monitoring presence and fear criminal prosecution. To play this role effectively, monitors depend on their neutrality, access to the polling sites, and open communication channels with the EMB. The instrument is not without its challenges, however. Given the passive nature of their mandate, international monitors may convey a false sense of security to endangered populations.

Election mapping includes the collection and visualization of data on basic election information, such as exit polling results and turnouts, as well as election-related incidents or violence. Through Web-based platforms, email, text messages, or more traditional communication methods, mapping instruments collect the observations of regular citizens to complement the views of professional monitors and triangulate official data. A tested methodology, multiple reporting channels, and robust verification mechanisms to ensure the credibility of reported incidents together form a best practice in the application of this instrument. The reports are commonly aggregated in database form and presented in visual maps indicating trends or patterns by location or time. The security of victims and monitors must be closely considered, as the information may be abused to crush dissent or punish disloyal behavior.[90] The requirement to verify large amounts of data and channel the information to generate a timely and effective response presents significant challenges.[91] Election monitoring and mapping are jointly analyzed because they operate under a similar logic. By deterring potential perpetrators and identifying areas of risk or irregularities, both facilitate a timely and effective security response.

Practice 7: Voter consultations. During the campaign period, voter consultations can reduce the risk of election violence by creating the perception among participating citizens that political candidates acknowledge their grievances and concerns. Direct consultations with broad segments of the electorate help ensure that political parties present campaign programs tailored to the needs and expectations of their support base, and simultaneously offer average voters an opportunity to air concerns. To fulfill a preventive function, the communication between political elite and the electorate must extend beyond supporter rallies or campaign activities, and must include interactions between candidates and those voters with legitimate grievances and frustrations who may otherwise seek more forceful ways to make their voices heard. Party platforms and voting questionnaires allow citizens to track changes in politicians' statements and hold them accountable even after results have been announced. As with other prevention tools, mass media play a central role as facilitator of voter consultations, underscoring the importance of their professionalism, accuracy, and independence. Local and international NGOs have been known to engage in dialogues between party officials and local communities as well. Public debates or call-in radio place campaign promises on the record, allowing media and voters to hold elected candidates accountable.[92]

Practice 8: Youth programming. Youth are often excluded from the political process and particularly vulnerable to recruitment by political actors to incite or commit violence. Dedicated youth programs are designed to reduce election violence by turning the most common perpetrators into constructively engaged participants in the economic and political system. Through education, training, and employment, youths are exposed to more opportunities to serve as positive change agents and help reduce the risk of violence. The attitudinal change youth programs aim for should reduce the ability of charismatic leaders to mobilize youth for violence.

To reduce their vulnerability to violent mobilization, youth should be informed about the electoral process and benefit from sustained employment and education programs, even between election cycles. Offering youth a voice to express their needs and concerns is a constructive approach. It is similarly deemed beneficial to engage youth directly in election administration as monitors, or even as political candidates through recruitment forums.[93] This preventive approach is more likely to succeed when informal groups, such as militias and gangs, are the most likely perpetrators, and arguably less likely to do so when government actors or security services commit violence.[94]

The list of practices results from a mapping exercise and is deliberately limited to ensure analytical parsimony. Although far from exhaustive, this selection features commonly applied prevention tools considered to affect certain attitudes, behaviors, and structures that help mitigate the risk or manifestation of election violence. Approaches with a specific focus on media, technology, or women, as well as detailed assessments of specific mechanisms considered under election administration, such as political party councils, codes of conduct, or antifraud measures, are not included.[95]

The assumptions regarding the potential impact of these instruments are plausible, as long as they are implemented according to best practice, informed by evaluations of relevant precedents, and preceded by a strategic risk assessment. For large peacebuilding actors with an established presence, assessments and evaluations are standard components of any conflict resolution effort. By identifying sources of risk and resilience and locating potential hotspots or areas in need, windows of vulnerability and opportunity can be recognized well in advance, enabling a more effective use of limited programming budgets. The assessment frameworks developed by some of the largest international players in this field, such as USAID's Election Security Framework or the IFES Preelection Technical Assessment, illustrate the recent progress made in developing resources for informed prevention. However, given variable funding levels or technical expertise in project management throughout the peacebuilding community, neither timely analysis nor systematic evaluations are particularly common. This gap blocks the transition from intuitive programming toward evidence-based PEV.

But even assessments and evaluations are no guarantee for effective programming. Prevention practice based on an accurate assessment of perpetrator motivations, fears, and incentives may still be overwhelmed by local security challenges and other contextual vulnerabilities. The determintion of local leaders to use violence or the competitive nature of the electoral system may still trump strategically sound efforts to keep the peace.

Evaluating the ability of prevention to overcome these challenges and to make a tangible difference in the level of risk or violence is the objective of this book. The following (and final) section presents both the applied research design and methodology for this study and an overview of the case chapters. The analytical framework was consistently applied across the five cases.

Research Design

Are the selected prevention practices able to achieve their intended outcome of mitigating election violence in conflict-prone democracies? To investigate this question, we use a small-N comparative analysis. The selected cases—Bangladesh, Honduras, Malawi, Thailand, and Moldova—share fundamental characteristics but vary on the dependent variable, specifically, the intensity of electoral violence. We explore whether prevention explains the variation.

Case Selection

Three basic criteria drove the selection of cases: the presence of a partial or imperfect electoral democracy, "middle-range risk" of political instability during the election period, and a recent election.[96] The selected cases are struggling or moderately fragile electoral democracies that Freedom House rated as "partly free."[97] All five have witnessed some form of election violence. Each saw a general, presidential, or parliamentary election, where the office of head of state or chief executive was directly or indirectly at stake in the twelve months before or during the data collection for this research.[98] Apart from security and access considerations, the selection of middle-range risk countries allows for better insight on the requirements for a positive outcome; middle-risk cases offer peacebuilding efforts with reasonable prospects that elections could be relatively stable or peaceful.

The selected cases entered their most recent electoral cycle in a state conducive to political violence. Despite similar preconditions for unrest, however, difference in the levels of election violence was considerable. It remains questionable whether this variation results from effective prevention programming, the contextual vulnerabilities, or a mix. Bangladesh's January 2014 election was marked by extreme levels of violence and several hundred casualties. Honduras's November 2013 election saw several dozen election-related assassinations. In contrast, Malawi's May 2014 election had few reported deaths but widespread tensions. The role of international and domestic prevention in determining these diverse outcomes remains an open question.

Data and Analysis

Our research hypothesizes that the variation in election violence is closely linked to the presence and quality of preventive practices in the given country. Prevention programming is assessed using a hybrid technique, combining traditional project evaluation techniques with a scientific research design—a variant of the most-similar system design. The presence and strength of prevention programming is estimated based on dataset analysis, evaluation reports, and field research, using semistructured interviews with key informants and stakeholder dialogues held through local civil society organizations. Researchers visited the countries for data collection either during or after the elections.

To systematically analyze the strength or weakness of PEV instruments, we use structured, focused comparison. For each case, eight violence-prevention tools were assessed using as 5-point coding rubric tailored to best practices. Rather than measure each tool as merely present or absent, this method allows for a more nuanced assessment of middle-range quality and reach. The scores of this independent variable refer to the quality and scope of implementation. Conclusions regarding the impact of prevention practices are gathered through a correlation analysis between these PEV scores and the levels of election violence. Understanding PEV practices as a configuration has powerful analytical potential. It allows the researcher to possibly identify a single, unique PEV configuration that produces peaceful elections, or, alternatively, multiple paths to the same outcome.

The 5-point scale for each prevention instrument (the independent variables) includes scores from 0 to 1, a score of 1 presenting ideal type implementation and of 0 indicating a weak or absent practice. The scoring levels indicate the extent in which preventive instruments were implemented according to best practice and the underlying theory of change, measured by the geographic extent of their use, and the quality and duration of implementation. The intensity of election violence, the dependent variable, is also measured in each case following a 5-point scale: 1 (extreme violence), 0.75 (high violence), 0.5 (violent repression), 0.25 (violent harassment), and 0 (no violence). Table 1.1 presents the indicators of each scoring level for security-sector engagement as an illustration. The full list of scoring tables for each prevention instrument is listed in the appendix.

Coding the prioritization of each tool, based on its presence and quality, enables creation of a fuzzy-set truth table, which is conducive to hypothesis generation and testing, and assessing causal conditions within the small case set. Conclusive statements about causality are not possible, but the selected approach allows us to identify the configuration of instruments that led to positive outcomes among our cases and extrapolate tentative generalizations.

Table 1.1 Security-Sector Engagement

SCORE	ENGAGEMENT
1.0	A clear regulatory framework for the provision of election security is in place, as are an integrated security-sector governance and capable, nonpartisan, and professional security forces that are accountable to civil authorities.
0.75	The security sector is mostly but not entirely effective in achieving the ideal because two criteria are fully met.
0.5	The security sector is partially effective in achieving the ideal because only one criteria is fully met.
0.25	The security sector is minimally effective in achieving the ideal.
0	The security sector has not at all achieved the ideal.

The instruments may reinforce each other and overcome challenging environments only as part of a holistic strategy. Conversely, the presence and strength of a particular prevention tool may offset or counteract another, leading to valuable lessons about the sequencing of interventions. In addition, the analysis determines the relevance of prominent hypotheses regarding election violence in the academic and policy literature for our case findings, exploring other exacerbating or mitigating conditions for election violence from a comparative perspective. The description of contextual vulnerabilities may indicate the required conditions for effective programming because they may overwhelm or neutralize the preventive measures taken.

To complement the comparative analysis process, tracing is used as an analytic tool to draw descriptive and causal inferences about the individual country cases. This approach pays close attention to the sequences and relationships among independent variables, conditions, and the dependent variable. Process tracing helps test the theory of change during the most recent election cycle and, if possible, assess levels of historical variation across elections. Using each variable's theory of change, the case authors take one of two approaches. In low-violence cases, they investigate the applied instruments through the prism of the theory of change: do the instruments change actor behavior or attitudes in expected ways, and at the anticipated time? In high-violence cases, they investigate why the tools, if present, failed to prevent violence and explore the two-part counterfactual: did weak practice fail to prevent the violence, and if so, how? And how could stronger prevention have prevented violence within the political and social context of the country?

Although the research design and methodology are appropriately tailored to the research question, our approach has its limitations. Given the multitude of risk environments, a small-N research design that focuses on middle-risk countries limits our ability to provide robust generalizations across the full universe of cases. Therefore, the understanding of causal conditions produced by this analysis cannot be confidently applied to all other cases without further specification of common characteristics. However, our conclusions will be directly applicable to other electoral democracies with comparable risk levels. If our analysis demonstrates that a particular combination of instruments corresponds with low-levels of election violence, there will be good reason to further investigate these promising approaches even in higher-risk cases.

Chapter Overview

Each case analysis and discussion follows an integrated approach based on the election, security context, and preventive efforts. Bangladesh (chapter 2) and Thailand (chapter 3) saw significant violence. Moldova (chapter 5) and Malawi (chapter 4) saw few if any. Honduras (chapter 6) showed a middle range.

The first assessment, by Geoffrey Macdonald, offers a rich overview of the January 2014 presidential elections in Bangladesh, a country with a long history of political violence. Assassinations, military coups, and street protests dot the country's tumultuous political history. The toxic electoral climate during the 2014 elections, in combination with weak or absent violence-prevention efforts, led to historically high levels of election violence. At least four hundred voters, party activists, election officials, and security personnel were killed in the resulting chaos. Bangladesh is one end of the scale considered in this volume: the highest absolute level of lethal election violence and an increase in electoral violence. Macdonald argues that its violence could have been mitigated or even prevented. The international community took a keen interest in resolving Bangladesh's political conflict. The weakness of state prevention structures, however, especially the police, combined with unique levels of antagonism between the primary political parties surely guaranteed the democratic process going up in flames.

In chapter 3, Duncan McCargo and Petra Desatova note how the February 2014 elections in Thailand proceeded amid unprecedented levels of intimidation and fear. The polls were effectively boycotted by the main opposition party, the Democrats. Massive street demonstrations with the self-proclaimed goal of protestors to shut down the capital city of Bangkok characterized the run-up to the snap election. The court's subsequent annulment of election results led to a military coup on May 22. Violence was significant in Bangkok and the Upper South of the country, but the voting proceeded normally elsewhere. Neither the army nor the police did anything to contain the protests; police passivity may have even contributed to increased violence levels. In all, around thirty people were killed, as many as during the 2005 general election. This number was within the "normal" Thai range, despite the smaller geographic reach and weaker implementation of prevention measures.

In chapter 4, Manuela Travaglianti observes that tensions in Malawi were widespread during the entire cycle of the 2014 elections but that only a few isolated casualties were reported. The limited violence that did occur resulted from frustrations with the management of the voting process, contestation of the results, and interparty campaign clashes. Malawi offers valuable insights on what makes violence an unappealing strategy for political actors and on the conditions that enable prevention to thrive. The most relevant preventive measures were preventive diplomacy and peace messaging, which influenced the preferences of competing actors toward peaceful campaigning and the resolution of disputes, and monitoring and mapping, which allowed stakeholders to record—and potentially address—instances of violence as they occurred. Malawi also shows that the impact of preventive measures depends heavily on the structural context in which they operate. In fact, it is unclear whether preventive instruments would have been effective had the elections produced a different result.

The Moldova 2014 elections, which Dominik Tolksdorf analyzes in chapter 5, took place amid significant regional instability and against the backdrop of violent parliamentary elections in 2009. Although the elections proceeded in a tense atmosphere of party rivalries and polarization, the election period remained free of significant violence; a large part of the electorate in fact seemed rather apathetic about the elections. Even the deregistration of the Patria Party, excluded from the contest few days before the election, did not trigger widespread unrest. Tolksdorf notes cases of voter intimidation, bribery, inflammatory language, and even manipulation of the election process by the governing party. Despite being imperfect, the close electoral race did not lead to violence, partly because of well-institutionalized preventive measures. The security-sector and monitoring efforts were key in helping stave off related violence. Other PEV instruments, however, such as voter consultations and youth programming, were largely absent. If more broadly employed, they could have further solidified the peaceful nature of the 2014 Moldova election.

In chapter 6, Elizabeth Murray presents the most challenging case in this comparative study, both analytically and logistically—Honduras. After the June 2009 coup d'état that removed President Mel Zelaya from power, Honduras returned to democratically elected rule with general elections in November of that year. Political polarization remained high in the aftermath of the coup, many anticipating that the 2013 elections would trigger significant violence. Although Honduras—which has the world's highest homicide rate—has extremely high levels of "common" violence, the violence surrounding the 2013 elections was not extraordinary. Suggested explanations include the electoral reform that permitted new political parties and specific initiatives intended to prevent electoral violence, including the widespread deployment of security forces, civic education campaigns, and high-level diplomatic pressure.

Individually, these cases offer a wealth of data on the measures taken to prevent election-related violence. Collectively, they yield additional insights on the effectiveness of the measures in similar risk environments globally. Based on the case data, chapter 7, the final of this volume, offers comparative insights on the effectiveness of common peacebuilding measures to prevent election violence. The analysis also examines prevailing hypotheses in the academic and political literature on election violence in the context of the five cases presented here, including the impact of electoral system design, or the history of violence. Chapter 7 also presents the book's core theoretical insights.

Notes

1.	Dorina Bekoe, "Conclusion: Implications for Research and Policy," in *Voting in Fear: Electoral Violence in Sub-Saharan Africa* (Washington, DC: U.S. Institute of Peace Press, 2012), p. 252.
2.	For a good overview, see Institute for Democracy and Electoral Assistance and the Carter Center, "Obligations and Standards: Towards Developing a Common Language for Electoral Integrity," UN Headquarters launch event, New York, October 28, 2014, http://webtv.un.org/watch/obligations-and-standards-towards-developing-a-common-language-for-electoral-integrity/3863241229001#full-text.
3.	Thomas Carothers, "Democracy Aid at 25: Time to Choose," *Journal of Democracy* 26, no. 1 (2015): 59–73.
4.	Ibid.
5.	United Nations Development Program, *Evaluation of UNDP Contribution to Strengthening Electoral Systems and Processes* (New York: UNDP, 2012), p. 18.
6.	Scott Straus and Charlie Taylor, "Democratization and Electoral Violence in Sub-Saharan Africa, 1990–2008," in *Voting in Fear*, p. 28.
7.	Thomas Carothers, *Aiding Democracy Abroad: The Learning Curve* (Washington, DC: Carnegie Endowment for International Peace, 1999), pp. 15–17.
8.	Philip Alston, "Report of the Special Rapporteur on extrajudicial, summary or arbitrary executions, Philip Alston, Addendum, Election-related violence and killings," United Nations Human Rights Council, May 21, 2010, A/HRC/14/24/Add.7, p. 4; David Gillies and Gerald J. Schmitz, "An Ounce of Prevention: Preliminary Implications for Policy and Practice," in *Elections in Dangerous Places: Democracy and the Paradoxes of Peacebuilding*, ed. David Gillies (Montreal: McGill-Queen's University Press, 2011), pp. 259–60.
9.	Jeff Fischer and Patrick W. Quirk, "Best Practices in Electoral Security: A Guide for Democracy, Human Rights and Governance Programming" (Washington, DC: U.S. Agency

for International Development/Creative Associates International, 2013), p. 10. Previous research shows that one in five elections in sub-Saharan Africa between 1990 and 2008 included significant violence. These include "generalized killing and violence directly tied to the electoral contest," as well as "repressive violence involving targeted assassinations and long-term high-level detentions combined with occasional cases of torture," the two highest violence categories as presented in the AEVD database (Straus and Taylor, "Democratization and Electoral Violence," p. 23).

10.   David C. Rapoport and Leonard Weinberg, "Elections and Violence," *Terrorism and Political Violence* 12, no. 3-4 (2000): 23–24, doi: 10.1080/09546550008427569.

11.   David Gillies, "Introduction: Electoral Democracy and the Paradoxes of Peacebuilding," in *Elections in Dangerous Places*, p. xxi. Figure provided by George Perlin, Queens University.

12.   Antonio Giustozzi and Silab Mangal, "Violence, the Taliban, and Afghanistan's 2014 Elections," Peaceworks no. 103 (Washington, DC: U.S. Institute of Peace Press, 2014), p. 7.

13.   Blas Enrique Barahona, "Informe Final de la Conflictividad y Violencia Política Electoral" (Tegucigalpa: Institución Universitario en Democracia, 2014), www.redpartidos.org/files/informe_violencia_electoral_2.pdf.

14.   On model of democracy, see "Tunisia Votes for First Directly-Elected President," NBC News, November 23, 2014, www.nbcnews.com/news/world/tunisia-votes-first-directly-elected-president-n254316; Paul Schemm, "Tunisia elections possible model for region," Associated Press, November 1, 2014, http://news.yahoo.com/tunisia-elections-possible-model-region-132610061.html; Leila Fadel, "With a Presidential Vote, Tunisia Seeks a Peaceful Transition," NPR News, December 19, 2014, www.npr.org/blogs/parallels/2014/12/19/371926650/with-a-presidential-vote-tunisia-seeks-a-peaceful-transition. On beacon of hope, see Pippa Norris, Ferran Martínez I Coma, and Max Grömping, "The Year in Elections: 2014" (Sydney: Electoral Integrity Project, February 2015), p. 21.

15.   "Good Voters, Not Such Good Guys," *Economist*, November 1, 2014, www.economist.com/news/europe/21629375-poll-results-were-promising-future-ukraine-dauntingly-difficult-good-voters.

16.   Kristine Höglund, "Electoral Violence in Conflict-Ridden Societies: Concepts, Causes, and Consequences," *Terrorism and Political Violence* 21, no. 3 (2009): 412–27, doi: 10.1080/09546550 902950290; Jeff Fischer, "Electoral Conflict and Violence: A Strategy for Study and Prevention," IFES white paper (Washington, DC: International Foundations for Electoral Systems, 2002); Dorina Bekoe, ed., *Voting in Fear: Electoral Violence in Sub-Saharan Africa* (Washington, DC: U.S. Institute of Peace Press, 2012); Alston, "Report of the Special Rapporteur"; Sead Alihodzic, "Elections, Violence, and Peace" in *Ballots or Bullets: Potentials and Limitations of Elections in Conflict Contexts*, ed. Andrea Iff (Bern: Swisspeace, 2011), pp. 27–35.

17.   Paul Staniland, "Violence and Democracy," *Comparative Politics* 47, no. 1 (2014): 100.

18.   The full UNDP definition reads as follows: "acts or threats of coercion, intimidation, or physical harm perpetrated to affect an electoral process or that arise in the context of electoral competition. When perpetrated to affect an electoral process, violence may be employed to influence the process of elections—such as efforts to delay, disrupt, or derail a poll—and to influence the outcomes: the determining of winners in competitive races for political office or to secure approval or disapproval of referendum questions." Timothy Sisk and Chris Spies, *Elections and Conflict Prevention: A Guide to Analysis, Planning, and Programming* (New York: UNDP, 2009), p. 4. An alternative definition, based on the work of Jeff Fischer (IFES Guide), and focusing on the different modalities of the violence and perpetrator motivations is provided by the U.S. Agency for International Development: "Any random or organized act or threat to intimidate, physically harm blackmail, or abuse an electoral stakeholder in seeking to determine, delay or otherwise influence the electoral process" (Fischer and Quirk, "Best Practices in Electoral Security," p. 42).

19.   Staniland, "Violence and Democracy," p. 106.

20.   Fischer, "Electoral Conflict and Violence," p. 3.

21. Alston, "Report of the Special Rapporteur," pp. 14, 5.
22. Alihodzic, "Elections, Violence, and Peace," p. 27.
23. Staniland, "Violence and Democracy," p. 101.
24. Although election day is not the most violent election phase, compared with the pre- and postelection periods, Straus and Taylor argue that it is the most violent day (Bekoe, "The Scope, Nature, and Pattern of Electoral Violence in Sub-Saharan Africa," in *Voting in Fear*, pp. 10–11).
25. Straus and Taylor, "Democratization and Electoral Violence," pp. 28–29. According to Straus and Taylor, tensions predominantly arise when decisions are made about who has the right to vote, when and if one can exercise the right to vote, which candidates are eligible to represent particular groups, the integrity of the registry, the credibility of results, or the process of filing grievances.
26. Leonardo Arriola and Chelsea Johnson, "Election Violence in Democratizing States," paper presented at the American Political Science Association annual meeting. Seattle, WA, September 2011.
27. Ibid., p. 29.
28. Rapoport and Weinberg, "Elections and Violence," p. 16.
29. Bekoe, "Scope, Nature, and Pattern," p. 4.
30. According to the Peace Alliance, $3.6 billion in economic growth was lost as a result of the 2007–2008 postelection violence in Kenya (http://peacealliance.org/tools-education/statistics-on-violence/).
31. Straus and Taylor, "Democratization and Electoral Violence," pp. 33–36; Bekoe, "Conclusion," pp. 244–46, 249–50.
32. Sisk and Spies, *Elections and Conflict Prevention*, pp. 15–17.
33. For a related conceptual framework mapping factors of election-related violence, see Alihodzic, "Elections, Violence, and Peace," p. 27.
34. The contextual vulnerabilities were selected during an author's meeting with the entire research team, aimed at identifying a diverse set of prominent theories in the literature on election violence.
35. Jeff Fischer, Karen Kaplan, and Elisabeth Bond, "Electoral Security Framework: Technical Guidance Handbook for Democracy and Governance Officers" (Washington, DC: U.S. Agency for International Development/Creative Associates International, 2010), p. 10.
36. Höglund, "Electoral Violence," pp. 422–23.
37. Peter Burnell, "Political Parties in Africa: Different, Functional and Dynamic? Reflections on Gero Erdmann's 'Party Research: The West European Bias and the African Labyrinth,'" in *Votes, Money, and Violence: Political Parties and Elections in Sub-Saharan Africa*, ed. Matthias Basedau, Gero Erdmann, and Andreas Mehler (Sweden: Nordiska Afrikainstitutet, 2007), p. 79.
38. Jonas Claes, "Atrocity Prevention at the State Level: Security Sector Reform and Horizontal Equality," Peace Brief no. 144 (Washington, DC: U.S. Institute of Peace Press, 2013).
39. Stewart Francis, "Horizontal Inequalities: A Neglected Dimension of Development," Wider Annual Lecture (Helsinki: UNU World Institute for Development Economics Research, 2001); Sisk and Spies, "Elections and Conflict Prevention," p. 11; Ted Robert Gurr, *Why Men Rebel* (Boulder, CO: Paradigm Publishers, 1970.)
40. Fischer, Kaplan, and Bond, "Electoral Security Framework," p. 10.
41. Alvin Rabushka and Kenneth A. Shepsle, *Politics in Plural Societies: A Theory of Democratic Instability* (Columbus, OH: Charles E. Merrill, 1972).
42. Donald Horowitz, *Ethnic Groups in Conflict* (Berkeley: University of California Press, 1985).
43. Minorities at Risk Project, University of Maryland, last updated July 28, 2014, www.cidcm.umd.edu/mar/about.asp.
44. Benjamin Reilly, "Understanding Elections in Conflict Situations," in *Elections in Dangerous Places: Democracy and the Paradoxes of Peacebuilding*, ed. David Gillies (Montreal: McGill-Queen's University Press, 2011), p. 10.

45. Common variations include first-past-the-post, alternative vote, or two-round system. On raised stakes, see Sisk and Spies, "Elections and Conflict Prevention," p. 9.

46. Gillies and Schmitz, "An Ounce of Prevention," p. 267.

47. Timothy Sisk, "Evaluation Election-Related Violence: Nigeria and Sudan in Comparative Perspective," in *Voting in Fear*, p. 47.

48. The adoption of the system that best reflects the composition of the electorate is a task for technical experts, though politicians are often tempted to change the rules of the game to consolidate power or exclude their opponents.

49. Close elections can be described as elections that are competitive—multiple candidates have a plausible chance of winning—or produce a result margin so close that uncertainty about a clear victor remains.

50. Emilie Hafner-Burton, Susan D. Hyde, and Ryan S. Jablonski, "When Do Governments Resort to Election Violence?" *British Journal of Political Science* 44, no. 1 (2014): 149–79, 57.

51. Edward D. Mansfield and Jack Snyder, "Democratic Transitions, Institutional Strength, and War," *International Organization* 56, no. 2: 297–337. Mansfield and Snyder find that once a system has made the complete transition to a "coherent democracy," the risks of violence "decline rapidly" (pp. 305–6).

52. Edward D. Mansfield and Jack Snyder, "Turbulent Transitions: Why Emerging Democracies Go to War," in *Leashing the Dogs of War: Conflict Management in a Divided World*, ed. Chester Crocker, Fen Osler Hampson, and Pamela Aall (Washington, DC: U.S. Institute of Peace Press, 2007); Arriola and Johnson, "Election Violence."

53. Bekoe, "Conclusion," p. 245.

54. Dawn Brancati and Jack L. Snyder, "Time to Kill: The Impact of Election Timing on Post-conflict Stability," *Journal of Conflict Resolution* 57 (2013): 822–53.

55. Höglund, "Electoral Violence," p. 241.

56. Claire Elder, Susan Stigant, and Jonas Claes, "Elections and Violent Conflict in Kenya: Making Prevention Stick," Peaceworks no. 101 (Washington, DC: U.S. Institute of Peace Press, 2014).

57. International IDEA, "An Overview of the Electoral Risk Management Tool (ERM Tool)," Support Document (Stockholm: International IDEA, 2013), pp. 6–7, www.idea.int/elections/ermtool/upload/Overview-Electoral-Risk-Management-Tool.pdf.

58. Jennifer McCoy, Larry Garbar, and Robert A. Pastor, "Pollwatching and Peacemaking," *Journal of Democracy* 2, no. 4 (1991): 102–14, 106.

59. Dorina Bekoe, "Preventing Electoral Violence: Greater Awareness, but Still Falling Short," USIP Winter Insights 2015 (Washington, DC: U.S. Institute of Peace Press, 2015), www.usip.org/the-prevention-of-election-violence.

60. Höglund, "Electoral Violence," p. 416; Fischer and Quirk, "Best Practices," p. 4.

61. USAID's "Electoral Security Framework" offers a description of parallel vote tabulation: "Observers record the results from a scientific sample of polling stations. Results are independently tabulated for comparison with the official results of the election authorities."

62. "The ACE Encyclopedia: Electoral Integrity," ACE Electoral Knowledge Network, 2013, www.aceproject.org.

63. The relationship between election fairness and election violence remains subject for debate. UNDP claims that "free, fair and transparent elections are less likely to experience election violence," but Liisa Laakso has found that "Elections declared as free and fair by election observers are no less violent." See "Insights into Electoral Violence in Africa," in *Votes, Money, and Violence: Political Parties and Elections in Sub-Saharan Africa*, ed. Matthias Basedau, Gero Erdmann, and Andreas Mehler (Sweden: Nordiska Afrikainstitutet, 2007), p. 224.

64. A theory of change presents the causal logic behind a strategy, program, or activity. In the case of election violence prevention, theories present the way programs may plausibly contribute to the intended outcome of violence prevention or reduction.

65. Fischer, Kaplan, and Bond, "Electoral Security Framework," p. 26.

66. Lawrence Woocher, "Field Guide: Helping Prevent Mass Atrocities," *U.S. Agency for International Development Field Guide* (Washington, DC: U.S. Agency for International Development, 2015), p. A-13.

67. Fischer and Quirk, "Best Practices," p. 23.

68. The quality of security-sector engagement will be coded in each of the selected cases, based on the question of whether the security sector has the capacity, professionalism, and neutrality to ensure election security.

69. Sisk and Spies, "Elections and Conflict Prevention," p. 4; Sisk, "Evaluation Election-Related Violence," p. 47.

70. Woocher, "Field Guide," p. A-7.

71. Election tribunals or courts may be created or mandated to adjudicate electoral disputes in an independent and transparent manner.

72. Fischer, Kaplan, and Bond, "Electoral Security Framework," p. 7.

73. Less comprehensive international intervention instruments include electoral verification, whereby the international community is mandated to verify an election or referendum, and electoral certification, in which an external actor, usually the UN, evaluates each stage of the electoral process and assesses its compliance to international good practices (Fischer, Kaplan, and Bond, "Electoral Security Framework," p. 20).

74. Fischer and Quirk, "Best Practices," p. 15.

75. Sean Dunne and Scott Smith, "Electoral Management during Transition: Challenges and Opportunities" (Stockholm: International IDEA, 2012), p. 8, www.idea.int/publications/electoral-management-during-transition/loader.cfm?csModule=security/getfile&pageid=53312.

76. Codes of conduct take the form of voluntary or enforceable guidelines for election stakeholders, like political parties, media actors or election observers. The code defines the rules of the game, such as by specifying the financial expenditures that are permitted, prohibiting hate speech or voter intimidation, or encouraging respect for the result announcement protocol.

77. The quality of election management and administration will be coded in each of the selected cases, based on whether the electoral management body has the capacity and independence to effectively manage the electoral process. The EMB functioning presents our primary indicator, but the quality of election administration depends on the overall strength of government institutions, the judicial branch, and security sector.

78. Boutros-Boutros Ghali, "An Agenda for Peace: Preventive Diplomacy, Peacemaking, and Peace-keeping," Report of the Secretary General, Document no. A/47/2771 (New York: United Nations, 1992), p. 5.

79. Ban Ki-moon, "Preventive Diplomacy: Delivering Results," Report of the Secretary General, Document no. S/2011/552 (New York: United Nations, 2011), pp. 11–12.

80. Ibid., p. 18.

81. The quality of preventive diplomacy will be coded in each of the selected cases, based on whether international actors intervene through preventive diplomacy during the electoral process.

82. Woocher, "Field Guide," p. A-15.

83. Ibid. The quality of peace messaging will be coded in each of the selected cases, based on whether a peace messaging campaign with broad societal and geographic reach is in place.

84. UN, "Women and Elections: Guide to Promoting the Participation of Women in Elections" (New York: United Nations, 2005), p. 56, www.eods.eu/library/UN.WomenAndElections.pdf.

85. Paul Collier and Pedro C. Vicente, "Votes and Violence: Evidence from a Field Experiment in Nigeria," *Economic Journal* 124, no. 574 (2014): 327–55; Jessica Gottlieb, "Can information that raises voter expectations improve accountability? A field experiment in Mali," unpublished manuscript, Stanford University, 2012.

86. UN, "Women and Elections," p. 59.

87. The quality of voter education is coded in each of the selected cases based on whether state or nonstate actors engage and empower citizens, including vulnerable communities, through civic and voter education programs throughout the country.

88. Fischer, Kaplan, and Bond, "Electoral Security Framework," p. 20.
89. In the Organization for Security and Cooperation in Europe, long-term observers spend six to eight weeks in-country.
90. Fischer and Quirk, "Best Practices," p. 32.
91. The quality of monitoring and mapping efforts are coded in each of the selected cases based on whether state or nonstate actors systematically monitor and map electoral violence and threats of violence.
92. The quality of voter consultations is coded in each of the selected cases, based on whether voter consultations and participatory political platforms allow voters to articulate their grievances and concerns, and hold parties and government officials accountable based on their campaign promises.
93. The quality of youth programming is coded in each of the selected cases, based on whether state or nonstate actors attempt to integrate youth into the electoral process and economy.
94. Woocher, "Field Guide," p. A-3.
95. Media are primarily considered as implementing actor of preventive activity, as they engage in several practices considered within this study (for example, peace messaging and civic education). As a related platform, social media can educate and serve as an organizational vehicle for peace, but can also spread hate speech or help mobilize for violence. Gender programs are not included in the evaluative study; in the context of elections, women are more commonly approached through broader development or civilian protection programming. Smaller technical instruments are pooled under election administration to keep the independent variables to a minimum.
96. The five cases were selected for this study based on specific criteria. First, we selected those countries with elections that occurred between October 1, 2013 and December 31, 2014, where the head of state and government (or simply the head of government) is at stake. Next, we included indexed scores from the Economic Intelligence Unit (EIU), Freedom House, and the Institute for Economics and Peace's 2014 Global Peace Index. We sorted these findings to pull cases from the "middle of the pack" through each of these indices. This middle is identified as a score between 70 and 130 on the 2014 Peace Index, a listing of partly free by Freedom House, and scores between 50 and 70 for political stability within the EIU. We were left with the following countries: Moldova, Malawi, Bolivia, Macedonia, Bangladesh, Nepal, Honduras, Thailand, and Turkey. These were further culled through consideration of geographic spread, access, and analytical bandwidth. Risk levels and actual election violence levels did not match consistently between the cases. Selected elections took place between October 1, 2013, and December 31, 2014, allowing the data collection to occur within the first year after election day.
97. All five countries are ranked with moderate or low fragility in terms of their political effectiveness and legitimacy. See Monty G. Marshall and Benjamin Cole, "Global Report 2014: Conflict Governance, and State Fragility" (Vienna, VA: Center for Systemic Peace, 2014), p. 45. The unconsolidated nature of these partial democracies entails a considerable level of risk. See Fischer, Kaplan, and Bond, "Electoral Security Framework," p. 9.
98. Recognizing the potentially high stakes and devastating impact local elections or other election types may have, the scope of this study is limited to national elections.

PART I

Preventive Failure or Vulnerable Context?

Map 2.1 Bangladesh National Map

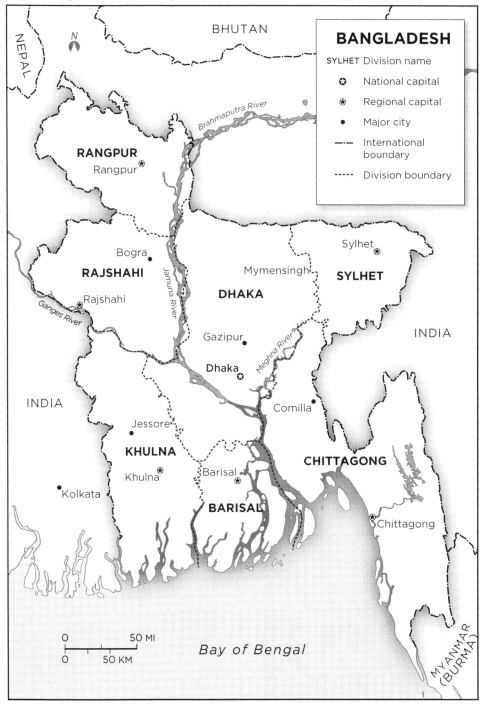

BHUTAN

NEPAL

N

BANGLADESH

SYLHET Division name
⊗ National capital
✳ Regional capital
• Major city
—·— International boundary
------ Division boundary

Brahmaputra River

RANGPUR
Rangpur ✳

Bogra •

RAJSHAHI

Ganges River

Rajshahi ✳

Jamuna River

Sylhet ✳

Mymensingh

SYLHET

DHAKA

INDIA

Gazipur •

Dhaka ⊗

Meghna River

Comilla •

INDIA

Jessore •

KHULNA

Khulna ✳

Barisal ✳

CHITTAGONG

Kolkata •

BARISAL

Chittagong ✳

0   50 MI
0   50 KM

Bay of Bengal

MYANMAR (BURMA)

2

Bangladesh

Political Intransigence and Weak Prevention

GEOFFREY MACDONALD

A fter her loss in the 1991 election, the combative leader of the Awami League (AL), Sheikh Hasina, declared to the victorious Bangladesh Nationalist Party, "I won't let (you) live in peace a single day."[1] So began Bangladesh's current democratic era, which has been marked by violence, successive political crises, and turbulent elections. The election in January 2014 was the most violent in the country's history. The opposition political party and its allies boycotted the poll, discouraging citizens from voting with beatings, murders, and Molotov cocktails hurled into buses. The ruling party responded to the unrest by deploying the partisan army and police, who often indiscriminately fired into crowds of protesters. At least four hundred were killed, including voters, party activists, election officials, and security personnel, in the months before, during, and weeks after the election.

The violence and tension, however, long predated the official electoral cycle. A series of controversial decisions by the ruling Awami League after its win in 2008 provoked a slow escalation of violence. Observers of Bangladesh's politics voiced concern about the growing risk for election violence at least a year and a half prior to the poll. In June 2012, the International Crisis Group wrote that if the incumbent party did not compromise with the opposition, Bangladesh "could face a protracted political crisis" that "threatens to erode Bangladesh's democratic foundations."[2] In August 2013, the Asia director for Human Rights Watch said, "Unless the government takes firm action to rein in the security forces, there is going to be a lot more blood on the streets before the year is over."[3]

Despite these concerns, Bangladesh's election violence could have been mitigated or even prevented. The tense political environment was exacerbated by the absence or weakness of conventional violence prevention. The election commission and security forces were co-opted by the ruling party, election monitoring and mapping was unsystematic, and voter-targeted programs—such as peace messaging, civic and voter education, voter consultations, and youth programming—were weak or effectively nonexistent. These otherwise commonly applied instruments to prevent election violence—PEV models—were not only weak in absolute terms during the 2014 general elections in Bangladesh, but also substandard in comparison with past elections.[4]

Political violence is not a new phenomenon in Bangladesh. Assassinations, coups, riots, intimidation, harassment, and corruption pervade the country's politics. Important contextual vulnerabilities, such as power centralization and social division, contribute to the risk of election-related violence, but the 2014 election was unique. Election-related violence was far more severe than in previous parliamentary contests. The difference is explained by two factors: first, the actions of the Awami League, which aggressively sought to consolidate its power and provoked a violent backlash from opposition parties; and, second, the poor implementation of prevention instruments, which were weaker than in previous elections. Although deficient violence-prevention tools cannot on their own explain Bangladesh's increased election violence, their weakness facilitated and in some cases even exacerbated tension and violent conflict.

History of Election Violence

Despite the prominence of political and election violence in Bangladesh, reliable data on conflicts, injuries, and deaths are scant. Estimates of the death toll for the January 2014 election cycle range from 150 to more than five hundred, most settling on at least four hundred.[5] This increase over the last three elections (the only reliable electoral data) is significant: 78 to 128 in 1996, 134 to 230 deaths in 2001, and 15 to 42 deaths in 2008 (see figure 2.1). Yet election violence is only one manifestation of Bangladesh's political violence, which includes assassinations, boycotts, strikes, protests, inter- and intraparty riots and killings, and state-sponsored murder and torture. Although the level of election violence during the January 2014 cycle was uniquely high, it was nevertheless situated within a long history of political and electoral violence that has come to define the country's political culture.

Figure 2.1 Prevention in Historical Perspective, Bangladesh

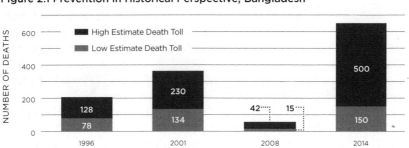

Source: Author's calculations

Post-Independence Era, 1971 to 1991

Contemporary PEV measures in Bangladesh attempt to address a problem that has numerous historical antecedents. Bangladesh's independence in 1971 came after a violent war of liberation from Pakistan. The ethnically and linguistically distinct Bengali Muslims in the eastern half of bifurcated Pakistan had long agitated for more rights. Following an election victory in 1971 for the Bengali nationalist party, the Awami League, the government in West Pakistan decided to invade the east to put down the incipient nationalist movement. Over the course of nine months, Pakistan's soldiers killed approximately three million Bengalis, indiscriminately massacred students and intellectuals, and raped approximately two hundred thousand women.[6] Several Bengali Islamic movements collaborated with the army's effort to prevent the breakup of Muslim Pakistan. The militia of one organization, Jamaat-i-Islami (known as Jamaat), carried out some of the most infamous massacres of the war. But the Pakistani army could not repress the independence movement and the war came to a quick and decisive end two months after India intervened and then presided over Pakistan's surrender to the newly formed nation of Bangladesh in 1971.[7]

Mujibur Rahman—known as Mujib—emerged from the war as a national hero and became the country's first prime minister. He shepherded through the national assembly a new constitution that followed the principles of so-called Mujibism: nationalism, democracy, socialism, and secularism. But his regime struggled to effectively govern the country and slowly centralized power. In the country's first defining act of political violence, a group of army officers stormed the presidential compound and assassinated Mujib and most of his family in August 1975. Only his two daughters, Hasina and Rehana, survived the attack. The assassination sparked a series of coups that brought political chaos to Bangladesh. General Ziaur Rahman (known as Zia) ultimately took power, formalizing his rule in 1977.

The next two decades cemented Bangladesh's burgeoning political culture of violence, instability, and authoritarianism. Zia formed the Bangladesh Nationalist Party (BNP) as his personal political vehicle and won election in 1979. His focus on economic development earned him widespread popularity, but his decision to not punish Mujib's assassins offended many Bangladeshis. Significantly, Zia also promoted Islamic nationalism to counter the secularism of Mujibism. The constitution was amended to include declarations of Islamic faith and solidarity with the broader Islamic world. Zia also allowed banned Jamaat leaders, including some accused of war crimes, to return to Bangladeshi politics under the banner of a different political organization. Zia's effort to build a national identity closely linked with Islam is an important part of his legacy.[8]

Zia's reign ended with his assassination in 1981 at the hands of a disgruntled liberation leader. The ensuing confrontation between the sitting vice president and the military led to a military coup in March 1982 that brought General Husain Muhammad Ershad to power. Ershad's administration was deeply repressive: political parties were banned, the press tightly controlled, and martial law imposed.[9] Like Zia before him, Ershad pursued Islamization policies that pushed the country in a conservative direction. By 1987, the Ershad regime was deeply unpopular and the opposition parties—the AL and BNP—were now unified against it. Both parties boycotted a new poll in 1988 that returned Ershad to power. Ershad eventually resigned office in November 1990 amid swelling unrest, beginning Bangladesh's present democratic period.

Democratic Era, 1991 to 2015

Intense political competition and election violence have continued to define the post-Ershad period of democratic politics. Elections have led to a cycling of power between the BNP and AL, which have both been implicated in political and electoral violence. Smaller parties have also played an important role in election competition and unrest. The four primary parties have subtle but important ideological differences that shape their often-combative rivalry.

- **Awami League**. Founded by Mujibur Rahman, the "father of the nation," the AL is Bangladesh's oldest political party. It is strongly associated with ethnic Bengali nationalism, the liberation war, secularism, and pro-poor rhetoric and policies. It also has a long relationship with the Indian Congress Party, which has earned it a negative reputation among political rivals for being pro-Indian. The Awami League has been in power from 1972 to 1975 under Mujib and from 1996 to 2000, 2008 to 2013, and 2013 to the present under Sheikh Hasina (Mujib's daughter). The AL has little internal democracy and is under the full control of Sheikh Hasina.
- **Bangladesh Nationalist Party**. Founded as the personal political vehicle of President Ziaur Rahman in 1978, the BNP enjoys popularity equal to that of the Awami League. It is associated with Bangladeshi nationalism, which is rooted in Islamic values rather than ethnicity, as well as with conservative free market policies. The party's close ties with former liberation opponents have led to criticism among rivals that it is pro-Pakistani and Islamist. The BNP was in power from 1979 to 1982 in the Zia era and again from 1991 to 1995 and 2001 to 2006 under Khaleda Zia, Zia's widow. Like the AL, the BNP has little internal democracy and is tightly controlled by its leader, Khaleda Zia.
- **Jatiya Party**. The Jatiya Party was founded by President Ershad in 1986 to formalize his political power. Today, the party has no discernable ideology but continues to win a relevant minority of the vote: 6.1 percent in 2008 and 11.3 percent in 2014. The height of its power was under Ershad's authoritarian rule, when it won two largely illegitimate elections in 1986 and 1988.
- **Jamaat-i-Islami**. Jamaat descends from the Pakistani party of the same name. It advocates an Islamic state in Bangladesh. Having opposed the breakaway of Bangladesh from Pakistan at the time, it connived with the Pakistani army to commit atrocities against liberation supporters. Jamaat's leaders fled to Pakistan after independence, but returned to Bangladesh under Zia's BNP rule. Jamaat is a minor national party, winning only 4.6 percent in 2008. However, it is also a highly organized cadre-based party that provides its traditional ally, the BNP, with street muscle during protests and elections.

Democratic competition between these four parties (and other smaller ones) has been highly dysfunctional. Parliamentary boycott is a constant—and debilitating—feature of Bangladeshi politics. Although the practice of boycotting is standard in parliamentary democracy, the extent of its practice in Bangladesh creates severe legislative paralysis. An analysis of parliamentary boycotts shows that nearly 43 percent of all parliamentary days were boycotted between 1991 and 2006.[10] The tactic has been used with increasing frequency over the years regardless of which party is in the opposition: the Awami League boycotted 29 percent of parliamentary days between 1991 and 1995; the BNP boycotted 40 percent between 1996 and 2000; and the Awami League boycotted 59 percent between 2001 and 2006. Invariably, the ruling party decries the boycott as undemocratic and the opposition claims that it is oppressed in some way, including the posting of illegitimate election results or the violation of parliamentary procedure. The resulting chaos and gridlock impede the legislative process and spill out into the streets in the form of outright violence.

Hartals are the street manifestation of parliamentary boycotts. A hartal is a general strike that aims to shut down every sector of the economy. Political parties commonly declare hartals to oppose the sitting government. A United Nations Development Program (UNDP) report on hartals in Bangladesh shows a dramatic spike during the democratic era: 64 percent of all hartals have occurred since 1991 (figure 2.2). Hartals and parliamentary boycotts are key elements of political expression in Bangladesh and exemplify the destructive political logic of nonparticipatory opposition. Rather than challenge the ruling party with a positive alternative vision, parties impede economic, social, and political progress to undermine the stability of the ruling administration.

Post-1991 political unrest has featured more than just parliamentary boycotts and hartals. Political assassination—a striking feature of pre-1991 Bangladeshi politics—has not felled a head of state in the democratic era. Other forms of conflict and violence, however, persist. Aminul Islam at the University of Dhaka compiled a list of political

Figure 2.2 Hartals in Bangladesh Since Partition

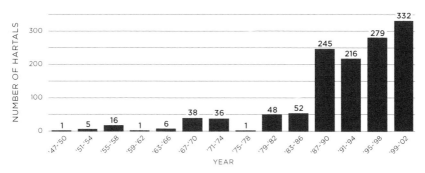

Source: Cecilie Brøkner, Dilara Choudhury, Lisa Hiller and Kathryn Uphaus, *Beyond Hartals: Towards Democratic Dialogue in Bangladesh* (New York: United Nations Development Program, 2005)

party conflicts during the first decade of the post-Ershad period.[11] He defines *conflict* broadly, as including attacks on political rallies, hartals and strikes, intraparty rivalry, protests, and physical violence. These types of conflict include both conventional political violence and election-related violence. Islam's study finds that conflicts during BNP and Awami League administrations constituted 44 percent and 38.25 percent respectively of the decade's total, which suggests that both parties were roughly equally violence prone in the 1990s.

When arranged to showcase election cycles, Islam's data illuminate the high propensity toward violence during periods of political competition. Election years became increasingly violent between 1991 and 2001 (figure 2.3), the number of party conflicts rising from 182 in 1991, to 453 in 1996, to 503 in 2001. The 1991 election was the high point of cooperation between the Awami League and BNP, which came together to oust Ershad and the Jatiyo Party. However, as the decade's democratic competition wore on, the two rival parties returned to fierce antagonism.

Political party youth wings are responsible for a significant amount of party conflict. Campus movements closely connected to party youth groups played an important role in agitating for language rights in the 1950s, independence in 1971, and a return to democracy in 1990. However, youth wings are now known for campus intimidation and brutal street violence. The youth wings of Jamaat and the Awami League, Chhatra Shibir and Chhatra League respectively, have been implicated in brutal acts of political violence. In 2012, a group of Chhatra League activists wrongly identified a pedestrian as an opposition member and hacked him to death with machetes in the street.[12] The following year, Shibir activists enforced a hartal with public beatings, petrol bombs, and attacks on police that resulted in dozens of deaths. These violent activities often increase during election cycles. Rather than represent political interests, youth wings are now often the primary perpetrators of political and election violence, operating at the direction of political party leaders.

Figure 2.3 Party Conflicts in Bangladesh

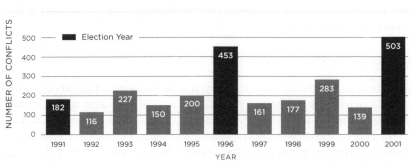

Source: Aminul Islam, "The Predicament of Democratic Consolidation in Bangladesh," *Bangladesh E-Journal of Sociology* 3, no. 2 (2006)

Hartals, protests, inter- and intraparty violence, and other deaths and injuries are often directly related to state repression, which is a significant form of violence in Bangladesh. Opposition parties argue that the ruling party uses the state security apparatus to harass, arrest, torture, and kill political opponents during and after election cycles. According to one study, the Awami League regime imprisoned fifty thousand BNP activists between 1996 and 2001. From 2001 to 2006, when the BNP held power, it allegedly carried out a similar mass-arrest campaign against AL activists.[13] Once arrested, regime opponents are often tortured and killed by the police or other security forces. While in custody, prisoners are sometimes burned with acid, have holes drilled into their legs, or endure mock executions.[14] Furthermore, political opponents are often killed in extrajudicial murders and so-called crossfire deaths, in which the security services claim the individual was killed while violently resisting arrest; the victims' bodies often show evidence of torture, however. According to the Dhaka-based human rights organization Odhikar, more than 2,400 people were killed extrajudicially and more than 1,500 in crossfire deaths between 2001 and 2014.[15] Such deaths occur both during and outside election periods.

Election violence is one facet of the multidimensional problem of political violence in Bangladesh. The post-independence period between 1971 and 1991 was marked by repressive military rule and the assassinations of Mujib and Zia. Since Ershad's fall, Bangladeshi politics has remained deeply unstable and often violent. Extreme party rivalry between the AL and the BNP has manifested itself in boycotts, hartals, protests, destruction of property, street brawls, killings, and state oppression. These activities often intensify during election cycles, but remain a constant presence.

2014 Election

Bangladesh's January 2014 election was unique not for the presence of violence, but rather for its scale. A set of controversial decisions made by the incumbent Awami League set in motion an escalating cycle of violent protest and state crackdown. On election day and throughout the pre- and postelection period, reciprocal violence killed hundreds and dramatically undermined the legitimacy of the process. This violence was framed around the long-standing secular-Islamist divide in Bangladeshi society, on which the AL and BNP rhetorically situate themselves. The religious tenor of political competition coupled with structural risk factors to significantly raise the stakes and tensions surrounding the election.

Contextual Vulnerabilities

Election violence in Bangladesh—and the preventive measures in place to stop it—are nested within important contextual vulnerabilities that can feed violent conflict. The two most significant are structural: power centralization and religious division. Constitutionally, Bangladesh has a centralized political system that rewards winners with access to virtually complete power and entirely excludes losers. Demographically, the political importance of the Hindu minority is controversial in an increasingly conservative Islamic-majority country. Both factors shape the risk environment for electoral violence.

Centralized power raises the stakes of elections and foments violence. Bangladesh uses a first-past-the-post electoral system and has single-member constituencies. This system creates a strong incentive for winner-take-all politics and single-party rule at the district and national levels. The consequences of an election loss are therefore enormous, because defeat results in full exclusion from power.[16] This problem is enhanced by the governmental structure—a unitary state with little autonomy provided to the local level. Despite some efforts at decentralization, the country's stunted vertical power sharing continues to concentrate authority at the national level. Furthermore, the judiciary has been a weak check on unconstrained executive power.[17] These factors combine with a winner-take-all electoral system to foster a zero-sum fight for power that often descends into violence. In Bangladesh, the significant spoils associated with national-level dominance are worth killing for.

An additional contextual vulnerability is religious division. Hindus are the most politically important minority group, currently making up approximately 9 percent of the population, which is a dramatic decline since the division of British India, before which they were approximately 30 percent. However, the exclusionary Islamic character of the Pakistani state and society precipitated a mass exodus from the country shortly after Partition. The secular Bangladeshi state founded by Mujib sought to protect its dwindling minority population, but the Islamization policies of Zia and Ershad alienated and endangered Hindus.

Politically, Hindus have gravitated toward the Awami League, which has continued to promote secularism and minority protections. Despite their minority status, disparate concentrations of Hindus are politically significant in particular areas, constituting majorities in some districts. Consequently, the BNP and its allies have tried to suppress or punish Hindu voters. During and after the 2001 parliamentary election, Hindu shrines were vandalized, women raped, and several killed; hundreds of Hindu families fled their homes.[18] A later investigation ordered by the Bangladesh High Court concluded that BNP ministers and MPs were involved in the attacks.[19] Political violence against Hindus is also closely related to land dispossession. A set of laws allows the government to confiscate the land of anyone who leaves the country or is declared an enemy of the state. Therefore, as Hindus are forcefully driven from their land, squatters quickly move in to occupy it.[20] One Hindu leader noted that elections "mean brutal violence against [the] minority, especially to [the] Hindu community."

Power centralization and social division are two important contextual vulnerabilities. They are not causes of violence but do shape the character of conflict. Centralized power enhances the spoils of victory and encourages ferocious political competition. The survival of politicians within patronage politics is based on access to state power, which in Bangladesh is provided through a single focal point: the national parliament. Attacks on Hindus are one manifestation of this issue. Localized Hindu majorities or large minorities have a significant influence over who gets access to state power, and Hindu's traditional support for the Awami League makes them a target of the opposition.

Political Centralization

The election violence in 2014 was precipitated by two AL decisions that heightened the political stakes of the election and exacerbated the historical secular-Islamic divide in the country. In 2009, the AL began organizing a war crimes trial that would indict, convict, and execute several members of the opposition-aligned Jamaat for crimes committed during the war of independence. Two years later, the League legislatively dismantled the caretaker government (CTG) system in place to prevent partisan rigging of national elections. These decisions combined to create an exceptionally tense and unstable political atmosphere entering the 2014 poll.[21]

Since independence, many Bangladeshis have called for an investigation into atrocities committed by West Pakistan sympathizers.[22] In 2009, the AL fulfilled its campaign pledge to begin organizing war crimes tribunals. A fact-finding commission was established and incriminated nine leaders of Jamaat. The party claimed that its members were unfairly targeted for political reasons, but the international community largely backed the International Crimes Tribunal (ICT). Officials from the U.S. government, European Union, and Human Rights Watch pledged to provide technical and legal support to ensure the independence of the process.

Domestic and international skepticism, however, grew as the tribunal proceeded. A controversial report by the *Economist* in December 2012 claimed illegal collusion involving the ICT chairman, the prosecutor, and the Awami League government.[23] The chairman was forced to resign. Other international observers also began to view the ICT as a political gambit designed to eliminate the opposition. Human Rights Watch's Asia director said the ICT had become "deeply problematic" and showed the government was "more concerned about winning votes than about following the rule of law."[24] Similarly, a leaked U.S. State Department cable from the time noted the "little doubt that hard-line elements within the ruling party [the Awami League] believe that the time is right to crush Jamaat and other Islamic parties."[25]

Some also called for internationalization of the trial to save its legitimacy. A former UN prosecutor concluded that Bangladesh did not have "the independent judicial and investigative capacity" to conduct impartial trials in accordance with international standards.[26] Nevertheless, Prime Minister Sheikh Hasina defended the process and continued with the ICT. In January 2013, Abul Kalam Azad was the first man convicted of crimes against humanity and sentenced to death. Throughout the remainder of the year, several former and current Jamaat officials were sentenced and executed.[27]

One such conviction sparked massive unrest that portended the election-related violence to come. In February, the ICT convicted Abdul Quader Mollah on multiple counts of crimes against humanity and war crimes, including rape and the murder of more than three hundred people. The court, however, sentenced him to life in prison instead of death. Outraged online activists and student organizations quickly began mobilizing. Two days after the verdict, more than one hundred thousand protesters gathered in Dhaka's Shahbag Square to demand both the execution of Mollah and all those convicted by the ICT as well as Jamaat's permanent ban from politics. Jamaat responded with large demonstrations and violent hartals, during which dozens were killed and hundreds injured in clashes with the police. In the end, the state changed course and executed Mollah in December 2013—less than a month before the election.

Amid the controversial formation and implementation of the ICT, the AL made a second inflammatory decision that raised political tension. After Ershad's fall in 1990, a caretaker government was implemented, requiring the incumbent party to turn over political power to a nonpartisan commission shortly before the election. This arrangement had no constitutional precedent, but quickly became a unique and successful feature of Bangladeshi elections. In 1996, the thirteenth amendment to the constitution codified the caretaker system.

However, a decade after being codified, the CTG system came under attack. Entering the 2006 election cycle, the AL and BNP could not agree on who should serve as chief adviser of the CTG. The League opposed the man ultimately selected and several of his staff members resigned due to a lack of transparency. The country was on the brink of state failure. In January 2007, the military intervened to break the political stalemate, declaring a state of emergency. The two-year military-backed caretaker government attempted to reform Bangladeshi politics. It controversially pursued corruption charges against AL head Sheikh Hasina and the sons of BNP chairwoman Khaleda Zia.

In 2008, the CTG yielded its power and held elections again. The Awami League won a resounding victory and began to agitate against the caretaker system that had targeted its leader. The Supreme Court then unintentionally assisted the League with its ruling that the caretaker system was unconstitutional. In July 2011, following the Court's lead, the Bangladeshi parliament—dominated by AL representatives—passed the 15th Amendment, which repealed vital elements of the caretaker government law and ended the system's mandate entirely. The opposition BNP, which had opposed the caretaker system when the AL first promoted it, declared its intention to boycott any election not held under a neutral authority. The League's refusal to reverse this decision—along with its continuation of the ICT—were provocative actions that set the stage for severe election unrest in 2013 and 2014.

Opposition Protest and State Reprisal

The short-term provocations and contextual vulnerabilities combined to create a combustible environment entering the election cycle in 2013. However, election-related protests and violence began as early as June 2011—two and a half years before election day—when the Awami League scrapped the caretaker government. The violence had two primary perpetrators. First, elites and activists from the BNP and its ally Jamaat violently enforced a series of election hartals during the campaign period and on election day. Violators of the boycott were often beaten or killed. In response, the AL—using its supporters and state security forces—cracked down on opposition rallies. In this indiscriminate chaos, all segments of society were vulnerable.

Odhikar and the Dhaka-based Election Working Group (EWG) provided the most systematic reporting on election unrest during the January 2014 election.[28] Odhikar documented 504 people killed and more than twenty-four thousand injured in 2013 during the lead-up to the election. In the eight months after, another 146 were killed and more than six thousand injured, fifty-three killed and 1,400 injured in January alone.[29] The count of hartals was also high in 2013, forty-five nationwide and 170 regional.[30] An EWG study focusing on approximately half the constituencies in December 2013 found evidence of political meetings disrupted by rival candidates and public or private property damage during campaigning, for which the Awami League was disproportionately responsible.[31]

Violence rose significantly in the observed constituencies after the summer. Between June and August only twenty-two cases were reported, and in October only seven. The trend then reversed: 190 incidents in November and 269 in December. When the perpetrators were identified, Jamaat was responsible for 40 percent, the BNP for 26 percent, and the AL for 18 percent. For the incidents about which victim information was available, the Awami League was targeted in 46 percent of the cases, Jamaat in 15 percent, BNP in 12 percent, and other parties in 22 percent.[32] Overall, EWG's reporting implicated the BNP and Jamaat in more violence than other parties.

The Election Commission was forced to suspend polling at hundreds of centers across the country because of violence, which often began the night before elections. In several instances, election officers were killed, polling centers bombed, and ballot papers burned.[33] The police response to such attacks also resulted in deaths, as ill-trained officers fired into crowds of violent protesters. Human Rights Watch describes petrol attacks used by the opposition: "On numerous occasions, opposition party members and activists threw petrol bombs at trucks, buses, and motorized rickshaws that defied the traffic blockades or were simply parked by the side of the road. In some cases, opposition groups recruited children to carry out the attacks.... Some of the victims were children."[34]

Polling centers were often attacked and rife with ballot stuffing. Official allegations of vote rigging were lodged in more than twenty districts. In one instance, a corrupt official allegedly stamped more than four hundred ballots in favor of the Awami League. At another center, voting was allowed after the specified closing time. Opposition candidates claimed that AL supporters took over polling centers across the country to cast fake ballots. Such allegations of fraud spurred attacks. In one instance, BNP supporters allegedly took away six ballot boxes from one polling center and attacked two more centers in the same constituency. Five voters were wounded in the chaos after police fired blank shots to disperse the attackers.[35]

A portion of the opposition violence was directed at minority communities—mostly Hindus but also Christians—who traditionally vote for the League. Prominent BNP and Jamaat leaders led looters in setting fire to more than a hundred houses and shops belonging to Hindu citizens in one district. In another area, reciprocal religious violence between Muslims and Hindus resulted in voter suppression and property destruction. After the election, opposition activists targeted Christian families in the district of Jamalpur, injuring fifteen in a series of attacks. This violence accompanied efforts before election day to suppress the Hindu vote through violence and intimidation.[36]

State forces and the Awami League were also accused of carrying out extrajudicial killings against opposition leaders. According to Odhikar, thirty-nine people were killed extrajudicially in January, eleven BNP leaders and fifteen Jamaat-Shibir activists among them. The police and other security units were implicated in many of these crimes, which included nighttime abductions and individuals being shot or beaten to death. Security forces claim these deaths occurred in the crossfire of gun battles. The Dhaka-based rights organization Ain O Salish Kendra reported more than two hundred extrajudicial killings during the 2013 election cycle.[37]

The Awami League also cracked down on the media. Bangladesh's Information and Communication Technology Act of 2006, which was amended in 2009 and 2013, gives the state wide latitude to punish dissent in the name of law and order. During the election tumult, the government closed down media outlets owned by opposition supporters. Editors and reporters were also imprisoned. Odhikar concluded that the act is "violating a democratic process" and being used to oppress human rights advocates and regime critics.[38]

In sum, the increase in election violence in 2013 and 2014 was related in part to a unique set of provocations that increased political tension. The violence, however, was likely exacerbated by the weakness or absence of violence-prevention tools during the election cycle.

Prevention in 2014

Violence-prevention tools both individually and in tandem can positively affect election stability. They can both improve the quality of election administration and moderate potentially violent actors. Overall, many of the most common PEV instruments in con- flict-prone democracies were generally weak or absent in Bangladesh's 2014 election cycle. The most institutionalized domestic tool was election management and adminis- tration, which still received a lackluster score because of partisanship and incompetence in 2014. The strongest overall was preventive diplomacy. The international community took a keen interest in resolving Bangladesh's political conflict. However, its large role indicates Bangladesh's weak domestic PEV practices and the consequent collapse into widespread violence. On the one hand was the partisan security sector, unsystematic peace messaging, incomplete election monitoring, and weak civic and voter education, youth programming, and voter consultation efforts (fuzzy set score: 0.25). On the other was extreme election violence (1.0).

The consistently weak prevention is in part unique to the 2014 election cycle, which was boycotted not only by opposition parties but also by many peacebuilding practi- tioners and diplomats, who refused to legitimize the process with their participation. Some previously strong instruments were substandard in 2014, such as election mon- itoring. However, many have been consistently weak or entirely absent during the post-Ershad democratic period. In short, the country's previously deficient PEV tools were effectively abandoned in 2014, which facilitated the most violent election in the country's history.

Security-Sector Engagement

An effective security sector is vital to guaranteeing security at the polls and protecting election materials by providing both deterrence and quick response. Yet the problems in the 2014 Bangladesh election cycle suggest that the sector—which includes the army, the police, and the Rapid Action Battalion (RAB)—was neither adequately prepared nor engaged. No clear regulatory framework is in place for security, governance of the sector is weak, and the sector is considered increasingly partisan—at times protecting its patrons regardless of who is in power.

During the 2014 election, security services at times used appropriate measures but also and frequently used excessive and deadly force. Witnesses claim that the police and RAB in particular used rubber bullets and live ammunition improperly and without justification. Protesters were shot dead amid street chaos and sometimes deliberately executed. Widespread vote rigging, ballot theft, and polling center destruction that went unimpeded by security forces are each alleged.[39] These acts of omission and commission contributed to the widespread violence.

Electoral violence, though, reflects broader problems with national governance and regulation. The Bangladesh Army is widely respected by the public, but at various times its domestic role becomes overtly political.[40] The military has cultivated an independent economic and political power base outside the control of civilian leaders, who often pander to the army for political support. During the election, Sheikh Hasina promised to provide "whatever [is] necessary in [the] future for a modern army."[41] These promises, along with guarantees to preserve the army's economic interests, worked to prevent military intervention at the height of election conflict with the opposition.[42]

The police are perceived as—and often are—corrupt, ineffective, and partisan. They are alleged to routinely abuse the Code of Criminal Procedure, make arrests without a warrant, detain citizens, and delay trials.[43] An editorial in Bangladesh's *Financial Express* was explicit that policing "has become an industry of producing victims of torture and fabrication of criminal charges against civilians and political opponents.... Corruption has replaced the chain of command within the police."[44] The Asian Human Rights Commission argues that "Arbitrary arrest, detention, fabrication of criminal cases, torture, and threats of extrajudicial executions are systematically used for extorting an unimaginable amount of money from the poor every year."[45] Odhikar reports that the police were responsible for nearly half of the 2,425 extrajudicial killings between 2001 and 2014.[46]

Despite high-profile success combating terrorism and illegal arms and drug smuggling since it was established in 2004, the RAB has been implicated in widespread human rights abuses during and outside election cycles. Odhikar reports that it is also responsible for nearly half of the documented 1,596 crossfire deaths since 2001.[47] RAB violence is at times directed against political opponents of the state, but is also part of a general abuse of power within the security apparatus.[48]

Politicization of security-sector governance impedes effective and accountable regulation. Although some opposition violence in 2014 was undoubtedly prevented—even corrupt security is better than anarchy—the often indiscriminate use of force and open partisanship certainly contributed to the unrest. By most accounts, the sector's violence and corruption increased during the Awami League's most recent tenure. A report on election violence during the 2008 election noted that "the security officers and/or police were very rarely recorded as being perpetrators... of the violence."[49] The evidence from 2013 and 2014 therefore indicates a rapid expansion of state-led election violence. Bangladesh's security sector presents little guarantee for election security (fuzzy set score: 0.25).

Election Management and Administration

An election management body is designed to deter violence by enforcing codes of conduct and by implementing a transparent and fair election process. The Election Commission of Bangladesh (ECB) has significant related de jure powers, but minimal de facto capacity. Election guidelines are clear and mostly comprehensive by international standards. They are, however, implemented unfairly, partially, or not at all. Rules regarding voter registration, party financing, codes of conduct, and security provision, and other election regulations are often violated with impunity for reasons that vary from lack of ability to partisanship.

During the 2013–2014 election cycle, opposition parties and many voters did not consider the ECB to be an independent body but rather a tool of the incumbent Awami League. The ECB's otherwise strong regulatory framework thus only partially met international standards. Bangladesh's unique caretaker system—an institutional addendum to the ECB—was also eliminated, which added to the perception of partisan election management. The Electoral Integrity Project, which assessed the quality of elections held between 2012 and 2014, called Bangladesh's contest a failure and ranked it at 113 of the 127 polls analyzed.[50]

The country's electoral legal framework is a sound one with respect to conducting democratic elections in line with international best practices. The constitution ensures citizens' political rights and guarantees freedoms of association, assembly, movement, and expression. Electoral legislation ensures the right to vote and to be elected in periodic elections under universal and equal suffrage by a secret vote.

Article 118 of the constitution provides for the Election Commission of Bangladesh, which consists of a chief election commissioner and not more than four election commissioners. The president is empowered to appoint the chief election commissioner and other election commissioners as necessary. The ECB exercises its functions as a formally independent body and is subject only to the constitution and other codified law. The constitution and Representation of the People Order (RPO) of 1972 assert that executive authorities are obliged to assist the ECB in the discharge of its functions. The ECB in turn has the power to require any person or authority to perform any necessary functions for the smooth functioning of an election.[51]

The constitution and RPO also assign specific electoral functions to the ECB. These guidelines create a comprehensive administrative structure vested with significant autonomy and authority; liberal rules for candidate nominations; controls on election expenses, campaign financing, and reporting of expenditures; detailed descriptions of polling procedures; instructions for counting and reporting of election results; and provisions related to election offenses and violations.[52]

Despite the ECB's reasonably well-developed and institutionalized powers, it has come under scathing criticism for being at times ineffectual and partisan. The Asian Human Rights Commission writes that it "has succumbed under the regime's desire to extend its power into perpetuity."[53] An interviewed senior official at Transparency International Bangladesh (TIB) claimed that the commission has a "hardware problem, not a software problem"—the commission's mandate is strong but its leadership is weak and corrupt. The ECB relies on the government for appointing commissioners, recruiting staff, discharging functions, maintaining law and order, and managing financial issues. ECB commissioners thus mirror the government's deeply partisan nature. In addition, another interviewee explained, the ruling party frequently stacks the ECB with openly partisan officials, often timed with the beginning of an election cycle.

The commission's mandated duties have been increasingly ignored as the body has become intensely partisan. TIB reports that Bangladesh's elections have been tainted by problems formally within the ECB's purview, including fake voter lists, irregularities in voter list preparation, population imbalances within constituencies, lack of party expenditure reporting, and poor distribution of voter identification cards. TIB also asserts that ECB officials have received corrupt promotions and potentially benefited financially through fraudulent disbursement of state and international funds for election-related programs and training.[54]

Local politicians and civil society leaders noted at the time numerous instances of the ECB's failing to carry out its mandate during the 2014 election. One representative from the Khulna City Corporation claimed the election commission ignored her complaints about opposition parties violating campaign law. A Khulna district adjutant said he believed "that 80 percent of election violence can be prevented if the candidates followed the election code of conduct [RPO]." Another claimed that the ECB has the power to implement a free and fair election, but not the capacity to challenge violent actors who undermine its efforts. Opposition political parties were equally critical. An official from the Bangladesh Jatiya Party said the 2014 election was carried out "by the incumbent Awami League in cooperation with the toothless electoral commission."

The commission's various deficiencies have occurred despite significant international technical assistance. In the lead-up to the 2014 election, the UNDP coordinated two projects to strengthen the ECB's capacity. These programs provided many necessary commodities, including security seals for ballot boxes, indelible ink markers, laptops, printers, and scanners, as well as technical assistance for training. The UNDP also developed training materials, handbooks, and guidelines for election officials, assisted in establishing the ECB's Media Centre, and conducted numerous staff training sessions on a variety of election-related topics.[55] These efforts were aimed at enhancing the professionalism and consistency of the election process, but clearly failed in the presence of intense partisanship.

The ECB's assent to the Awami League's elimination of the caretaker system fed the perception of the commission's partisanship, which in turn enflamed the opposition's violent street protests. Indeed, one ECB staff member claimed that his position within the election commission restricted his ability to speak out in support of the caretaker system. The role of the CTG as a sui generis PEV tool is difficult to assess, however. Available data on party conflicts show violence remaining the same or escalating during election cycles administered under the CTG in 1996 and 2001.[56] This likely indicates the difficult task the CTG has faced: bringing order to a tumultuous political system when the stakes and tensions are highest. One cannot accurately estimate the extent of conflict it prevented. Given the hyperpartisan atmosphere in which it was eliminated in 2011—and the resulting hartals and election boycott—it is undeniable that the CTG's absence intensified election violence even though its presence had a mixed role.

In sum, the ECB is legally empowered with functions that indicate a strong mandate. Its formal independence is limited, however, and the informal and often corrupt infiltration by incumbent party officials has dramatically undermined its autonomy and capacity (fuzzy set score: 0.25).

Preventive Diplomacy

When efforts are sustained and targeted, preventive international diplomacy can pressure political elites to make difficult compromises or moderate overheated rhetoric. In Bangladesh, various international actors engaged in early and robust preventive diplomacy. Eight months before the election, the UN sent a special envoy to facilitate negotiations throughout the election cycle.[57] It was joined by the United States, which issued strongly worded condemnations of the preelection violence and political intransigence. After the election, the UN, United States, and other Commonwealth countries rebuked the process and called for new elections. Yet despite significant international leverage, preventive diplomacy failed.[58]

The international community intervened diplomatically as violence escalated. Most prominently, the UN was actively engaged in conflict mediation during the year leading up to the election. Oscar Fernandez-Taranco first visited the country in May 2013 as the secretary-general's special envoy and met with the Awami League's Sheikh Hasina, the BNP's Khaleda Zia, the chief election commissioner, and other political leaders to call for more constructive dialogue in pursuit of free and fair elections.[59] His efforts, however, failed to change the political dynamic.

As chaos escalated, Fernandez-Taranco returned to Bangladesh seven months later to deliver a letter from Ban Ki-moon that called for constructive dialogue and a nonviolent election. He again met with political leaders to urge compromise.[60] The same month, the UN high commissioner for human rights condemned Bangladesh's main parties: "Whatever their differences, political leaders on both sides must halt their destructive brinkmanship... they must... use their influence to bring this violence to an immediate halt and seek a solution to this crisis through dialogue."[61]

The United States, which has important economic influence in Bangladesh, was also closely attentive to the situation. In September 2013, U.S. Secretary of State John Kerry wrote letters to Prime Minister Sheikh Hasina and opposition leader Khaleda Zia. According to news reports, Kerry's private letter said, "The USA along with the international community is concerned about the political situation in Bangladesh." He also encouraged the respective leaders "to engage in constructive dialogue to find a way forward towards free, fair and credible elections."[62] In Washington, the State Department spokesperson said that "nonviolence is essential to any solution" in Bangladesh.[63]

Similar statements from the State Department continued. About two weeks before election day, it issued a press release condemning the violence, urging peaceful participation, pressing the parties to compromise, and declaring its intention to withhold U.S. observers.[64] This last action was an attempt to delegitimize the electoral process, thereby forcing the AL to postpone the election or negotiate with the BNP.

The League, however, ignored the pressure and persisted with the election, declaring a democratic mandate at its conclusion. The day after the election, the State Department issued another strongly worded condemnation, expressing disappointment in the election, which did not appear "to credibly express the will of the Bangladeshi people." It encouraged the parties to engage in "immediate dialogue" and recommended new elections "as soon as possible." It also called on political leaders "to ensure law and order and refrain from supporting and fomenting violence, especially against minority communities, inflammatory rhetoric, and intimidation."[65]

Other members of the international community joined in. The European Union High Representative for Foreign Affairs and Security Policy Catherine Ashton issued a press statement calling for new elections and denouncing "the acts of violence which occurred in the run-up to and during the elections and particularly attacks against the most vulnerable populations, including women and children as well as religious and ethnic minorities.... the people of Bangladesh were not given an opportunity to express fully their democratic choice" because of dysfunctional electoral conditions.[66]

The UN and Canada also went public. A spokesperson for Ban Ki-moon said the secretary-general was saddened that parties could not come to an agreement to produce "peaceful, all-inclusive" elections, which were instead "characterized by polarization and low participation." Echoing this sentiment, the Canadian Foreign Minister John Baird said his country advocates "a new national election and urges all parties to reach an agreement soon that would allow the next election to be truly participatory, with results that all Bangladeshis will see as credible."[67] India, however, supported the election process, provided two election observers, and endorsed the outcome. Russia and China did the same.

In sum, robust preventive diplomacy efforts were made before and after the election. The various official public statements were not purely altruistic, however. The international community, particularly the United States, has important economic, security, and geostrategic interests in Bangladesh and the wider region. Regardless of intent, however, preventive diplomacy efforts were robust in 2013 and 2014 (fuzzy set score: 1.0).

Peace Messaging

A successful peace-messaging campaign can reduce conflict by promoting nonviolence in the election cycle and across the country, thereby altering attitudes toward conflict. Peace messaging in Bangladesh, however, is neither geographically widespread nor robust where it is launched. Campaigns remain ad hoc, isolated, and—in 2014—reactionary. The government began a general social media campaign for peace only after election violence erupted. In Bangladesh, the messaging barely met international standards and had no discernable effect on violent behavior.

The Sheikh Hasina government carried out the most geographically widespread messaging effort of the 2014 election. Using text messages, the election commission contacted citizens to promote unity and peace, counter misinformation, and warn about the consequences of violence. It also urged citizens to vote: "Please go to cast your vote without any fear and hassle."[68] However, given the widely held perception that the commission was a partisan tool, the messages seemed to have limited effect.

Other than the ECB's, no systematic messaging campaign was attempted during the preelection period. A senior official at the Dhaka-based Center for Policy Dialogue asserted that no real peace movement activities occurred during the election cycle. Despite a few informal dialogue sessions that were held, he argued, civil society organizations in Bangladesh are often overtly partisan and unable to conduct legitimate peace-messaging campaigns or dialogue sessions. A staff member of the International Republican Institute (IRI) confirmed the lack of any systematic campaign.

Many observers of Bangladeshi politics are skeptical that a voter-focused peace-messaging campaign would effectively counter elite mobilization for violence, but some support the approach. The U.S. State Department's Bureau of Conflict and Stabilization Operations began organizing peace-messaging programs in Bangladesh after the election, which include dialogue sessions with local democratic stakeholders and public service announcements on television and social media that promote peaceful conflict resolution. A former city councilor advocated this approach, saying a countrywide "say no to violence" public awareness campaign was needed.

In sum, the 2014 election saw limited peace messaging, in part because such campaigns have no historical precedent in the country (fuzzy set score: 0.25).

Civic and Voter Education

An effective civic and voter education program can reduce violence by educating voters on democratic procedures and responsibilities, empowering vulnerable communities, and enhancing the legitimacy and transparency of the electoral process. Yet such efforts in the 2014 election cycle were weakly organized and had limited breadth. In the past, nongovernmental organizations (NGOs) have mobilized some civic and voter education campaigns, but the controversy surrounding the 2014 election impeded similar efforts. Civic and voter education is not ordinarily strong in the country. International NGOs and political observers lament the poor quality of voter education in Bangladesh and often argue it should receive more funding.

The ECB engaged in minimal voter education efforts, using text messages to encourage voter registration and to provide information about voting procedures. An IRI program officer argued that, because of the turmoil surrounding the election, normal civic education efforts were either reduced or did not take place at all. Similarly, field staff at the International Foundation for Electoral Systems (IFES) confirmed that civic education programming was drastically cut despite the clear needs. Before violence began to spiral out of control, IFES teamed with People Against Violence in Elections on a workshop that focused on democratic norms, free and fair elections, the role of the election commission, and conflict mediation. These workshops, however, were isolated and infrequent.

Many voters, government administrators, and politicians argue that greater civil society involvement in election education could lessen violence. Those involved in local activism claimed that election violence decreased in areas where civil society groups worked to resolve political disputes. One government official said that developing an education system should be treated as an "emergency" for free and fair elections. Religious exchanges during the 2014 election cycle also brought limited but important conflict reduction. In the Tala upazila in the Sathkhira district, a local Muslim leader regularly presides over a Hindu holy festival and a notable Hindu community leader helps arrange a Muslim religious program. Such efforts have been successful in alleviating interreligious tension and could be replicated.

The severely limited presence of civic and voter education in 2014 differed from previous elections. The Election Working Group has promoted issue-based voting, nonviolence, candidate accountability, and increased women's participation since 2006. Its programming includes various outreach efforts, including distribution of voter guides at newspaper stands, tea stalls, and during Friday prayers. The group also attempts to raise awareness on the registration process, particularly among ethnic and religious minorities and in low-income communities.[69] Such activities were limited during the 2014 campaign, however. Voter education efforts were minimal and failed to reach a significant portion of the population (fuzzy set score: 0.25). Activists and observers note that ignorance and apathy about the election process remain rampant.

Election Monitoring and Mapping

Effective election monitoring and mapping can reduce violence by deterring potentially violent actors, identifying areas of risk, and facilitating a rapid security response to violent incidents. In 2014, Bangladesh's election monitoring was unsystematic and significantly weaker than in previous elections. Domestic observer organizations scaled back their preelection and election day activity. The international community—including the United States, European Union, and international NGOs—refused to provide or train election observers to protest an electoral process tainted by Awami League partisanship. This differed from previous elections, during which international and domestic observers spanned the country, often present in all districts and constituencies. In 2008, local civil society conducted a sophisticated monitoring and mapping campaign. However, during the 2013–2014 election cycle, monitoring and mapping efforts only partially met international standards.

Local NGOs conducted the most substantial observation efforts, which were still weaker than in previous elections. The election organization Janipop observed elections in six of three hundred constituencies, including two on election day.[70] The EWG carried out observations before and during the election in selected constituencies. Long-term observers were deployed in 140 constituencies in fifty-three of sixty-four districts across the country. Some instances of violence were documented, but no systematic program of mapping and reporting could prevent future violence. On election day, EWG sent observers to seventy-five of three hundred constituencies in forty-three of sixty-four districts. This deployment was smaller than intended because of violence, uncooperative local administers, and security forces keeping observers away from the polls following the orders of local MPs.[71] In contrast, EWG's 2008 observation effort used 178,000 monitors across all three hundred constituencies.[72]

Odhikar halted its monitoring and mapping program in 2014 in response to state coercion. For the December 2008 election, it used the Election Violence Education and Resolution (EVER) monitoring tool developed by the IFES. EVER is a multifaceted framework that investigates and documents the type of violence, its perpetrator, and its motivation. Documented violence was reported to party and security officials to assist in conflict mitigation strategies. These activities—though limited in geographic scope—met the international standard for electoral monitoring and mapping. After the election, however, Odhikar's director was jailed and similar efforts were not replicated for the January 2014 election; the government claimed that Odhikar had fabricated its data on police violence.

International NGOs also ended their monitoring and mapping programs, following the lead of the international actors protesting the election; the Indian government, which supported the election, sent two observers. The Washington-based National Democratic Institute engaged in only limited efforts to train monitors in 2014 and cancelled its scheduled monitoring activities for election day, which it had conducted during parliamentary elections in 1991, 1996, 2001, and 2008. It had trained citizen observers in advance on impartial and transparent election observation. Given the insecurity leading up to the election, however, these observers were not systematically deployed.[73] The IRI also abandoned its observer efforts, which in 2008 had included a high-level observer mission for parliamentary elections.

In sum, monitoring and mapping activities during the 2013–2014 election cycle were deeply flawed: voters and local officials complained of inadequate monitoring efforts,[74] violence and political obstruction undermined EWG's partial monitoring effort, and international observers boycotted the election (fuzzy set score: 0.25). This was all a distinct departure from the 2008 election.

Voter Consultations

By creating the perception of accountability, campaign consultations between voters and candidates can alleviate animosity and reduce the tendency to violence. Voter consultations, though, were effectively absent in the 2014 election cycle. As in previous elections, NGOs held only perfunctory sessions and these efforts never achieved the seriousness or systematization that that had the potential to reduce political disaffection, an interviewee reported. Abysmal voter turnout, which according to some sources declined from 87 percent in 2008 to 22 percent in 2014, is symptomatic of the absence of constructive party engagement with the electorate (fuzzy set score: 0.25).[75]

Youth Programming

Given the prominent role youth often play in election violence, employment and training programs that target them can have important pacifying effects. Yet despite the urgent need, related programming remains largely absent. Specific organizations, such as the Bangladesh Youth Leadership Center, provide leadership and skills training that include the promotion of toleration, diversity, and inclusiveness. Another, Jaago, focuses on primary education for underprivileged children. Although other comparable groups exist, no systematic or direct effort is in place across the country to improve the economic well-being and democratic values of youth. Since the 2014 election, some groups have begun to hold youth dialogue sessions about social issues. The Dhaka-based Bangladesh Institute for Peace and Security Studies held an interfaith dialogue for youth on issues of social harmony between religious groups. This and similar efforts, however, remain geographically isolated.

The absence of youth programming is striking given the widespread belief in its necessity. The secretary of the Communist Party in a southern district claimed that unemployed youth use their "muscle" for generating income: they are paid by political parties to enforce hartals or protest in the street. An official from the Chittagong City Corporation said that student politics must be reformed. Constraining or banning campus politics has received increasing attention, particularly after the 2014 election, during which the youth wings of Jamaat and the Awami League were active perpetrators of violence. Nevertheless, the most was not made of youth programming in 2014 (fuzzy set score: 0.25).

Assessing Prevention

Bangladesh's 2014 election is a difficult case study when it comes to assessing the success of prevention tools. Because most instruments were weak or absent, their positive affect cannot be fully evaluated. However, Bangladesh does confirm the counterfactual of this book's hypothesis: in the absence of strong prevention, levels of violence were high. Moreover, for seven of eight instruments, the counterfactual holds: expected positive behavior of a strong practice does not occur but the negative counterpart of a weak or absent practice does. This counterfactual does not necessarily indicate that a stronger tool would have had the desired impact, only that no impact was discernable without the tool present. What negative activity occurred in the absence of the prevention tool designed to stop it?

Security-Sector Engagement

In the absence of a nonpartisan security sector, party activists in Bangladesh clashed in pre- and postelection protests and opposition party cadres looted polling stations. In addition, given poor governance and regulation, the security services often used disproportionate force, contributing to election violence.

Election Management and Administration

In the absence of a nonpartisan election management body to enforce party codes of conduct and mediate party disputes, technical violations of Bangladesh's election law went unaddressed and opposition parties rebelled against the election process.

Preventive Diplomacy

Despite strong preventive diplomatic intervention by intergovernmental organizations and prominent international powers, Bangladeshi political elites defied predicted behavior and continued to engage in bickering and violence. This paradoxical outcome is explored further.

Peace Messaging

In the absence of an inclusive and widespread peace-messaging campaign, Bangladesh's party elites were able to mobilize supporters for violent protests and property destruction without having to overcome the enhanced normative cost such actions face when effective peace programs are present.

Civic and Voter Education

Because only limited and ad hoc civic and voter education efforts were in place to legitimize the democratic process, party elites in Bangladesh were able to more easily mobilize
supporters to violently oppose the election.

Monitoring and Mapping

In the absence of a systematic monitoring and mapping program to identify violence-prone areas, Bangladeshi authorities and security forces were slow to respond to
violence. Party supporters seeking to carry out violence, harassment, or intimidation
were enabled to do so.

Voter Consultations

In the absence of close connections between political parties and voters, Bangladesh's
parties are viewed as corrupt vehicles for elite power. Ordinary citizens have little incentive
to participate in the process or attempt to hold election officials accountable. Disillusioned
and frustrated citizens joined or passively supported the disruption of an electoral process
that did little for them.

Youth Programs

In the absence of programming to create economic opportunities and democratic buy-in
among youth, young Bangladeshis were prey to political party youth wings, such as Shibir
or Chhatra League, that provided payment and purpose to a poor and disenchanted population. Bangladeshi youth were thus routinely implicated in election-related violence.

The speculated causal relationship between strong prevention practices and low levels
of violence is further affirmed by the correlation of historically weak PEV practices in 2013
and 2014 with the country's highest amount of election violence. Of the eight prevention
tools, four were weaker than in past elections, three were the same, and one—preventive
diplomacy—was stronger (table 2.1). Although this assessment is less systematic than that
for the 2014 election, the negative trend lines of PEV quality and the spread and duration
of implementation in Bangladesh are in little doubt. This finding offers additional counterfactual evidence for the hypothesis: not only did weak prevention instruments correlate
with high levels of violence, as predicted; but the 2014 election cycle's relatively weaker
PEV tools also correlated with relatively higher violence.

Although the strength of each instrument is important, theoretical and empirical interaction effects are as well. In Bangladesh, the uniform weakness of prevention tools created
interactions that likely exacerbated election violence. One way to organize and understand this interaction is to focus on the implementing actor, which creates a typology of
state-centered, civil society–centered, and international actor–centered tools. The categories are not mutually exclusive, but they provide a useful organizing principle.

The security sector and election management are primarily state-centered. NGOs and
international assistance can of course enhance these efforts, but the state has the primary

Table 2.1 Prevention in Historical Perspective, Bangladesh

PEV MODEL	SCORE	2014 ROLE	OVER PAST ELECTIONS
Election Management and Administration	0.25	Election regulations partially implemented; ECB politically co-opted, CTG eliminated	Weaker
Security-Sector Engagement	0.25	Police, army, RAB, and courts co-opted	Weaker
Preventive Diplomacy	1.0	United Nations, U.S. involvement; international condemnation of results	Stronger
Peace Messaging	0.25	Post-hoc ECB efforts weak and partisan; No significant CSO programming	No Change
Civic and Voter Education	0.25	ECB text messages, early IFES programming	Weaker
Monitoring and Mapping	0.25	Limited local observation mission; international monitoring revoked	Weaker
Voter Consultations	0.25	Extremely weak, but minimally present	No Change
Youth Programming	0.25	Some minimal skills training but not election related	No Change

Source: Author's compilation

responsibility for instituting and maintaining security and election law. In Bangladesh, the partisanship and incompetence of both tools compounded their individual weaknesses. The ECB's independent mandate was for the most part hijacked by the Awami League, which constitutionally altered the election process by eliminating the caretaker government and stacking the commission with party functionaries. Part of the ECB's purview is election security, but because the ruling party is in de facto control, it had no incentive to do so and no alternative nonpartisan institution was in place to stop the violence. The role of the security sector and the ECB as prevention tools was therefore undermined by the same problem of state co-optation, which created a highly negative interaction effect. Strengthening the mandate and independence of the election commission against the interest of the political party in power at that time is therefore vital for future elections. The ECB's weakness compounded the fears of the opposition, which took to the streets in violent action that the security sector could not control.

Civil society actors, including the media, universities, and international NGOs that train local civil society groups and operate independent programs, are important players. Although the state has an important role, civil society often coordinates peace messaging, civic and voter education, election monitoring, voter consultations, and youth programming. In Bangladesh, both the partisanship and disengagement of civil society in 2013 and 2014 had a negative interaction effect. The potentially moderating impact of youth and voter education and peace messaging was absent. Violence grew in extent and ferocity before and during the election, and no robust monitoring efforts were in place to document and potentially deter it. The goal of grassroots prevention efforts is of course not necessarily to avert violence, but their unvarying weakness compounds the negative impact of any single instrument's deficiency. This is particularly true in Bangladesh, where the government did not operate as a nonpartisan body and therefore could not fill the gap left by civil society's inaction.

However, it seems unlikely that stronger civil society–centered prevention programs would have substantially reduced the chaos in 2013 and 2014. That violence was led by opposition political elites who were responding violently to the Awami League's actions. The weakened integrity of this tool created a cascade effect that likely would have overwhelmed even robust programming. Yet these types of prevention tools could make a difference. In particular, stronger monitoring and mapping would facilitate faster and potentially preemptive action to secure polling stations under attack or pacify violent crowds. Civil society PEV instruments, however, would likely have primarily addressed the symptoms of the violence rather than the causes.

Preventive diplomacy is the only purely international PEV practice in that, by definition, only foreign countries or international organizations can intervene as diplomatic actors. As noted, the international community took a strong interest in resolving Bangladesh's election impasse and violence. Preventive diplomacy, though, is often tied to the weaknesses of the other prevention tools. If an independent election commission implemented sound election laws, a nonpartisan security sector punished violent actors, and a vibrant and apolitical civil society sector trained citizens on democratic values, international intervention would likely not be necessary. Instead, violence in Bangladesh spiraled out of control and international actors felt compelled to intervene.

However, their diplomacy failed to induce conciliation, prevent violence, or force a new election after the Awami League declared victory. The most direct answer for this failure is the general inability of international actors in the face of weak political institutions. The infrastructure for a successful and peaceful election was simply not present. Moreover, an oppositional political culture had already been activated by the time international actors intervened. The BNP had anticipated that an election boycott featuring violent hartals would compel concessions in its favor. The AL believed the BNP's violent protests were undermining the opposition's popularity. Each side therefore believed violence was in its interest. Because no strong domestic prevention tools were in place to challenge this bellicosity, the international community was impotent. Preventive diplomacy was attempting to force a compromise that did not interest either party.

An additional complicating factor was India's negative and implicitly provocative diplomacy. The incumbent Awami League is considered pro-Indian, secular, and anti-Islamist, which endears it to the Indian government. India is also competing with China for regional influence, which makes it eager to maintain close ties with the government in Dhaka. Consequently, India countered prevailing international opinion and supported the Hasina government's preelection intransigence and resulting election victory. A week after the election, Indian Prime Minister Manmohan Singh called Sheikh Hasina to wish her "success in the endeavor to strengthen democratic institutions in Bangladesh."[76] As mentioned earlier, India became one of only three major powers—along with Russia and China—to recognize the AL victory.

In sum, the weakness or absence of PEV programming correlated with the expected outcome: high levels of violence. The evidence, though, is not conclusive that stronger engagement would have prevented violence. However, coupling a nonpartisan and effective election commission and security sector with expanded election monitoring would likely have had important mitigating effects. Adding substantive peace messaging, civic and voter education, voter consultations, and youth programming might have made a marginal contribution to peace.

Conclusion

Election violence has been common throughout Bangladesh's history. Beginning with a violent independence movement against Pakistan, Bangladeshi politics has become synonymous with assassinations, boycotts, hartals, riots, murder, military intervention, and state repression. Even within this context, however, the January 2014 election was exceptionally violent, more deadly than any before it. Several hundred people died amid the violent protests, state suppression, and campaign conflict. Understanding what exacerbated traditional drivers of political and electoral violence in Bangladesh and what positive role stronger prevention could have played is therefore critical.

The January 2014 election cycle was unique for two reasons: first, the Awami League's action against the opposition, and, second, the weakness of conventional PEV instruments. The AL's decision to implement the war crimes tribunal and abrogate the caretaker government system had a markedly deleterious effect on political stability. The secular-Islamic schism that has defined Bangladeshi politics since independence widened considerably. The BNP and its Islamist allies in Jamaat felt under siege from a ruling party ostensibly seeking a one-party state. Key opposition leaders were executed as the institutional mechanism for nonpartisan elections was dismantled. The resulting BNP decision to boycott the election and announce hartals—however ill-advised in hindsight, because it likely would have won the election—created an untenable and inevitably violent situation. To retain its power, the AL appeared to be undermining the country's democracy. Bangladesh's long-standing cycle of political violence therefore recurred at an even larger scale.

Although the political context of the election significantly raised the probability of violence, the weakness of PEV tools likely exacerbated it. The partisan character of the election commission and the security sector was also particularly harmful. These two institutions play an important and interconnected role in preserving transparency and security during an election. Additionally, the absence of systematic election monitoring enabled violent players to act with impunity. Nonexistent youth programming could not mitigate the influx of mostly young men into violent youth wings that follow party commands. Finally, other preventive tools—such as civic and voter education, voter consultations, and peace messaging—were not used to alleviate tension and foster democratic values. The decision of international actors and local civil society groups to withdraw existing prevention programming only facilitated violence and failed to stop the election. In this environment, even strong preventive diplomacy could do little. The deadliest election in Bangladesh's history, then, was caused by the confluence of two factors: an extraordinary level of antagonism between the two primary parties and historically weak prevention measures.

Notes

1. Kamrun Nahar, *Political Violence in Bangladesh: Nature, Causes and Consequences* (Dhaka: Shrabon Prokashani, 2013), p. 28.

2. International Crisis Group, "Executive Summary – Bangladesh: Back to the Future," June 13, 2012, www.crisisgroup.org/en/regions/asia/south-asia/bangladesh/226-bangladesh-back-to-the-future.aspx.

3. Human Rights Watch, "Bangladesh: Security Forces Kill Protestors," August 1, 2013, www.hrw.org/news/2013/08/01/bangladesh-security-forces-kill-protesters.

4. The strength or weakness of prevention during the 2014 election was primarily evaluated during two fieldwork trips in July and November 2014, which included more than forty key-informant interviews with election officials, politicians, journalists, academics, CSO leaders, diplomats, and students. In addition, two focus group dialogues including key election stakeholders were conducted in October and November 2014. This chapter benefited from the research assistance of the Bangladesh Institute for Peace and Security Studies in Dhaka, Ian Proctor, Nirabh Koirala, and the comments and suggestions from this volume's collaborators.

5. Jason Burke, "Bangladesh opposition parties vow to continue protests as violence mars polls," *Guardian*, January 6, 2014, www.theguardian.com/world/2014/jan/05/bangladesh. The Dhaka-based human rights organization Odhikar reported 504 killed in political violence between January and August 2013. Other news sources reported around three hundred killed over the course of the year. See Mahfuz Anam, "A Picture and a Train," *Daily Star*, November 29, 2013; Maher Sattar, "Bangladesh's Year of Violence," *Diplomat*, August 13, 2013. No definitive count of those killed has been established.

6. Bangladesh's government estimates the death toll at more than three million, whereas some independent research indicates only about a half million. Some Pakistani sources deny the events altogether.

7. Owen Bennett Jones, *Pakistan: Eye of the Storm* (New Haven, CT: Yale University Press, 2009).

8. David Lewis, *Bangladesh: Politics, Economy and Civil Society* (Cambridge: Cambridge University Press, 2011).

9. Ashok Kapur and Ygendra Malik, "Bangladesh: Government Institutions," *Government and Politics in South Asia*, 7th ed. (Boulder, CO: Westview Press, 2014).

10. Percentages calculated from data in M. Moniruzzaman, "Party Politics and Political Violence in Bangladesh: Issues, Manifestation and Consequences," *South Asian Survey* 16, no. 1 (2009).

11. S. Aminul Islam, "The Predicament of Democratic Consolidation in Bangladesh," *Bangladesh E-Journal of Sociology* 3, no. 2 (2006).

12. Mahdin Mahboob, "Time to ban student politics?" *Dhaka Tribune*, February 2, 2014, www.dhakatribune.com/op-ed/2014/feb/02/time-ban-student-politics.

13. Moniruzzaman, "Party Politics," pp. 94–95.

14. HRW, "The Torture of Tasneem Khalil: How the Bangladesh Military Abuses Its Power Under the State of Emergency," *Human Rights Watch* 20, no.1 (February 2008), www.hrw.org/reports/2008/bangladesh0208/bangladesh0208web.pdf.

15. Odhikar, "Total Extra-Judicial Killings from January 2001–August 2014," 2015, http://odhikar.org/statistics/killed-by-law-enforcement-agencies/; Odhikar, "Crossfire/Gunfight from 2001–August 2014," 2015, http://odhikar.org/statistics/killed-by-law-enforcement-agencies/.

16. Harry Blair, "Party Overinstitutionalization, Contestation, and Democratic Degradation in Bangladesh," in *Routledge Handbook of South Asian Politics: India, Pakistan, Bangladesh, Sri Lanka, and Nepal*, ed. Paul Brass (London: Routledge, 2013).

17. The Upazila Parishad Act 2009 and Union Parishad Act 2009 are recent attempts to decentralize Bangladesh's power distribution. Sara Hossain, "Confronting Curtailments: Attempts to Rebuild Independence of the Judiciary in Bangladesh," in *Routledge Handbook*.

18. Amnesty International, "Bangladesh: Attacks on Members of the Hindu Minority," Document no. ASA 13/006/2001 (London: Amnesty International, 2001), www.amnesty.org/en/documents/asa13/006/2001/en/.

19. Anbarasan Ethirajan, "Bangladesh 'persecution' panel reports on 2001 violence," BBC News, December 2, 2011, www.bbc.co.uk/news/world-asia-15987644.
20. Minorities at Risk, "Assessment for Hindus in Bangladesh," last modified December 2006, www.cidcm.umd.edu/mar/assessment.asp?groupId=77102.
21. Ahrar Ahmad, "Bangladesh in 2013: Year of Confusions, Confrontations, and Concerns," *Asian Survey* 54, no. 1 (2013): 190–98.
22. The overthrow and assassination of Mujib delayed any trial for war crimes committed during independence. Subsequent BNP governments have fought war crimes investigations. Despite the controversy surrounding the trials, Jamaat's role in the 1971 violence is well documented.
23. "Discrepancy in Dhaka," *Economist*, December 8, 2012, www.economist.com/blogs/banyan/2012/12/bangladesh.
24. Human Rights Watch, "Bangladesh: Government Backtracks on Rights," February 1, 2013, www.hrw.org/news/2013/02/01/bangladesh-government-backtracks-rights.
25. Joseph Allchin, "The Midlife Crisis of Bangladesh," *Foreign Policy*, December 21, 2012, www.foreignpolicy.com/articles/2012/12/21/the_midlife_crisis_of_bangladesh?page=full&wp_login_redirect=0.
26. Sir Desmond de Silva, "The Bangladesh War Crimes Tribunal should be internationalised - for the sake of the nation's future," *No Peace Without Justice*, October 25, 2014, www.npwj.org/ICC/Bangladesh-War-Crimes-Tribunal-should-be-internationalised-sake-na-tion%E2%80%99s-future.html.
27. Among the other most prominent Jamaat officials sentenced were Abdul Quader Mollah, Delwar Hossain Sayeedi, and Golam Azam.
28. The Election Working Group is a network of more than thirty local civil society organizations that advocate and pursue free and fair elections and good governance.
29. Odhikar, "Political Violence: January 2001–August 2014," 2015, http://odhikar.org/statistics/statistics-on-political-violence/; "Human Rights Monitoring Report, January 1–31, 2014," 2015, http://odhikar.org/category/reports/monthly/.
30. Odhikar, "Hartal–2013," 2015, http://odhikar.org/statistics/statistics-on-hartal/.
31. Election Working Group, "Eye on Election" (Dhaka: Election Working Group/The Asia Foundation, December 14–26, 2013).
32. Ibid.
33. Odhikar, "Political Violence."
34. Human Rights Watch, "Democracy in the Crossfire" (New York: HRW, 2014), p. 2, www.hrw.org/reports/2014/04/29/democracy-crossfire.
35. Odhikar, "Political Violence."
36. Ibid.
37. "Killed; Obviously in 'Shootout,'" *Daily Star*, February 25, 2014, www.thedailystar.net/killed-obviously-inshootout-12908.
38. Odhikar, "Political Violence."
39. Bangladesh Institute of Peace and Security Studies, "Preventing Electoral Violence: Lessons from Bangladesh" (unpublished report commissioned by the United States Institute of Peace, January 2015).
40. The most obvious example is during the 2007 to 2008 military-backed caretaker government.
41. "Hasina solicits forces' support, promises 'to give whatever necessary,'" *Bangladesh Chronicle*, October 12, 2013, www.bangladeshchronicle.net/2013/10/hasina-solicits-forces-support-promises-to-give-whatever-necessary/.
42. The army has significant economic interests closely tied to the state. For example, the Sena Kalyan Sangstha (SKS) is a state-run business enterprise run out of the Ministry of Defense, which is heavily invested in various sectors of the economy, including textiles, food production, and real estate. The SKS board of directors is composed of military personnel who make personal fortunes from the company. SKS is only one example of the army's significant state-organized business interests, which are vulnerable to political attack. Therefore, although the

army has significant political leverage, civilian politicians can commandeer military support to maintain the status quo in exchange for continued economic and institutional benefits.

43. M. Jashim Uddin, "Security Sector Reform in Bangladesh," *South Asian Survey* 16, no. 2 (2009): 209–30.

44. Shahiduzzaman Khan, "Why police reform is badly needed," *Financial Express*, August 12, 2012, www.thefinancialexpress-bd.com/old/more.php?date=2012-08-12&news_id=139925.

45. Asian Human Rights Commission, "Bangladesh: Rights Disappeared," December 10, 2014, www.humanrights.asia/news.php?id=AHRC-STM-205-2014. The Asian Human Rights Commission is a human rights organization based in Hong Kong.

46. Odhikar, "Total Extra-Judicial Killings."

47. Odhikar, "Crossfire/Gunfight."

48. The corruption and lack of accountability that pervade the security sector are exacerbated by a weak and corrupt judiciary. In November 2007, the judiciary was formally separated from the executive branch. However, the courts have continued to face political pressure. The World Economic Forum, which rates judicial functions, gives Bangladesh poor scores for judicial independence, government favoritism, undue influence, and extraction of bribes. Bangladesh ranks less than 130 globally on all indicators of judicial quality. Transparency International's Corruption Perceptions Index rates it at 145 of 175. Oversight over the security sector is a primary responsibility of the judiciary. Therefore, its ineffectiveness and corruption aggravates and indeed promotes political corruption and violence.

49. Odhikar-IFES, "Election Violence Education and Resolution," Bangladesh, February 16, 2009, www.ifes.org/sites/default/files/odhikar_ever_rpt2009.pdf.

50. Pippa Norris, Ferran Martinez I Coma, and Max Gromping, "The Year in Elections, 2014," HKS working paper no. RWP15-008 (Cambridge, MA: Harvard University, February 2015). The report assessed the strength of eleven indicators of quality elections: electoral laws, electoral procedures, district boundaries, voter registration, party and candidate registration, media coverage, campaign finance, voting processes, and vote count.

51. Bangladesh Institute, "Preventing Electoral Violence."

52. Ibid.

53. Asian Human Rights Commission, "Bangladesh: Rights Disappeared."

54. Shahzada M. Akram and Shadhan Kunar Das, "Bangladesh Election Commission: A Diagnostic Study," Transparency International Bangladesh, 2006, www.ti-bangladesh.org/beta3/images/max_file/rp_ES_ElectionCommission_06.pdf.

55. Bangladesh Institute, "Preventing Electoral Violence."

56. S. Aminul Islam, "The Predicament of Democratic Consolidation in Bangladesh," *Bangladesh E-Journal of Sociology* 3, no. 2 (2006), www.bangladeshsociology.org/BEJS%203.2%20Sardar.pdf.

57. The focus of preventive diplomacy efforts on elite, as opposed to local, actors seems appropriate given the top-down nature of election violence in Bangladesh. Election violence is generally organized and mobilized by political elites.

58. Bangladesh's exports receive duty-free access to EU markets. It also receives discounted import taxes in Canada. Collectively, Western markets constitute a major source of Bangladesh's export revenue.

59. United Nations, "Mr. Oscar Fernandez-Taranco, Assistant Secretary-General for Political Affairs, visited Bangladesh," Press Release, December 9, 2012, www.bd.undp.org/content/bangladesh/en/home/presscenter/pressreleases/2012/12/09/bangladesh-mission-by-mr-oscar-fernandez-taranco-assistant-secretary-general-for-political-affairs-6-9-december-2012-.html.

60. "Taranco meets Hasina, Khaleda today," *Financial Express*, December 7, 2014, http://print.thefinancialexpress-bd.com/2013/12/07/7697/print.

61. "UN rights chief condemns 'shocking' Bangladesh poll unrest," *DnaIndia.com*, December 1, 2013, www.dnaindia.com/world/report-un-rights-chief-condemns-shocking-bangladesh-poll-unrest-1927872.

62. "Don't waste time, Kerry writes Hasina, Khaleda," *Daily Star*, September 9, 2013, http://archive.thedailystar.net/beta2/news/kerry-asks-hasina-khaleda-for-talks/.
63. U.S. Department of State, "Question Taken at the September 9, 2013 Daily Press Briefing," September 10, 2013, www.state.gov/r/pa/prs/ps/2013/09/214048.htm.
64. U.S. Department of State, "Continued Concerns on Bangladesh Elections," Press Statement, December 22, 2013, www.state.gov/r/pa/prs/ps/2013/219058.htm.
65. U.S. Department of State, "Parliamentary Elections in Bangladesh," Press Statement, January 6, 2014, www.state.gov/r/pa/prs/ps/2014/01/219331.htm.
66. European Union, "Declaration by the High Representative Catherine Ashton on behalf of the European Union on the Legislative Elections in Bangladesh," Press Statement, January 9, 2014, www.consilium.europa.eu/uedocs/cms_data/docs/pressdata/en/foraff/140315.pdf.
67. Fabzee, "UN, US, Canada And Commonwealth on Bangladesh Election," *Priyo News*, January 7, 2014, http://news.priyo.com/2014/01/07/un-us-canada-and-commonwealth-bangladesh-election-96927.html.
68. Bangladesh Institute, "Preventing Electoral Violence."
69. Asia Foundation, "Elections in Bangladesh," 2012, www.asiafoundation.org/resources/pdfs/BGElections2012Final.pdf.
70. Nazmul Ahsan Kalimullah, chairman of Janipop, email interview, February 10, 2014. The six constituencies were Dhaka (2), Gazipur (1), Munshiganj (1), and Chittagong (2).
71. Election Working Group, "Preliminary Statement on 10th Parliament Elections Held on Janutary 5, 2014," January 6, 2014.
72. Asia Foundation, "Elections in Bangladesh."
73. "Bangladesh," National Democratic Institute, www.ndi.org/bangladesh.
74. Dialogue Session on Election Violence, November 2014.
75. Ellen Barry, "Low Turnout in Bangladesh Elections Amid Boycott and Violence," *New York Times*, January 5, 2014, www.nytimes.com/2014/01/06/world/asia/boycott-and-violence-mar-elections-in-bangladesh.html.
76. Indian Ministry of External Affairs, "Prime Minister congratulates Sheikh Hasina on her assumption of the office of Prime Minister of Bangladesh," Press Release, January 12, 2014, www.mea.gov.in/pressreleases.htm?dtl/22727/Prime_Minister_congratulates_Sheikh_Hasina_on_her_assumption_of_the_office_of_Prime_Minister_of_Bangladesh
International actor-centered models.

Map 3.1 Thailand National Map

MYANMAR
(BURMA)

LAOS

VIETNAM

Chiang Mai

Lampang

Vientiane

NORTHERN
REGION

Udon Thani

NORTHEASTERN
REGION

Nakhon
Sawan

Ubon
Ratchathani

CENTRAL
REGION

Nakhon
Ratchasima

Andaman
Sea

Bangkok

Thon Buri

Chon Buri

EASTERN
REGION

CAMBODIA

Phnom
Penh

Gulf of
Thailand

Ranong

SOUTHERN
REGION

THAILAND

YORO   Department name

⊛   National capital

●   Selected major city

—·—   International
         boundary

-----   Province boundary*

▬▬▬   Regional boundary

*THAILAND HAS SEVENTY-SIX
PROVINCES AND ONE METROPOLITAN
AUTHORITY (BANGKOK).

0   100 MI

0   100 KM

Hat Yai

3

Thailand

Electoral Intimidation

DUNCAN MCCARGO AND PETRA DESATOVÁ

Thailand's snap general election of February 2, 2014, was among the most troublesome contests in the country's history. Called under duress, it followed massive street protests against the government of Yingluck Shinawatra, sister of former premier Thaksin Shinawatra. Thailand's politics had been growing intensely polarized for some years, especially after Thaksin was ousted in the 2006 military coup. Pro-Thaksin forces continued to win elections after the coup but were strongly opposed in certain segments of Thai society, notably the Bangkok middle class. The country's main opposition party, the Democrats, went so far as to boycott the 2014 election, and protest groups aligned with the opposition conspired to subvert the election process in a number of ways. Candidate registration was prevented in some parts of the country; the run-up to the election was marred by violent clashes; most of the polling stations in Bangkok and the upper south were closed on January 26, the day set for advance voting; and voting on February 2 was disrupted, especially in the south. The election was subsequently annulled by the Constitutional Court, and on May 22 Yingluck's Pheu Thai Party was removed from office in a military coup.

Unprecedented levels of intimidation, fear, and various forms of nonlethal violence had characterized the election.[1] The death toll was significant as well, at about thirty.[2] These developments reflected significant failings in the mechanisms that could have helped prevent election violence. No well-thought-out strategy was in place to mitigate the highly charged atmosphere. The few international and local preventive efforts were piecemeal and had little positive impact. This chapter argues that better election management, more systematic election monitoring, and above all a strong security-sector commitment to preventing intimidation would have increased the prospects for a more peaceful election.

Despite the prevalence of intimidation, however, fatalities were no higher than in 2005 (see figure 3.1). At the same time, applied models for preventing election violence (PEV models) were for the most part limited or absent: security-sector engagement was

Figure 3.1 Thailand Election Fatalities

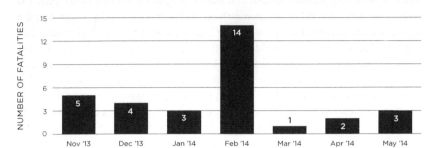

Source: Erawan Emergency Center, January 19, 2015, supplemented by news reports; Prajak Kongkirati, "Bullets, smoke bombs, mass clashes and polling: conflict and violence in the February 2, 2014 general election" unpublished undated paper, c. January 2015

largely ineffective, election management and administration was weak, civic and voter education campaigns were absent, monitoring and mapping was piecemeal at best, and voter consultations were nonexistent. Despite a few weak and unsuccessful efforts at preventive diplomacy and partisan peace messaging the picture for the study of preventing election violence was fairly grim. The larger project behind this study asks why priority models often fail in high violence scenarios. The question here is how strong prevention models could have prevented violence in the Thai social and political context.

History of Election Violence

The norm in Thailand since 1975, election-related violence was widely anticipated in 2014—especially given the highly charged political conditions. Nationalism scholar Benedict Anderson famously argued that the rise of such violence in fact marks the coming of age of elections in developing democracies, indicating that political power may actually change hands as the result of polling.[3]

Invaluable data on Thai election violence gleaned from an extensive review of newspaper sources are collected in a database compiled by Prajak Kongkirati in 2013 for Australian National University. The database is populated by violent incidents in the period from the day after parliament was dissolved until a month after election day for fourteen national elections between 1975 and 2011.[4] Only physical violence against people, both injuries and fatalities, or the property of election-related actors is included.

Voter intimidation, though it is difficult to quantify and is omitted in the Prajak study, is another form of election violence that can seriously thwart prospects for peaceful elections, both disrupting the election process and often heralding an escalation of physical violence.[5]

Throughout the period, preelection violence was by far the most common—accounting for more than 86 percent of the violence between 2001 and 2011, for example.[6] The clear implication is that violence is most useful in setting the tone for an impending election, removing potential threats, and intimidating or eliminating challengers. The main trend since the 1970s has been a sharp decline in election day violence, and a smaller increase in postelection violence to 12 percent for the 2001–2011 period. This suggests that one factor underpinning violence was "settling scores"—for example, punishing vote canvassers who had double-crossed candidates by taking money from both sides, or failing to distribute cash intended for vote-buying. Prajak argues that more effective PEV strategies have at times helped mitigate postelection violence: for example, he recommends the improved vote counting and complaints procedures used by the Election Commission (EC) in the 2005 elections.[7] Reducing election violence has been facilitated under the changed conditions since 2006 because Thai elections now entail greater real choice between alternative policy and political platforms, seen in the standoff between pro-Thaksin and anti-Thaksin forces. However, when polarization reaches an extreme form it may generate new modes of violence, incited this time not by provincial godfathers, but by national political figures who use overheated rhetoric to assail their opponents.

Unfortunately, Prajak omits data for the 2006 election—which, like that of 2014, was boycotted by the opposition and later annulled—from his work. Yet the overall level of election violence has changed relatively little over thirty-two years: an average of sixteen deaths and eighteen injuries. During the fourteen elections prior to 2014, the total fatalities dropped to single figures only twice, and exceeded twenty only three times: 1992, 2001, and 2005 (see figure 3.2). The high figure for September 1992 surely reflects the intense polarization following the so-called bloody May protests of that year, but the reason for high levels of violence in the two Thaksin victory elections is less obvious. Prajak attributes them to the highly competitive political atmosphere of this period, when Thaksin fought a controversial "war on influential people" aimed at curbing the power of provincial politicians and creating space for his candidates to appeal to the voters using populist policy platforms. The low levels of violence during the highly contested 2007 and 2011 polls are also quite surprising, although martial law was in effect in twenty-six provinces in 2007. The regional election monitoring body Asian Network for Free Elections (ANFREL) ascribed the lack of violence that year to a postcoup climate of fear in which free speech was harshly suppressed.[8] The low levels of injuries during the fourteen elections prior to 2014 suggest that election violence was mostly targeted. Assassination attempts amounted to more than 50 percent of the total 463 violent incidents during elections in this period.[9]

On the face of it, the 2006 military coup and subsequent national political polarization did not increase electoral violence. In fact, until 2014, the opposite was true. The recent trend in Thai politics has been toward high electoral polarization, but extremely aggressive public rhetoric has been mirrored by an overall decline in political murders. Prajak argues that this trend shows how the more ideological character of Thai politics "stifled and marginalized provincial bosses, thereby decreasing the demand for violence."[10] Given this background, it may be unsurprising that only thirty people were actually killed in events relating to the February 2014 elections, despite the unprecedented fear and numbers of attempts to disrupt the election process. In 2014, the

Figure 3.2 Thailand Election Fatalities, Historic

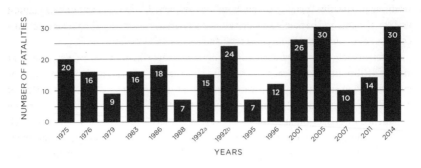

Note: 1992a and 1992b were separate elections held in March and September of that year.

Source: Prajak Kongkirati, "Bosses, Bullets and Ballots" (PhD diss., Australian National University, 2013), tables 2.11, 4.3, 6.1; data supplied to authors by Erawan Emergency Center, January 19, 2015, supplemented by news reports; Prajak Kongkirati, Bullets, smoke bombs, mass clashes and polling: conflict and violence in the February 2, 2014 general election, unpublished undated paper, c. January 2015

dominant mode of violence shifted from attacks on rival candidates and canvassers to large-scale attempts to intimidate voters—approximately six million of whom were affected—election officials, and those who supported holding the polls. This shift has, however, resulted in an unprecedented increase in election-related injuries, from sixteen in 2011 to 459 in 2014.[11]Although large-scale physical violence that resulted in fatalities was limited, this cycle was rife with other forms of election violence—including intimidation—that stronger prevention models could potentially have prevented.

Roots of Political Polarization

The February 2014 general election in Thailand was highly charged and took place in an intensely polarized political context. Thailand—formerly Siam—was historically an absolute monarchy. This changed in 1932, when the political system was opened up after a "revolution" staged by an elite group of military officers and civilian officials who called themselves the People's Party but were not supported by any mass mobilization of the populace.[12] From the outset, the new system of government proved highly contested as rival emergent cliques jostled for power and royalists sought to retain as much of their former influence as possible. By the end of the 1950s, the pattern began to change: the military formed a strategic alliance with the monarchy, greatly boosting the standing and prestige of King Bhumibol. Civilian political forces were marginalized until the 1970s—which saw mass student-led demonstrations on the streets of Bangkok—after which parliamentary politics staged a gradual comeback.

By the 1990s, Thailand superficially resembled many other countries in the Asia-Pacific, where rapid economic growth, the rise of a new middle class, the emergence of a dynamic provincial business sector, and an incredibly rapid social transformation was leading to a much more open and democratic political order. This openness was symbolized by the relatively progressive "people's constitution" of 1997, which codified a raft of new political and social rights and backed up a range of independent agencies, including a constitutional court, an election commission, and a national human rights commission.[13]

Unfortunately, this apparent democratic transition was only skin-deep. The dark side of Thai politics for decades had been a chronic instability, manifested in a vicious cycle featuring successively a military coup, redrafting of the constitution, a period of relative normalcy during which electoral politics was able to function, and then the emergence of crisis—often heralded by huge mass rallies in central Bangkok—which triggered another military coup. The result was that Thailand has experienced more military coups—and drafted more constitutions in recent decades—than any country in the world.[14]

The people's constitution was supposed to lay this vicious cycle of instability to rest. In practice, however, the new constitution coincided with the 1997 economic crisis, which saw the value of the Thai baht collapse and forced the country into the unwelcome arms of the World Bank and the International Monetary Fund. The primary beneficiary of Thailand's new mood of economic nationalism was the billionaire telecommunications tycoon Thaksin Shinawatra, who had already made a couple of unsuccessful attempts to build a political power base.[15] His new party, Thai Rak Thai (Thais Love Thais), brought up electable politicians from across the party spectrum and achieved overwhelming victories in the 2001 and 2005 general elections.

Thaksin's primary support base lay among the urbanized villagers of the north and northeast, many of whom spent most of their time working in Bangkok and other areas of the country with dynamic industrial and service sectors.[16] They were upwardly mobile and ambitious for themselves and for their children, weary of decades of royalist paternalism. By targeting rural-based voters and demonstrating that they could be mobilized for political purposes, Thaksin was undermining the traditional support base of the monarchy and tapping into the same areas of the population that supplied most of the conscripts for Thailand's armed forces. Over time, Thaksin began increasingly to alienate the Bangkok establishment. Thaksin was ousted from power in the military coup of September 19, 2006, and apart from a brief spell in 2008 has lived in self-imposed exile ever since, based mainly in Dubai.[17]

Attempts to eradicate Thaksin's influence recurred: his political parties were legally dissolved in 2007 and 2008; he and most of his lieutenants received a five-year ban on holding political office in 2007; and he was given a jail sentence in 2008 on corruption-related charges. Despite all this, a pro-Thaksin party won decisively in the 2007 general election. Nevertheless, tensions still ran deep in the highly polarized political order. In late 2008, the pro-Thaksin government was ousted from power by a series of backroom maneuvers that allowed the Democrat Party's Abhisit Vejjajiva to become prime minister. Street protests were followed by the pro-Thaksin red shirt movement in 2009 and 2010. The 2010 protests were in turn violently dispersed by the military, resulting in more than ninety fatalities. In August 2011, following another strong electoral showing, Thaksin's sister Yingluck Shinawatra became prime minister, apparently as a result of an elite pact under which she agreed both to not challenge the privileges of the military or the monarchy, and to keep her brother away from Thailand. Yingluck's government presided over a degree of normalcy until late 2013, when it apparently violated the tacit understandings behind the elite pact.

Key Developments

In the final weeks of 2013, anti-Thaksin protests started once again on the streets of Bangkok, this time triggered by ill-considered attempts on the part of the Yingluck government to push an amnesty bill through parliament for all those who had been charged of political offenses in the wake of the 2006 coup. It was an open secret that the main beneficiary of the legislation, approved by the lower house on November 1, would have been Thaksin himself. Under pressure from vociferous protests, the government withdrew the proposed legislation before it was promulgated.

This time the anti-Thaksin movement was spearheaded by a group calling itself the People's Democratic Reform Committee (PDRC).[18] Its leader was Suthep Thueksuban, former deputy prime minister (2008–2011) and former secretary-general of the opposition Democrat Party. Violent clashes broke out between pro- and antigovernment protesters on November 30, resulting in five fatalities and more than a hundred injuries. The PDRC demanded that Yingluck dissolve parliament and call fresh elections, which she did on December 9. The PDRC, however, then escalated its protests, calling for a wholesale reform of the political system and the permanent exclusion of the Shinawatra family from public life. The Democrat Party proceeded to announce a boycott of the elections, doubtless hoping that this would delegitimize the process and force Yingluck from power.

Further violent clashes between police and demonstrators took place at the Thai-Japanese Stadium on December 26, where protesters tried to disrupt the candidate registration process and three more people were killed. The PDRC protests culminated in the Bangkok Shutdown movement of January 13, 2014, when demonstrators occupied eleven major sites across the capital—paralyzing traffic, curtailing commerce, and driving tourists away in the height of the season. Each protest site was equipped with a stage for speakers and musicians and included hi-tech sound and video systems. Some of Thailand's top entertainment stars gave nightly free concerts at the rallies, which attracted a large following among middle-class Bangkokians.[19] The popularity of the protests, however, gradually waned after various incidents of violence—including twenty-eight people being injured by a grenade attack at the Victory Monument site on January 19—and growing complaints from the big companies underwriting their expenses that the extended demonstrations were harming business. PDRC leader Suthep abruptly called off Bangkok Shutdown at the end of February, and the remaining protesters moved to an off-street location in Lumpini Park on March 3.

Because of the disruption by the PDRC and its allies, conducting the 2014 general election was difficult. The scale of the likely problems became apparent on Sunday, January 26, the designated day for early voting. On this date, those who would not be in their home areas were supposed to be able to cast their ballots. More than two million people had registered for advance voting, including just under one million in Bangkok. Polling on the day, though, was disrupted in ten provinces, mainly in Bangkok and the upper south; did not take place in eighty-seven of the country's 375 constituencies; and was prevented or halted in forty-nine of Bangkok's fifty administrative districts, which do not correspond to its thirty-three parliamentary seats. Those people unable to cast preregistered advance votes were not eligible to vote on election day itself.[20] More than 97 percent of advance votes were by absentee voters—people who were living away from the places where they were registered to vote, many of whom were pro-Pheu Thai "urbanized villagers." In other words, disrupting the advance voting process directly affected Yingluck's core vote. On the night of the early voting, speakers at the PDRC stages were jubilant about the degree of disruption they had caused. One speaker declared that people he had seen trying to vote that day did not love Thailand in the same way that he and his audience did. Indeed, he was sure that most of them were not Thai at all but instead Cambodians with fake voter identifications. For the protesters, voting was now far from a civic duty or a political right: it had become instead an act of national betrayal.

On election day, 127 of Thailand's 375 constituencies saw disruptions (see figure 3.3). No voting at all was conducted in nine provinces in the upper south: Songkhla, Trang, Phatthalung, Phuket, Surat Thani, Ranong, Krabi, Chumphon, and Phang-nga. It went ahead unhindered in the insurgency-affected Malay majority provinces of Pattani, Yala, and Narathiwat, where local political leaders apparently made clear to PDRC-leaning government officials that they would not tolerate any attempts to interfere with polling. Nor did voters in the populous north or northeast, both Thaksin strongholds, encounter any problems, and polling was disrupted in only five of 127 constituencies in the central and eastern regions.

During the early voting there were violent clashes between PDRC protesters and pro-government groups: one PDRC leader was shot dead and ten people were injured at a polling station in Bang Na (in Eastern Bangkok) on January 26. The day before the election, a dramatic gunfight broke out on the streets in Laksi district (Northern Bangkok) between redshirts and PDRC supporters who had been preventing the distribution of ballot boxes. Seven people were wounded, including three journalists.[21] On election day, disruption in the capital was confined largely to three districts where polling was halted: Ratchathewi, Laksi, and Din Daeng.

Figure 3.3 Geographic Spread of Fatalities in Thailand

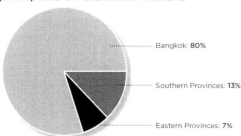

Bangkok: **80%**

Southern Provinces: **13%**

Eastern Provinces: **7%**

Source: Author's calculation

Protesters occupied the Ratchathewi District Office—the ballot box distribution center for the eighty-six polling stations across the district—from early morning. A large PDRC sound truck was stationed outside the district office; a succession of speakers addressed a crowd of hundreds from the top of the vehicle, urging them to make sure that no voting took place. Inside the official compound, white ballot boxes were laid out in rows rather like tombstones, "guarded" from a distance by dozens of PDRC supporters intent on ensuring that they did not leave the district office.[22] One of the officials in charge of the polling seemed resigned to canceling the ballot. Meanwhile, a local school principal who was supposed to serve as director of one of the polling stations complained that too few volunteers served on the polling station committees. Thirty of the eighty-six polling stations had no committees at all, only directors. Normally, some of the polling officials would be sent by the district office to make up the shortfall, but this time the task had been delegated largely to schoolteachers.

Protesters and district officials, most of whom appeared to be PDRC sympathizers, colluded actively. One senior official repeatedly declared his unhappiness that they had been asked to hold the election, which he considered illegitimate. Indeed, it later transpired that voting tents—normally erected the day before an election—had not been set up at polling stations in the district. Little serious effort to hold the election was actually made in Ratchathewi; the loud cheers that went up from the crowd when local officials announced the cancellation of polling in the district were just the culmination of an elaborate charade.[23] Overall, what happened in Ratchathewi was atypical: 6,155 of the capital's 6,671 polling stations opened on voting day; 516 (less than 8 percent) did not. But this form of structural violence—complicity between election officials and protesters to prevent and obstruct the polling process—epitomized the fraught nature of the electoral process in Thailand.

Following the election, the Democrat Party compounded matters when it took legal action to have the polls invalidated on the basis that they were illegitimate. Ultimately, the Constitutional Court did retroactively declare the February 2 election invalid, on the grounds that voting had not taken place in all constituencies on the same day. As International Crisis Group noted, "The decision did not mention the actions of anti-government protesters that prevented the election from taking place on the same day throughout the country."[24] Yingluck herself was ousted as premier on May 7. But even her departure was not enough to stabilize the situation. Thailand's military declared martial law on May 20 and then staged a full-blown coup d'état two days later.

The most striking features of the February 2014 elections included the boycott by the opposition Democrat Party and the anti-election demonstrations and disruptive tactics by the PDRC, a movement with very close ties to the Democrats. In effect, the Democrat boycott rendered the elections meaningless, ensuring that even a strong win for the Pheu Thai Party (PTP, or For Thais Party) could not offer Yingluck a viable way to restore her authority in the wake of the amnesty bill crisis and the Bangkok Shutdown protests. In short, the 2014 election was bound to fail.

Judged as a short-term instrumental measure, the boycott was highly successful, putting Thaksin and Yingluck on the defensive and preventing them from capitalizing on their main strength—popularity at the polls. But by boycotting elections and supporting

Photo 3.1 Respect My Veto poster at PDRC rally site

Photo Credit: Duncan McCargo

Photo 3.2 Protestors celebrate successful polling disruption

Photo Credit: Duncan McCargo

a shift to rally politics, the Democrats were violating their own long-standing insistence on supporting the constitutional order; arguably, polling boycotts themselves constituted a form of electoral violence. The willingness of the main opposition party to subvert the electoral process helped create the conditions for a disrupted election, and made violence an extremely likely outcome.

The presence of large numbers of PDRC-aligned protesters in Bangkok—and others in many parts of the south—made conducting a peaceful and orderly election extremely difficult. Emotions were running high, not only among those who regularly attended the PDRC rallies, but also among sympathizers who sported Thai-flag-themed clothing and accessories throughout the period. In such a climate, even expressing support for holding an election was regarded in many circles as an expression of social deviance that bordered on the treasonous. Saying anything positive about Yingluck or Pheu Thai was even more difficult.

At the same time, the conditions in central Bangkok and the upper south were quite different from those in the rest of the country. Support for Yingluck and Pheu Thai remained strong in the north and northeast, where there were few attempts to disrupt polling. For those living in the capital, the firm support of most voters for the election was both invisible and inaudible—a testament to the large gaps in geography, income, ethnicity, class, information and perception that characterized Thailand's polarized political order. The badly written (or perhaps well-written) electoral laws, which stated that a new government could not be appointed if any fewer than 95 percent of parliament could take their seats, meant that disrupting the ballot in a relatively small number of constituencies allowed protesters to sabotage the entire election.

Expectations of further electoral disruption and violence were widespread in Thailand before February 2014, reflecting the extremely political polarization in the country, the mass demonstrations under way for more than three months, the eleven key blocked intersections in Bangkok for three weeks prior to the election, and the series of violent clashes in the run-up to the polls. The mass violence of April and May 2010—in which more than ninety people were killed—was nearly four years in the past, but they were a reminder that street protests in the capital could easily spill over into bloodshed. Holding elections in February 2014 was rather gratuitous: the Yingluck government still had nearly eighteen months in office. In retrospect, nothing was gained by her dissolving parliament; holding an election was simply an additional step in opposition attempts to challenge the authority of the ruling party and lay the groundwork for removing Yingluck from office without an election, facilitating an eventual military coup.

The election process included a series of troubling incidents and triggers for disruption and instability. The opposition—both the Democrat Party and those aligned with the PDRC—engaged in constant verbal personal attacks on Yingluck, Thaksin, and the ruling Pheu Thai Party, often using misogynistic language.[25] In an attempt to bolster the image of the election, pro-government groups mounted a Respect My Vote campaign, using the slogan "Don't look down on the people." The PDRC countered with Respect my Veto posters that ridiculed the PTP and cast aspersions concerning Yingluck's supposedly ACDC sexuality.

Other important triggers for instability included the persistent legalism of those who opposed the election. Initially, the PDRC and the Democrats loudly demanded that Yingluck dissolve the parliament and call an election. But, having achieved this goal, they then began a series of challenges—submitted to the Election Commission and the courts—aimed at delaying the polls. Once the election had been held, the opposition promptly complained that it was invalid and sought to have it annulled. They accused the Yingluck government of abusing its power by spending money on holding an election, even though the opposition had demanded the election and the government had never sought it. This alleged abuse of power was one basis of the calls for Yingluck's impeachment.

Electoral System

Thailand's electoral system has undergone regular changes over the past two decades: a multimember constituency system was replaced by a combination of single member constituencies and proportional representation in 1997, and further modifications came in 2007. Broadly, these changes have favored larger parties; smaller parties struggled to win seats, and several of them merged with larger parties or were unable to re-form when they were banned by the courts; relatedly some parties have been banned since 2006 for alleged election fraud. The result was a virtual two-party system, in which a large pro-Thaksin party has competed at election times mainly with the old-established Democrats. This system favors majoritarian governments, which has fueled political polarization and with it the potential for election violence. For most of this period, the Democrats have been the more popular party in Bangkok, especially among higher- and middle-income voters; the two major parties have never been all that far apart in the proportional representation vote. However, pro-Thaksin parties easily won the 2001, 2005, 2007, and 2011 elections based on their consistently stronger appeal to constituency voters in the populous north and northeast regions of the country. Thus the ideological divide between the two main parties was also a class and regional divide.

Electoral outcomes are only one factor in determining who holds political office in Thailand; support from the military and the monarchical network are almost equally important. Governments and prime ministers have changed with great frequency in recent decades in the wake of elections, the collapse of governments following no-confidence debates, coalition reshuffles, judicial ousters, and military coups: seven prime ministers between 2006 and 2014 alone.

Contextual Vulnerabilities

Contextual vulnerabilities define the context or risk environment in which preventive efforts operate, based on the existing literature about the drivers of election violence. In the Thai case, they include overcentralization, internal contestation among state agencies, incomplete democratic consolidation, and polarized civil society.

Centralization

Thailand has a highly centralized political order in which power and resources are overwhelmingly in the hands of the Bangkok elite. In this respect, power structures mirror horizontal inequalities in society. Elected local government is in place at the subdistrict, municipal, and provincial levels, but local politicians are closely overseen by the bureaucracy and have limited freedom of maneuver. Most important, their capacity to raise local tax revenues or to determine local legislation is highly restricted. Provincial governors, all of whom are appointed in Bangkok and sent out to the provinces, still hold considerable authority and prestige. Local army and police commanders, also centrally appointed, are especially powerful. Wealth is overwhelmingly concentrated in and around Bangkok, which is also home to virtually all of the country's top schools, hospitals, and universities.

This centralization fuels resentment in the regions, especially in those with long-standing grievances against Bangkok: the northeast (Isan, where most people are of Lao ethnicity), the north (Lanna ethnicity), and the deep south (Malay ethnicity). Although ethnic grievances against the Thai state have in recent years generated serious violence only in the deep south, in late 2013 and early 2014 pro-Thaksin groups in the north and northeast began to articulate regionalist and separatist aspirations, a development that alarmed the military. The twenty million people of Isan have a history of rebellion against Bangkok. The region has long suffered from relative socioeconomic deprivation, and Isan people are typically patronized and discriminated against by central Thais. Regionalist sentiments in northern Thailand are less intense, but have been boosted by Thaksin's origins in Chiang Mai, which Bangkok has refused formally to recognize as the country's second city.

Internal Contestation

Thailand's state elites are characterized by intense contestation among the legislature, the bureaucracy, the police, the army, and what is known as the network monarchy,[26] a loosely structured power grouping that includes the judiciary and senior bureaucrats. In recent years, parliament and the police have been dominated by pro-Thaksin forces, and the military and bureaucracy have been broadly aligned with the Democrat Party and the monarchy. Whenever pro-Thaksin forces gained the upper hand through elections, other components of the elite have sought to remove them from office without the bother of an election. Thailand is thus a remarkably disunited unitary state, partly because elections provide the winners with overwhelming control over state resources. Intense intra-elite contestation is thus one of the major drivers of the country's political instability: if the "wrong" party is in power, the other side will stop at nothing to remove it from office. In recent years uncertainty about lower house electoral outcomes has been scant: pro-Thaksin parties have consistently won.

Incomplete Consolidation

Normally, a country that has successfully conducted two general elections after the end of an authoritarian regime may be considered to have passed through the consolidation phase. In Thailand's case, this milestone was arguably passed in mid-1995, after the second election following the military coup of 1991 and Black May crackdown of 1992. Certainly, the milestone was more than passed by 2005, by which time Thailand had successfully promulgated the more liberal 1997 constitution and peacefully conducted five general elections. But the 2006 military coup overturned all previous assumptions. The relatively smooth 2007 and 2011 elections could not gloss over the disturbing 2008 and 2009 mass protests, or the violent repression of the 2010 redshirt demonstrations. Some

scholars have argued that Thailand is a clear example of a reverse trend toward authoritarianism, in contrast to the global trend toward democracy in the 1980s and 1990s.[27]
Regardless of whether Thailand should be termed an autocratizing state or an anocracy,
it shares many of the features of such states: unstable governments and a propensity to
switch abruptly into rally mode.[28] Most important, changes of government in Thailand
result as frequently from military coups, judicial outcomes, or clandestine elite maneuvers
as from election outcomes.

Lack of Civil Society Space

In the 1990s, Thailand was widely praised for having a vibrant civil society and a relatively
free media, and for providing abundant public space in which to debate much-needed
social and political reforms. The more recent picture, though, has been less positive.
During his time in office between 2001 and 2006, Thaksin sought actively to curtail
dissenting media voices and co-opt critical elements of civil society. By the 2006 coup,
highly partisan pro- and anti-Thaksin newspapers and satellite TV channels were fast
gaining ground, and during the 2014 elections were exceptionally polarized. The main
role of this one-sided reporting and commentary was to exacerbate tensions around the
election and promote a culture of defamation and verbal violence.

Prevention in 2014

This study evaluates eight of the most widely used practices for the prevention of election
violence, and examines the extent to which they mattered in each of the elections under
review in this volume. The objective is to better understand the extent to which election
violence may be preventable using targeted peacebuilding efforts.

Security-Sector Engagement

Ensuring orderly elections generally requires overt commitment from a relatively neutral
security sector. Rivalry between the military—broadly aligned with the conservative establishment—and the generally pro-Thaksin police force meant that the security forces were
fragmented and partisan. As a result, the security sector failed consistently to safeguard
election procedures, its actions ranging from candidate registration to distribution of
ballot boxes and indeed polling itself. The sector did not operate in a nonpartisan way or
follow clear rules of engagement. These failures contributed to a climate of intimidation and
violence throughout the election cycle.

Responsibility for security enforcement during the February 2014 election was shared
among the police, the army, and the Centre for the Administration of Peace and Order
(CAPO) later replaced by the newly formed Centre for Maintaining Peace and Order
(CMPO).[29] Primary responsibility for security enforcement lay with the police and CAPO,
which was tasked with addressing the antigovernment protests. In the past, the army
would occasionally be involved in elections, either to provide extra security or in some
cases to help with vote counting in the event of a staff shortage at polling stations.[30] As the

violence began to escalate in January 2014, the government set up the CMPO to enforce the emergency decree and asked the military for help with election security.

In practice, the Royal Thai Army, with its long history of coups and other political interventions, was by far the most powerful component of the security sector, and was actively courted by both sides throughout the conflict. As early as December 11, 2013, PDRC leader Suthep Thueksuban called on the military to join the protesters' side and to help them oust Yingluck's government and install an unelected People's Council that would reform the country before any election took place.[31] A number of prominent retired military officers joined Suthep's calls for the army to side with PDRC, raising more questions about the army's claims to neutrality.[32] Following deadly clashes at the Thai-Japanese Stadium, the military changed its public position on the conflict. Army Commander General Prayut Chan-ocha, who had previously claimed that a military coup would not solve anything, said on December 27, "The military does not shut or open the door to a coup, but a decision depends on the situation."[33] This was effectively a green light for the PDRC, increasing the likelihood of further violence that could be used to justify military intervention.[34] As one columnist explained, having failed to bully the military into openly siding with the PDRC, Suthep was left with "no choice but to organise another, larger rally. That would heighten the chance of violence. And the situation could get out of hand."[35] Pro-government supporters, an interviewee said, were allegedly instructed by Thaksin not to get involved in violent clashes because that would mean the end for the Yingluck government. As time wore on, it became increasingly apparent that the military did not support the election, and was usually nowhere to be seen when protesters turned up to disrupt polling.

The Royal Thai Police has a generally poor reputation and is seen by most Thais as both highly corrupt and of doubtful competence. Nevertheless, the police have rarely been centrally involved in the fatal shooting of political protesters: this has been the domain of the army. Thaksin Shinawatra is a former police officer, and for the most part the police have been supportive of pro-Thaksin governments, in contrast to the more royalist and pro-Democrat military. From the very start of the PDRC protests, the police were directed to exercise utmost restraint and so reduce the risk of precipitating a coup.[36]

However, the response to violence during candidate registration at Thai-Japanese Stadium revealed serious weaknesses in police security enforcement. Three fatalities (two policemen and one protester), more than 150 injured (including twenty-three policemen), allegations that live rounds were used by the police to deter protesters, and a picture of four policemen beating an unarmed protester, all told stories of police failings.[37] Although the escalation of violence could not be solely blamed on the police—hard-line factions of the Network of Students and People for Reform of Thailand (NSPRT) were believed to have initiated the violence—the indiscriminate use of force against protesters could not be justified.[38] Lame attempts by senior police officers to blame abuses on a third party made matters worse, and General Adul's eventual acknowledgment of police culpability came too late.

Following the events at Thai-Japanese Stadium, pressure on the police from the antigovernment side increased. On January 22, just days before advance voting, hard-line protesters tore the signage from the front of the Royal Thai Police Headquarters in central Bangkok and defaced the gates with insulting graffiti. Police commanders watched the entire episode on CCTV from their control room inside the headquarters. General Adul never flinched: his admirable restraint undoubtedly averted a riot that could have plunged the country into chaos. At the same time, the line between restraint and passivity was fine. Satit Wongnongtaey, a core PDRC leader, criticized the police for their unwillingness to help the protesters during a violent incident at a Bang Na temple on the January 26 that left a leader of the People's Army to Overthrow the Thaksin Regime (Suthin Taratin) dead and another ten protesters wounded. Allegedly the military had to step in to help the protesters.[39] Police inaction gave the protesters another pretext for calling on the military to intervene. "We don't want them to seize power," Suthep claimed. "We only need them to help protect the people. We can seize the power ourselves."[40]

Following this disruption, which largely determined the fate of the February election before it even took place, the regional election monitoring organization ANFREL criticized the police for doing little to ensure that voters' rights were protected.[41] ANFREL observers reported that heavily outnumbered police made no efforts to prevent PDRC protesters from obstructing the ballots and instead stood by watching the protesters close down polling stations. Although the police were right to have exercised restraint at key junctures in the run-up to the election, police passivity may have contributed to increased violence during the polling itself. General Chaisit Shinawatra, who served as army chief under his cousin Thaksin, described the situation as a "quiet coup," remarking that neither the army nor the police did anything to contain the protests.[42]

After advance voting closed, Foreign Minister Surapong Tovichakchaikul condemned the disruption and simultaneously blamed the EC for "failing to ask for help from the government to provide safety for voters."[43] Yet under the emergency decree, CMPO had a mandate to limit people's movements, set curfews, and censor the media: the government did not need to await any request from the EC. As one volunteer explained, it seemed that the government sometimes wanted the "violence to come from the other [PDRC] side" because this would make it look more legitimate. The emergency decree thus made no difference to the situation on the ground: no visible additional security measures were put in place. The government designated parts of Bangkok as prohibition zones, but the protesters largely ignored them and the security forces did nothing to enforce them.[44] In reality, the Yingluck government had little capacity to enforce the emergency decree, given the reluctance of the security forces to cooperate, and the very real prospect that clamping down on anti-election protesters would have triggered more violence. Although previous governments had staged clampdowns on protests (notably in April 2010), doing so was less of an option for elected pro-Thaksin administrations. It would have been difficult to deploy the security forces more effectively unless the military had been ready to take a tough line to ensure that the election went ahead.

The government's decision to invoke emergency legislation was fiercely contested by a number of senators, who filed a case with the Constitutional Court claiming that the measures were unnecessary, and by the National Human Rights Commission. A civil court ruling on February 19, 2014, stripped the government of most of its powers under the emergency decree on the grounds that they violated the rights of protesters to gather freely as granted by the 2007 constitution.[45] This ruling rendered the state of emergency meaningless, leaving the government with no powers to contain postelection violence.

The security sector during the February election was characterized by minimal effectiveness and a lack of proper governance, especially of the military, over which the prime minister had no real control. Given the lack of legitimacy enjoyed by the police in the eyes of antigovernment protesters, only nonpartisan and transparent joint security-sector engagement led by the army could have created the conditions for a more peaceful election. The unwillingness of the military to perform this role was an important factor accounting for high levels of violence (fuzzy set score: 0.25).

Election Management and Administration

Sound management is an extremely important factor underpinning the success of any election process. Primary responsibility for this election was in the hands of the Election Commission, which was extremely tentative about holding the polls, and kept seeking opportunities and pretexts for postponement. The 2007 constitution gave the EC significant powers to ensure that elections were conducted fairly and peacefully: it could suspend political rights of candidates, investigate allegations, issue election regulations, and control and oversee election budget allocation. The EC can also request security enforcement to prevent election violence at and around the polling station—something not done during the February 2014 election.[46] No efforts were made to change venues to prevent disruption and the related violence, one interviewee indicated, even when widely predictable. Similarly, after the disrupted candidate registration, the EC did not extend the registration period to allow candidates to register in the affected constituencies left without candidates. This decision alone effectively sabotaged the February election because it meant that the required 95 percent of seats for a quorate parliament could not be achieved. The EC's ambivalence about holding the election was arguably the single biggest obstacle to preventing election violence.

The Yingluck government was engaged in a constant tug of war with the EC to ensure that the election went ahead. As late as January 28, Somchai Srisuthiyakorn, the election commissioner in charge of managing the election, was calling for a postponement of polling for three to four months.[47] In effect, holding the election became a pro-Yingluck move and postponing it became a pro-Democrat/PDRC move. Opposition calls for postponement were part of attempts to make the country increasingly ungovernable, and to force Pheu Thai from office nonelectorally or even unconstitutionally.

Persistent anti-election statements by EC members generated widespread skepticism about the integrity and political biases of the commission, led by a new team of commissioners who assumed office only on December 13, 2013. No one seriously doubted the technical capacity of the EC to stage the election.[48] The big questions concerned the commission's willingness to do so. The EC was accused by one commentator of having a "hidden agenda" to delay the election, and the commissioners were criticized by some of their predecessors for an alleged lack of political neutrality.[49] Many constituencies in the south and in Bangkok had too few polling station officials to manage the election process because many local people who normally performed this function had resigned or simply failed to carry out their assigned duties.[50] ANFREL officials felt that the EC was trying to prevent the election, rather than to prevent election violence, and did not mind the disruption of the polling. One informant argued that the EC could have taken various steps to make the election more workable, but declined to accept any advice.

The EC also knew very well that for the election to be valid it had to be completed within a single day nationwide, a key argument used by the Constitutional Court to nullify the February election on March 21, 2014.[51] Thus the EC was in no particular rush to set early dates for the election reruns in constituencies where the polling was disrupted or completely absent.[52] The new dates for the election reruns in disrupted constituencies were eventually scheduled for late April but no agreement between the government and the EC had yet been reached as to whether a new royal decree was needed to open candidate registration in constituencies with no candidates, given that the Constitutional Court had nullified the election.[53] As one of the volunteer observers aptly put it, the EC's big-picture election management was "a joke." Nevertheless, the election process was managed quite smoothly in many areas of the country, thanks largely to the dedication of provincial EC officials. The technical capabilities and competencies of the commission were excellent.

The Election Commission's mismanagement was the biggest hurdle to holding the February 2014 election.[54] A well-functioning election management body confers legitimacy on an election process and alleviates frustrations. In the Thai case, however, the EC's overt bias and obvious reluctance either to proceed with the election or to ensure the security of voters fueled the frustration of the pro-government side and inflamed the passions of antigovernment protesters (fuzzy set score: 0.25).

Preventive Diplomacy

The international community did make significant efforts to help deter or mitigate violence during the February 2014 election cycle. These efforts were rather sporadic and low profile, however, and had little positive effect on the level of political stability. No coordinated international response was made to the increasing violence, especially during the preelection build-up.

Siam-Thailand was never formally colonized, and its governments have long resisted any lecturing from the international community, especially on questions relating to politics and governance. Thailand has a dynamic economy, has not been a significant aid recipient in recent decades, and is thus largely immune from external political conditionalities. Although Foreign Minister Surapong Tovichakchaikul asserted that more than forty countries had expressed their support for the February 2014 election within a week after the dissolution of government, much of this support was allegedly generated by the foreign minister himself, by lobbying fellow Association of Southeast Asian Nations (ASEAN) members and the diplomatic community in Bangkok.[55] Government critics took Surapong to task for "using foreign diplomats as a human shield for the government's political manoeuvrings."[56] Leaks about Surapong's lobbying activities were orchestrated by pro-PDRC elements in the Foreign Ministry, many of whose diplomats made little secret of their contempt for Thaksin, Yingluck, and their own minister.

The lack of visible coordinated efforts by the international community to put pressure on the opposing factions made it relatively easy for commentators to question international support for the election.[57] Only the Swiss and Swedish ambassadors to Thailand sought more direct involvement with the election, when they offered to act as observers.[58]

The eruption of violence at Thai-Japanese Stadium during the candidate registration on December 26, 2013, which resulted in three deaths and more than 150 injuries, was largely overlooked by the international community. Neither the U.S. Department of State nor the UK government, both close allies of Thailand, commented publicly on these events—which may have encouraged the opposition to believe that their election-blocking tactics would not generate much international criticism.[59] At the same time, efforts at preventive diplomacy did go on behind the scenes.

Thailand enjoys a complex relationship with the United Nations (UN), and hosts a large contingent of UN agencies and officials. Former prime minister Thaksin spoke for many Thais when he famously declared (concerning a proposed investigation into his controversial war on drugs policy), "the UN is not my father."[60] Nevertheless, during the period surrounding the 2014 election, UN Secretary-General Ban Ki-moon made several mediation attempts, phoning Yingluck Shinawatra and the Democrat Party leader Abhisit Vejjajiva in a bid to bring the opposing sides together and reach a peaceful resolution to the country's political crisis.[61] The UN secretary-general then issued a statement saying that he was "very concerned that the situation could escalate in the days ahead" and urged "all involved to show restraint, avoid provocative acts and settle their differences peacefully, through dialogue."[62]

As the political crisis deepened, he made another effort to offer Thailand UN assistance in resolving the situation peacefully, by sending the UN Development Program (UNDP) chief Helen Clark to Bangkok. Clark met separately with both Yingluck and Abhisit. Yingluck was willing to work with the UN; but Abhisit made clear that the Democrats were entirely unwilling to hold any talks. Clark's visit received no media coverage and was never made public, though it was common knowledge in Bangkok diplomatic circles, and among community leaders in the deep south, who had hoped that Clark would pay a visit to the troubled region.

In late February, Surapong made a telephone call to the UN secretary-general requesting the UN to intervene—a final bid to salvage Yingluck and her government.[63] The failed 2006 election was still very much alive in the country's memory: by involving the UN, Surapong was hoping he could prevent another military coup.

A desire for mediation also featured on the European Union (EU) agenda, as revealed in a short policy report commissioned by the European Parliament in February 2014. The report suggested a number of policy options, but these efforts never materialized.[64] Humanitarian Dialogue, a Swiss-based nongovernmental organization (NGO) with close links to the Norwegian and Swiss embassies, made attempts to promote dialogue in collaboration with Thai establishment groupings such as the Reform Now Network. Their dialogue meetings, though, consisted mainly of second-tier players who had no real influence over the government, the Democrats, or the PDRC. Following the election day events, the UN and the United States condemned the protesters' attempts to block voting as undemocratic—preventing voters from exercising their basic rights—and called for a peaceful resolution of the situation.[65] Clearly, protesters were doing anything they could to create a political vacuum that would allow for another military coup or at least another intervention from above: the installation of an unelected government.

The U.S. Embassy in Bangkok was subject to severe criticism from the opposition forces after Washington expressed its support for the snap election. A statement issued by the State Department on December 9, 2013, declared that the United States "strongly supports democratic institutions and the democratic process in Thailand," encouraging the country to "resolve political differences peacefully and democratically in a way that reflects the will of the Thai people and strengthens the rule of law."[66] The PDRC viewed this statement as a sign that the United States was siding with the Shinawatra family. Nitithon Lamleua, the leader of the NSPRT, attacked the United States at a public rally for its constant calls for democracy and human rights. He also threatened to occupy its embassy in Bangkok if the U.S. government did not stop siding with the Yingluck government—threats that brought back dark memories of the 1979 Iranian embassy siege.[67] Having the backing of the international community was an important bargaining chip against the power held by the military and a source of political legitimacy. This helps explain the antagonism of NSPRT protesters toward the United States after it expressed its support for the February elections.

Ahead of the disruptions on advance voting day, PRDC leader Suthep Thueksuban sent an open letter to Barack Obama, assuring the American president that the PDRC's antigovernment campaigns would be violence-free. However, the clashes between the protesters and Red Shirts at a polling station in Bang Na on January 26 that left one PDRC leader dead and ten people injured showed the thuggish side of Suthep's "peaceful" protests.[68]

Opposing factions' eagerness to "explain" Thailand's domestic political situation to the world showed that international opinion did indeed matter. Some credit needs to be given to the international community for the various efforts made to support a free and fair election, especially given the obstacles it faced in doing more. At the same time, these efforts varied in quality (fuzzy set score: 0.75).

Peace Messaging

Peace messaging can be an important tool to raise awareness about the possibility of election violence and help defuse tensions. Quite a bit of self-proclaimed peace messaging went on in the period leading up to the February 2014 election, often carried out by ad hoc groups and networks that had emerged out of the ongoing political standoff. Most were created in the first half of January 2014, coinciding with the Bangkok Shutdown campaign that made the threat of violence imminent. The campaigns were largely reactive but enjoyed a relatively wide geographical reach through social media.

A Facebook group called YaBasta Thailand was founded by Kittichai Ngarmchaipisit and a group of his friends to campaign against election-related violence.[69] The group's full name—YaBasta Thailand: Stop protests that create conditions for violence—suggests that it was formed primarily in response to antigovernment protesters who were seen as the main drivers of violence. YaBasta organized candlelit vigils to commemorate peacefully those who lost their lives in violent events with the message Enough Is Enough. Banners carrying this message were displayed at their events, and throughout Bangkok. Besides the vigils, YaBasta initiated both a Post-it campaign and the Respect My Vote poster campaign. To brand themselves within Thailand's color-coded politics, the group donned white T-shirts and used largely white props. The campaigns were especially popular with younger generations and students who often used their schools or universities to organize the vigils.[70]

Although the activities of YaBasta were mostly confined to Bangkok, its social media profile helped spread their messages beyond the capital. YaBasta developed an almost nationwide network of supporters who posted photographs of their own candlelit vigils to the group's Facebook page. However, despite YaBasta's avowedly peaceful agenda, some images from the candlelit vigils show banners using offensive language toward the PDRC, the Democrat Party, the Election Commission, the National Anti-Corruption Commission, and the National Human Rights Commission. Unsurprisingly, according to one interviewee, such sentiments only fueled rumors that YaBasta was just another front for the Pheu Thai Party.

Another group with a peace-messaging agenda was the Network of 2 Yeses and 2 Nos established on January 10, 2014. The network was a grouping of prominent academics, intellectuals, and other highly respected Thais—including some leading figures from the NGO sector—with different political stances but at least four common standpoints: no to a coup and no to violence (two nos)—and yes to elections and yes to democratic reform (two yeses).[71] Given the high profile of leading members, the group received extensive media coverage. However, feelings were mixed about the network's manifesto. The group was praised by some as a long-awaited and sensible middle ground that could help build bridges in Thailand's highly polarized society.[72] For others, it was a group promoting pro-government propaganda. An article by Sombat Kusumawali of the National Institute of Development Administration in *Manager Online*—a strongly pro-PDRC newspaper—harshly criticized the group, saying that its 2 Yeses and 2 Nos painted the PDRC protesters in a bad light, as an undemocratic mob yearning for a coup, that uses violence, and has no regard for voters' rights.[73] However, the network drew support not only from intellectual and academic circles but also from rural areas.[74]

Other groups, such as the Network of Servants for Thailand's Peaceful Reform (NSTPR) and Reform Now Network (RNN) were more reform than peace oriented, and their initiatives cannot be seen as apolitical either. For instance, the NSTPR, comprising 185 prominent public Thai figures, had strong pro-PDRC sentiments: a number of its members also spoke at PDRC rallies against the government and the Shinawatra family.[75]

In Thailand's highly polarized climate, for any peace-messaging group to succeed it would have to refrain from expressing public support for the election and to campaign only on the need to end violence. The credibility of each group, and their campaigns, was fiercely questioned—and often deliberately undermined—by people on either side of the divide. Overall, the quality, geographical scope, and implementation of peace messaging were patchy during the 2014 election process (fuzzy set score: 0.50).

Civic and Voter Education

In previous elections, the Election Commission carried out extensive campaigns to inform voters of their rights and responsibilities, and to disseminate information about how to take part in the polls. For example, in 2007 it sent informational booklets to every household in Thailand, recruited celebrities to spread the word, and used radio and television extensively.[76] By contrast, the run-up to the 2014 elections offered little evidence of voter education activities.

Because expectation was scant that the February election would be a game changer, interviewees indicated, neither the political parties nor the EC were eager to invest significant time or money to educate voters. The traditional role of celebrities as election ambassadors was less evident given the level of polarization: many celebrities openly voiced their support for the PDRC activities and even encouraged people to join National Picnic Day—a PDRC-led anti-election celebration held on election day.[77]

Most Thais are well aware of how to vote (partly because they have a great deal of practice) and in recent years the number of invalid votes cast in error has been relatively low. During the 2006 snap election, the Democrat Party actively encouraged voters in its southern heartlands to cast a Vote No (that is, to vote for no one). According to interviewees, this helped create the political deadlock that contributed to the election's being annulled and opened up the way for the September 2006 coup. During the February 2014 election, the Democrat Party instead urged people not to vote at all. Voter education was largely absent during the 2014 election, instead giving way to anti-election activities (fuzzy set score: 0).

Monitoring and Mapping

Election monitoring and mapping can help mitigate violence by increasing transparency and highlighting potential flashpoints. Thailand's election monitoring "business" is a complex network of professional and personal affiliations that span the governmental and nongovernmental sectors. During the February 2014 elections, the network operated at only a fraction of its usual capacity, a factor that surely contributed to the widespread violence and intimidation.

Thailand has little tradition of permitting missions of international election observers; global organizations such as the Carter Center, the EU, and the International Republican Institute have never undertaken a full monitoring mission in the country. Starting with the September 1992 election, Thailand launched a home-grown monitoring agency known as PollWatch, which had close ties to the then vibrant local NGO community.[78] In September 1998, PollWatch joined forces with around a hundred NGOs to create P-NET, a volunteer monitoring network. In successive elections, the Election Commission issued permits for registered election observers in each province, and sometimes provided funding for PollWatch and P-NET monitoring activities. Nevertheless, the heyday of PollWatch was in the 1990s, before the creation of the Election Commission: the Thai NGO community never really recovered from the political polarization that followed Thaksin's rise to power in 2001.

In February 2014, PollWatch and P-NET did not carry out any official election monitoring. The organization's acting director, Sakool Zuesongdham, explained in an interview that he found the election legally questionable and believed the government should have resigned rather than dissolving parliament. He also felt that the election was both "too risky to achieve its goal" and "meaningless" given the tense political situation. Warin Taemjarat, a P-NET board member, also argued that the February 2014 election should not have been held because it created divisions and violence. He believed that the PDRC had every right to disrupt the election process.

The EC did not register PollWatch or P-NET observers to monitor the election. Sakool explained in an interview that PollWatch had become reluctant to ask for funding from the EC because of previous misunderstandings. During February 2014, some PollWatch officials carried out informal election monitoring but not in a systematic way. Leading figures in PollWatch and P-NET were sympathetic to the PDRC and hostile to the Yingluck government, which helps explain why PollWatch made little attempt to mobilize observers. With some justification, PollWatch could argue that conditions were not safe for their volunteer monitors to observe the polling; at the same time, however, the absence of independent monitors made voting conditions significantly less safe. Former leading P-NET members included current EC commissioner Somchai Srisuthiya-korn—who during his tenure as P-NET's coordinator refused to monitor the 2006 snap election that was followed by the coup that deposed Thaksin Shinawatra—and General Saiyud Kerdphol, who was also a founding member of ANFREL and a vociferous opponent of the Shinawatra family. Saiyud led a group of retired military officers calling for a military intervention to depose the Yingluck government before the February election.[79] Thai election observation bodies thus have a history of anti-election sentiments.

The only quasi-international monitoring agency permitted formally to observe Thai elections is the Asian Network for Free Elections, established in 1997. Physically based in Bangkok, ANFREL had a Thai executive director for many years and is a predominantly Southeast Asian body. PollWatch's hostility toward the February election made it also increasingly difficult for ANFREL to monitor the situation. Although ANFREL publicly distanced itself from anti-election sentiments shared by Sakool Zuesongdham and other P-NET members, according to one interviewee, a rift ran deep within the organization and Thailand's NGO sector as a whole. One early ANFREL election report contained extremely Bangkok-centric, patronizing, and inappropriate views of the Thai rural electorate, similar in tone to the rhetoric of the PDRC.[80] In a January 2014 interview, ANFREL Director Ichal Supriadi (an Indonesian national) expressed a desire for the election to go ahead, arguing that any postponement would need to be based on a stronger justification and accompanied by a clear timeframe.[81] ANFREL also made explicit demands for investigations into the violent incidents that occurred since the beginning of the protests in November 2013, and for the election rerun. ANFREL called on the Election Commission to "better prepare" for the election rerun "moving proactively forward with a plan to hold the elections as is constitutionally mandated"—an implicit criticism of the EC's anti-election stance.[82]

Western embassies in Thailand, according to one interviewee, were also generally reluctant to provide donations to ANFREL—unlike in previous years—because most diplomats believed that the election was not going to resolve the crisis. Even those donors who initially promised support later pulled out, apparently fearing that they might be accused of legitimizing a flawed election process. Despite limited funding, ANFREL did carry out some modest election monitoring in 2014: altogether it deployed ten international observers, thirty-five local observers across the country, and an additional thirty-two observers in Bangkok. Beyond Bangkok, the number of observers was entirely inadequate, enabling ANFREL to monitor the situation in only thirty provinces of seventy-six.[83]

The EU sent a two-person Expert Electoral Mission to observe the February election.[84] This was a low-profile exercise: no mainstream media in Thailand reported on its presence, its focus was confined to some limited "technical" issues, and its report was never published. The mission had little direct contact with the Election Commission.

Some independent monitoring and mapping was carried out by a Bangkok-based NGO, Thai Violence Watch (TVW), funded mainly by the UNDP. Its monitoring commenced with the start of the Bangkok Shutdown campaign on January 13. During the advance voting and on election day, it sent observers to polling stations and to high risk areas such as Lak Si, where an hour-long shootout took place on February 1. Despite a limited geographical reach, TVW monitored PDRC rally sites systematically twice a day during the preelection period and once a day after the election until after the May 22 coup d'état.[85] This was arguably the most systematic monitoring effort carried out for the February 2014 election.

In terms of mapping, TVW published its findings daily on its website evaluating potential risks, using its own coding system. Besides the usual factors, such as the use of weapons, physical violence, and property damage, TVW also analyzed softer forms of violence, such as hate speech, and included these in its coding rubric of violence. It also published numerous diagrams and maps on its website illustrating the scope and form of violence as it unfolded. Based on their observations, TVW issued a set of recommendations ahead of the February 2 to election advising stakeholders—including the security forces, EC, protesters, media, and on-ground medical personnel—on how to reduce the risk of violence, and outlining the major risk areas.[86]

Independent election monitoring efforts were also undertaken by a group of volunteers coordinated under the Citizen Media Network, a department within Thai Public Broadcasting Service (Thai PBS). Following the Bangkok Shutdown campaign, the Citizen Media Network (CMN) deployed approximately thirty active volunteers nationwide to observe and report the situation. However, none were trained observers. Many were university students and unable to conduct systematic observations. The observers would phone in their findings to CMN, which would then liaise with Thai Violence Watch—with which it worked closely—and Thai PBS News. Due to the high risk of violence and safety concerns, CMN discouraged students from direct involvement in observations at major PDRC rallies and polling stations within Bangkok. In other provinces, where the risk of violence was significantly lower, students were encouraged to participate in monitoring activities.

Although the monitoring and mapping efforts of ANFREL, the EU, Thai PBS, and Violence Watch were extremely commendable, they were confined mainly to the Bangkok area and parts of the south, were not systematic, and did not cover the entire election cycle (fuzzy set score: 0.25).

Voter Consultations

A range of fora were organized at which different political proposals concerning reform were discussed and presented. Some were initiated by nonpolitical groups such as an alliance of seven private-sector and business organizations, the RNN and the NSTPR, and the Network of 2 Yeses and 2 Nos.[87] Party rallies were also held around the country, especially by the PTP, at which policy platforms were elaborated. But whether these activities amount to the kinds of voter consultations that fit the rubric of a PEV model is questionable.

The PDRC protests, especially in the early stages, created opportunities for voter consultations—the Democrat Party could have capitalized on the popular discontent and built its policy platforms around PDRC demands, shifting political contestation from the streets to the ballot boxes: for better or worse, according to interviewees, the party chose not to do so. Similarly, PDRC leaders could have formed a new political party and contested the election: again, they did no such thing. Despite the number of political fora during the election period, then, none of them amounted to proper voter consultations (fuzzy set score: 0).

Youth Programs

In theory, creating programs to involve young people in election processes should reduce the risk of their taking part in political violence. High school and other students have traditionally been involved in assisting at polling stations during Thai elections, but did not in February 2014. Those P-NET and ANFREL members who observed recalled seeing very few students at work. This differed from previous elections, several interviewees reported, for which students were trained to check voter lists at polling stations and were even present during vote counting.

On October 24, 2013, Pheu Thai Party established a Pheu Thai Youth Institute to solicit and exchange ideas from young people between fifteen and thirty on political issues and agendas. Prime Minister Yingluck, Thaksin's son Phanthongthae, and former Thaksin-era minister and party secretary Phumitham Wetchayachai comprised the institute's advisory board.[88] The institute set up a Facebook page, inviting youth to share their views in an effort to attract young people to politics and nurture a future generation of politicians. In December 2013, the Council of University Presidents of Thailand proposed a project to involve students in studying and observing the coming February 2 election and any forthcoming political reform project.[89] It is unclear whether this proposed project was ever implemented. Both PDRC rallies and pro-election candle-lighting ceremonies were held on a number of university and college campuses around Thailand.

Whereas in previous elections, schools had often staged activities in support of the voting process, doing so proved more difficult in 2014. One school director who tried to organize a street rally in support of the election found himself facing a mass protest from three hundred students demanding his removal.[90] Although attempts were made to engage the young generation in politics, these programs were neither systematic nor geographically widespread (fuzzy set score: 0.25).

Assessing Prevention

Thailand's February 2014 elections are not readily comparable with previous national polls, given that the election was boycotted, blockaded, never completed, subject to intense legal challenges and controversy, and soon afterward annulled. As one interviewee explained, "There wasn't really any election." Nevertheless, some conclusions may be drawn from an analysis of this nonelection election. Most of the PEV models were weak or absent. Because two sources attest to thirty fatalities, election violence was deemed significant.

Historical comparison shows that though most PEV models were weaker during the February 2014 election, the associated levels of electoral violence were similar to those in 2005 (see table 3.1). Fatalities were within the normal range, though intimidation and harassment reached unprecedented heights. Only three of eight PEV models were no weaker during the 2014 election: preventive diplomacy, peace messaging, and voter consultation. Preventive diplomacy and voter consultations remained unchanged: the former was unlikely to change given long-standing Thai sensitivities, and the latter has never really existed in Thailand.

- **Peace messaging.** The only PEV model that strengthened was peace messaging. High levels of voter intimidation and the imminent threat of violence prompted many people to create independent peace-messaging

Table 3.1 Prevention in Historical Perspective, Thailand

PEV MODEL	SCORE	2014 ROLE	OVER PAST ELECTIONS
Security-Sector Engagement	0.25	Highly partisan, reluctant to act, weak governance	Weaker
Election Management and administration	0.25	Strong anti-election sentiments, mismanagement	Weaker
Preventive Diplomacy	0.50	Some international behind-the-scenes mediation but limited effectiveness and reach	No Change
Peace Messaging	0.50	Adhoc groups with various peace messages but contested credibility	Stronger
Civic and Voter Education	0	NA	Weaker
Monitoring and Mapping	0.25	Geographically limited and not systematic	Weaker*
Voter Consultations	0	NA	No Change
Youth Programming	0.25	Little involvement of youth	Weaker

*Weaker overall, despite some strengths.
Source: Author's compilation

groups, especially after the start of the Bangkok Shutdown campaign. Even though it may have been too late for these groups to have a real impact on the increasingly violent situation, an interviewee explained, they created awareness and spread their peace messages across the nation through social media channels, attracting support further afield. Although the strongest PEV element during the election was peace messaging, even it was not consistent across the country and failed to counter a pervasive belief—especially among the Bangkok middle classes and southern Democrats—that disrupting the polls was perfectly reasonable, or even public-spirited.

- **Election management and administration**. Weak election management was at the core of the troubles afflicting Thailand's abortive February 2014 election. The failure of the Election Commission to demonstrate a strong commitment to holding the polls, and to defend the relevant mechanisms and processes, helped encourage a climate in which the election was seen as peripheral to the country's larger political problems. Some of the disruption could have been averted had the EC been more committed to resisting PDRC efforts at generating confusion. Instead, the EC's willing-ness constantly to raise the possibility of postponements played into the hands of those who did not want to the election to take place successfully, encouraging anti-election groups to commit increasingly aggressive acts of intimidation. On this occasion, the military assistance seen in previous elections was not forthcoming—partly because the EC never requested it. Another alternative would have been to ask P-NET, other NGOs, or even universities to provide volunteers—but again, the EC failed to make any such request. A stronger and less partisan EC would thus have been able to ensure that the election was more likely to go ahead, and even to avert the prospect of violence.

- **Security-sector engagement**. More constructive participation by the secu-rity forces could have helped ensure a smoother electoral process, especial-ly if the military and police had been able to prevent the intimidation of prospective candidates from registering in the upper south. The politici-zation of the military, and army commander General Prayut's categorical refusal to rule out a coup, encouraged the PDRC to disrupt the election. PDRC leader Suthep made open calls for the military to take sides, and in the wake of the coup it became clear that collusion between the protesters and the army had been extensive.

The appointment of Labor Minister Chalerm Yubamrung to head the CMPO and oversee election and national security during the PDRC protests was an unfortunate choice; the outspoken former police officer's combination of bluster and incompetence boded ill for the future of the ad-ministration he was allegedly trying to secure. In the end, the failure of the Royal Thai Army—the only security agency with the legitimacy to secure support from antigovernment protesters—to robustly defend the election process was the crucial factor in fueling violence and intimidation.

- **Preventive diplomacy.** Although the international community did express concern about the situation in Thailand, major actors such as the UN, EU, and United States saw little prospect of preventive diplomacy measures' successfully reducing the unfolding conflict. This belief was closely linked to the view that the election might not take place, that it was unlikely to produce a complete result, that it was very likely to be annulled—and that even if it were successful, it would do nothing to affect the intense polarization that characterized Thai politics.

  Given the shortcomings of preventive diplomacy, international interest was scant in supporting monitoring efforts, voter education, or youth campaigns—especially given that many of the local NGOs that would normally take the lead in such activities were themselves tacitly supporting a boycott. The relative absence of these models was also a direct result of the studied inaction of the Election Commission, which generally provided both funding and administrative leadership for such activities, and a security sector that remained unwilling to intervene in support of the polling. All three sides thus colluded in a shared desire to thwart the 2014 election, which was crucial in creating the conditions for violence. As this study shows, a previously competent election management body and elements of civil society can mobilize in support of violence-inducing anti-election activities that are made possible by a passive security sector. In the end, even the stronger prevention models—peace messaging and preventive diplomacy—were unable to offset these negative interaction effects.

- **Levels of violence.** In spite of the many shortcomings of the PEV models, Thailand's 2014 election did not involve exceptional mass violence: the number of fatalities was in line with previous elections. No one expected this election to be decisive in determining the outcome of the ongoing power struggle. High levels of violence—fifty or more fatalities—have only occurred in clashes directly arising from extended street protests. The decision of the PDRC to end their protests at the beginning of March helped deescalate the standoff to some degree. Throughout the election process, tensions were extremely high, and an atmosphere of intimidation was disturbingly palpable. At the same time, however, the stakes were lower than might have appeared. Ultimately, the conflict was likely to be resolved in the courts, by a military coup, or by a further round of street demonstrations—not at the ballot box.

- **Contextual vulnerabilities.** In the end, levels of violence were primarily a function of contextual vulnerabilities at the time of the election. The incomplete nature of Thailand's democratic consolidation meant that those seeking to influence the country's political direction could do so by attempting to provoke disorder, and so facilitate conditions for a military coup. Given the acute levels of political polarization, fueled by the two-party system, regional inequalities, and a weak civil society, a violent election was likely—but an election was unlikely to be the way for power to change hands. Contextual vulnerabilities during the 2014 election thus made the historically stronger PEV models more susceptible to partisan interests and abuse of power than ever before. From a counterfactual perspective, conscious efforts to strengthen rather than weaken the applied prevention would have helped mitigate at least some of the effects on the 2014 election.

Conclusion

To date, Benedict Anderson has been proved wrong in what he wrote in 1990:

> This reality, or rather the part of it with which I am here concerned, is that in the 1980s political killing in Siam has assumed a completely unprecedented character, one which is, oddly enough, probably a positive omen for the future. For it seems tied to the eclipse of a longstanding tradition of military-bureaucratic dictatorship and its supersession by a stable, bourgeois parliamentary political system.[91]

The reality that unfolded was rather different. First, the military dictators were not eclipsed, but instead staged three further seizures of power over the next twenty-five years. Second, the parliamentary political system has proved profoundly unstable and incapable of decisively superseding traditions of dictatorship. Third, political murders continue to assume new and more ominous forms, none of them in the least positive.

But what also emerged was a relatively robust set of prevention instruments: in particular, an Election Commission that was technically quite competent (if never entirely independent), regular rounds of civic and voter education, and youth programs. Despite their professional shortcomings and high levels of politicization, neither the military nor the police had a track record of serious meddling in the election process. PollWatch, P-NET, and ANFREL, for all their limitations, did invaluable supporting work to monitor elections, assisted to some extent by international funders and embassies. The numbers of election-related murders remained relatively low.

In 2014, mechanisms that had worked passably well in elections since September 1992 failed. This resulted in unprecedented levels of electoral disruption, voter intimidation, and fear. Fortunately, larger-scale fatalities did not ensue as a result of the shambolic election process, largely for negative reasons: no one believed that the election would be a game changer. This conclusion reflects the specific politics of the Thai case, in which changes of government in recent years have resulted just as frequently from military coups and judicial interventions as from electoral outcomes. The purpose of disrupting the February election was to usher in a new political order in which electoral politics would be downgraded and a more conservative, authoritarian mode of governance would be institutionalized. This process has been under way since the May 22, 2014, military coup, with consequences that are so far impossible to predict.

Altough it is impossible to prove that stronger PEV models would have curtailed violence further, more systematic monitoring and mapping, and a firm commitment by the security forces to prevent voter intimidation would certainly have increased the chances of a more peaceful polling process.

Notes

1. This chapter draws on fieldwork during the 2014 election and on telephone interviews during January and February 2015. A number of internal official documents were supplied anonymously, not by interviewees. We would like to thank all our interview informants, Prajak Kongkirati, and the Erawan Emergency Center for their generous help, and Jittip Mongkolnchaiarunya for research assistance in Thailand.

2. Authors' figure based on data supplied by the Erawan Emergency Center, January 19, 2015, supplemented by news reports. Prajak Kongkirati also suggests a total of thirty killed, though he uses a different dataset and a slightly different period. See "Krasunpheun khwanrabuet kanpata muanchon lae khuhaleuktang: khwamkatyaeng lae khwam runraeng nai kanleuktang tua pai wan thi 2 kumphaphan 2557" [Bullets, smoke bombs, mass clashes and polling: Conflict and violence in the February 2, 2014, general election], unpublished paper, January 2015. ICG gives a figure of twenty-eight killed. See "A Coup Ordained? Thailand's Prospects for Stability," Asia Report no. 263 (Brussels: International Crisis Group, December 3, 2014), p. 1. *Thai Rath* newspaper offered an alternative figure of twenty-five on May 20, 2014, "St. triam thim pheat fao rawang wang lang prakat 'kotaiya kansuk'" [Ministry of Public Health prepares a team of doctors to be on standby after the martial law has been declared], www. thairath.co.th/content/424050. Both figures are based on a period from November 30, 2013, to May 15, 2014.

3. Benedict Anderson, "Murder and Progress in Modern Siam," *New Left Review* 181 (1990): 33–48.

4. Prajak Kongkirati, "Bosses, Bullets and Ballots: Electoral Violence and Democracy in Thailand, 1975–2011" (PhD diss., Australian National University, 2013), p. 21.

5. Election violence is based on numbers of fatalities in line with this volume's comparative framework.

6. Kongkirati, "Bosses, Bullets and Ballots," p. 175.

7. Ibid., pp. 160–61; see also Paul Chambers, "Consolidation of Thaksinocracy and Crisis of Democracy: Thailand's 2005 General Elections," in *Between Consolidation and Crisis*, ed. Aurel Croissant and Beate Martin (Berlin: LIT Verlag, 2006), p. 290.

8. Asian Network for Free Elections, "Post-Election Summary Report" (Bangkok: ANFREL, December 25, 2007), p. 31, cited in Prajak 2013, p. 165.

9. Kongkirati, "Bosses, Bullets and Ballots," pp. 121, 173.

10. Prajak Kongkirati, "The Rise and Fall of Electoral Violence in Thailand: Changing Rules, Structures and Power Landscapes, 1997–2011," *Contemporary Southeast Asia* 36, no. 3 (2014): 409.

11. Prajak Kongkirati, "Thailand in no(transition): The anti-election movement, the 2014 military coup and democratic breakdown," *Southeast Asia Research Centre* working paper no. 168 (Hong Kong: Southeast Asia Research Centre, August 2015), p. 19.

12. For a detailed account of the Siamese revolution, see Chris Baker and Pasuk Phongpaichit, *A History of Thailand* (Cambridge: Cambridge University Press, 2014), pp. 115–23.

13. The political reform movement of the 1990s is examined in Duncan McCargo, ed., *Reforming Thai Politics* (Copenhagen: NIAS, 2002).

14. For an analysis of Thai political developments following the 1932 revolution, see Federico Ferrara, *The Political Development of Modern Thailand* (Cambridge: Cambridge University Press, 2015).

15. See Pasuk Phongpaichit and Chris Baker, *Thaksin* (Chiang Mai: Silkworm, 2009); Duncan McCargo and Ukrist Pathmanand, *The Thaksinization of Thailand* (Copenhagen: Nordic Institute of Asian Studies, 2005).

16. See Naruemon Thabchumpon and Duncan McCargo, "Urbanized Villagers in the 2010 Thai Redshirt Protests: Not just poor farmers?" *Asian Survey* 51, no. 6 (2011): 993–1018.

17. On the 2006 coup, see "Thailand's 'Good Coup': The Fall of Thaksin, the Military and Democracy," ed. Michael Connors and Kevin Hewison, *Journal of Contemporary Asia* 38, no. 1 (2008); and Pavin Chachavalpongpun, ed., *"Good Coup" Gone Bad* (Singapore: ISEAS, 2014).

18. Strictly speaking, several of the protests (and associated rally sites) were not directly organized by the PDRC, but were linked to other anti-Thaksin groups.

19. PDRC supporters were reportedly generally better off and better educated than the average Thai. See "Profile of the Protestors: A Survey of Pro and Anti-Government Demonstrators in Bangkok on November 30, 2013" (Washington, DC: Asia Foundation, December 2013), www.asiafoundation.org/resources/pdfs/FinalSurveyReportDecember20.pdf; "Profile of the 'Bangkok Shutdown' Protestors: A Survey of Anti-Government PDRC Demonstrators in Bangkok" (Washington, DC: Asia Foundation, January 2014), www.asiafoundation.org/resources/pdfs/THPDRCSurveyReport.pdf.

20. EC claims that 440,000 were unable to vote were contradicted by their data: the real figure was much higher. See ANFREL, "Briefing on the Thai Election of 2 February 2014," unpublished document (Bangkok: ANFREL, February 3, 2014).

21. See "Shoot out at Laksi," ANU College of Asia and the Pacific, February 11, 2014, http://asiapacific.anu.edu.au/news-events/all-stories/shoot-out-laksi#.VKxDLSvF98E; Kocha Olarn, "Trapped in a gunfight: CNN producer's harrowing account of Thai election violence," CNN, February 3, 2014, www.cnn.com/2014/02/03/world/asia/thai-protests-gunfight-kocha/.

22. Duncan McCargo wishes to thank Michael Connors, who joined him during these observations, for this comparison.

23. For a discussion, see Duncan McCargo, "The Thai Malaise," *Foreign Policy,* February 18, 2014, www.foreignpolicy.com/2014/02/18/the-thai-malaise/.

24. ICG, "A Coup Ordained?" p. 15.

25. See, for example, Thin Lei Win, "The din of misogyny at Bangkok protests," Thomson Reuters, January 17, 2014, www.trust.org/item/20140117102903-gcbzr/.

26. See Duncan McCargo, "Network Monarchy and Legitimacy Crises in Thailand," *Pacific Review* 18, no. 4 (2005): 499–519.

27. See, for example, Joshua Kurlantzick, *Democracy in Retreat* (New Haven, CT: Yale University Press, 2013), pp. 233–35.

28. For regime trends, see Monty G. Marshall, "Polity IV Individual Country Regime Trends, 1946–2013," Center for Systemic Peace, June 6, 2014, www.systemicpeace.org/polity/polity4.htm.

29. The Centre for the Administration of Peace and Order was established in 2009 to monitor maintenance of peace and order. See "What is CAPO?" *Political Prisoners in Thailand,* April 5, 2010, https://thaipoliticalprisoners.wordpress.com/2010/04/05/what-is-capo/. CMPO was established after the government issued a sixty-day emergency decree on January 21, 2014. CMPO then replaced CAPO, overseeing national security and enforcing the emergency decree.

30. "Kkt. chiang mai pho jai leuaktang riaproi khat napkhanaen set 11 khet phrung ni yen" [EC Chiang Mai is satisfied with orderly election and expects to finish counting votes in 11 constituencies by tomorrow evening], *Manager Online,* April 2, 2006, www.manager.co.th/Local/ViewNews.aspx?NewsID=9490000044255.

31. See "Game reaches dead end PM pleads for justice as PDRC pushes on with its ultimatum," *The Nation,* December 11, 2013, www.nationmultimedia.com/politics/Game-reaches-dead-end-30221807.html.

32. Paritta Wangkiat, "Army's old guard to join anti-govt push," *Bangkok Post,* December 21, 2013, www.bangkokpost.com/news/politics/385956/army-old-guard-to-join-anti-govt-push; "Military must choose the side of righteousness," *The Nation,* December 21, 2013, www.nationmultimedia.com/politics/Military-must-choose-the-side-of-righteousness-say-30222603.html; "Retired military chiefs call on top brass to back public," *The Nation,* December 17, 2013, www.nationmultimedia.com/politics/Retired-military-chiefs-call-on-top-brass-to-back--30222277.html; "Old soldiers pledge support for PDRC," *Bangkok Post,* December 12, 2013, www.bangkokpost.com/news/politics/384491/former-soldiers-pledge-support-for-pdrc.

33. ThaiTVnews2014, "Prayut pb. thb. kham to kham pathiwat mai mi pit mai mi poet" [Prayut, Army Commander in Chief's exact words: a coup is neither off nor on], *YouTube* video, 5:33, December 29, 2013, www.youtube.com/watch?v=UO4Mo-Bk-Zk [no longer available].

34. "Reds discuss pro-govt rallies in Isaan next week," *The Nation*, January 8, 2014, www.nation-multimedia.com/politics/Reds-discuss-pro-govt-rallies-in-Isaan-next-week-30223739.html.

35. Thanong Khanthong, "Top brass now hold all the cards," *The Nation*, December 13, 2013, www.nationmultimedia.com/opinion/Top-brass-now-hold-all-the-cards-30221955.html.

36. The risk of violence that could lead to civil unrest or even civil war was a justification for the 2006 military coup. See "Thai coup proceeding 1," *YouTube* video, 3:33, September 20, 2006, www.youtube.com/watch?v=dOW0Ffsm8rg.

37. C. M. Phillips, "A partisan police force?" *The Nation*, December 29, 2013, www.nationmul-timedia.com/opinion/A-partisan-police-force-30223174.html; *Bangkok Post,* "Old soldiers pledge support for PDRC."

38. Panya Thiosangwan and Noppadon Sritaweekart, "Police on defensive over Dec 26 conflict: Top officer admits existence of rooftop team at labor ministry on the day," *The Nation*, January 3, 2014, www.nationmultimedia.com/politics/Police-on-defensive-over-Dec-26-conflict-30223390.html.

39. "Poet clip patha deuat wat Sri Iam ying sa nan! 'Suthin Tharathin' dap" [Watch a video clip of the Sri Iam temple shooting! Suthin Tharathin is dead], *Sanook News*, January 26, 2014, http://news.sanook.com/1430683/.

40. "Suthep won kongthap chuai khumkhrong prachachon" [Suthep begs the army to help protect people], *Thai Rath*, January 26, 2014, www.thairath.co.th/content/399068.

41. "'ANFREL' sadaeng khwam sia jai to kkt. mai chuai eua leuatang luan na" ['ANFREL' expressed dissatisfaction with the EC not helping advance voting], *Prachatai*, January 27, 2014, www.prachatai.com/journal/2014/01/51439.

42. "Thaksin tell family, keep low profile," *Bangkok Post*, December 25, 2013, www.nationmulti-media.com/politics/First-family-keeps-low-profile-30241498.html.

43. "PDRC claims victory in blocking advance votes most polling stations in the south and Bangkok forced to close but few problems in north, Isaan," *The Nation*, January 27, 2014.

44. EU Election Expert Mission, Interim Report No. 1 (unpublished manuscript, 2014).

45. "Kham sang san phae – ph.r.k.chuk choen" [Civil Court order – Declaration of a State of Emergency], *Khaosod,* February 21, 2014, www.khaosod.co.th/view_news.php?newsid=-TUROd2Iyd3dNakl4TURJMU53PT0.

46. "Constitution of the Kingdom of Thailand," *Government Gazette*, August 24, 2007, www.moph.go.th/ops/minister_06/Office2/1%5B1%5D.pdf .

47. "EC: Postpone the Poll for 3–4 Months," *Bangkok Post,* January 28, 2014, www.bangkok-post.com/most-recent/391915/allow-time-for-agreement-on-electoral-reform-says-election-commission.

48. See Pippa Norris, Ferran Martínez i Coma, and Max Grömping,"The Year in Elections, 2014: The World's Flawed and Failed Contests" (Sydney: Electoral Integrity Project, February 11, 2015), p. 26.

49. Attayuth Bootsripoom, "Does the EC have a hidden agenda over poll date?" *The Nation*, January 16, 2014, www.nationmultimedia.com/politics/Does-the-EC-have-a-hidden-agenda-over-poll-date--30224413.html.

50. "The momentum is swinging toward reform," *The Nation*.

51. Bangkok Pundit, "Thai court nullifies February election," *Asian Correspondent*, March 21, 2014, http://asiancorrespondent.com/120816/court-expected-to-rule-today-whether-to-void-the-february-2-election/; "Sarup sathanakan 2557: kan khatkhwang kanchai sitthi doi phak prachachon thi put hang su kan yu amnat" [Summarizing the situation in 2014: Obstructing the voters' rights by a section of people who paved the way to power seizure], *Prachatai*, February 4, 2015, www.prachatai.com/journal/2015/02/57742.

52. Kongkirati, "Thailand in no(transition)," p. 17.

53. Saksith Saiyasombut and Siam Voices, "Thai government, Election Commission clash over catch-up poll dates," *Asian Correspondent*, February 12, 2014, http://asiancorrespondent.com/119490/thai-government-election-commission-clash-over-catch-up-poll-dates/.

54. See Norris, Martínez i Coma, and Grömping, "The Year in Elections, 2014," 26. In addition to election mismanagement, the PDRC movement's intimidation campaign was another important factor that contributed to the failure of the February election.

55. These included the United States, Russia, China, the United Kingdom, Germany, France, Australia, Canada, EU, and ASEAN member states. See "40 countries 'back Thai election,'" *Bangkok Post*, December 14, 2013, www.bangkokpost.com/most-recent/384826/surapong-world-backs-thai-polls. Technically speaking, between December 9, 2013, and May 22, 2014, all ministers and even the prime minister were "caretaker" ministers. "The perils of personalised Thai diplomacy," *The Nation*, January 2, 2014, www.nationmultimedia.com/opinion/The-perils-of-personalised-Thai-diplomacy-30223307.html.

56. "Govt seeks ASEAN backing for election," *Bangkok Post*, December 13, 2013, www.bangkokpost.com/news/politics/384548/govt-seeks-asean-backing-for-election.

57. Both the *Bangkok Post* and *The Nation* adopted a broadly pro-PDRC and anti-election stance throughout this period. While these newspapers have very small readerships inside Thailand, they helped undermine the international legitimacy of the election. This was not the case for leading Thai language daily newspapers such as *Matichon* or *Thai Rath*, which were much more supportive of the election. See Duncan McCargo, "The Thai Malaise," *Foreign Policy*, February 18, 2014, www.foreignpolicy.com/2014/02/18/the-thai-malaise/.

58. "Govt seeks ASEAN backing," *Bangkok Post*.

59. For the Department of State's press release archive, see "Press Releases: December 2013," *Diplomacy in Action*, www.state.gov/r/pa/prs/ps/2013/c60414.htm. For the UK government press releases and statements, see "Thailand: Ánnouncements," *Gov.uk*, www.gov.uk/government/announcements?keywords=&announcement_filter_option=all&topics%5B%5D=all&departments%5B%5D=all&world_locations%5B%5D=thailand&from_date=&to_date=.

60. "'Not-my-father': Thaksin retracts UN jibe," *The Nation*, March 5, 2003, www.nationmultimedia.com/home/NOT-MY-FATHER-Thaksin-retracts-UN-jibe-75037.html.

61. "UN leader launches Thai mediation effort," *Bangkok Post*, January 11, 2014, www.bangkokpost.com/news/politics/388991/un-leader-launches-thai-mediation-effort; "Govt thanks Ban; Abhisit sends letter to UN," *The Nation*, January 13, 2014, www.nationmultimedia.com/politics/Govt-thanks-Ban;-Abhisit-sends-letter-to-UN-30224106.html.

62. "Press Conference by Secretary-General Ban Ki-moon at United Nations Headquarters," UN Press Release, January 10, 2014, www.un.org/press/en/2014/sgsm15577.doc.htm.

63. "Ban Ki-moon asked for Thai crisis help Surapong to propose UN involvement to CMPO," *Bangkok Post*, February 26, 2014, www.bangkokpost.com/news/politics/397077/ban-ki-moon-urged-to-help-fix-thai-conflict.

64. Marika Armanovica, "Kingdom of Thailand: A distressing standoff," DG EXPO/B/PolDep/Note/2014_25 (Brussels: European Parliament, Directorate-General for External Policies, February 26, 2014), p. 6, www.europarl.europa.eu/RegData/etudes/briefing_note/join/2014/522334/EXPO-AFET_SP(2014)522334_EN.pdf. The report made a number of proposals, including calling on both sides to refrain from violence, encouraging civil society groups to support democracy, urging all stakeholders to engage in dialogue, and using regional fora to engage parliamentarians (p. 16).

65. "UN opposes vote blocking in Thailand," *Bangkok Post*, February 5, 2014, www.bangkokpost.com/news/politics/393321/united-nations-will-not-condone-any-action-that-undermines-the-democratic-process-in-thailand; "US warns Thailand against coup d'etat," *Bangkok Post*, February 5, 2014, www.bangkokpost.com/news/politics/393221/us-warns-thailand-against-coup-d-etat.

66. U.S. Department of State, "Political Tensions in Thailand," Press Release, December 9, 2013, www.state.gov/r/pa/prs/ps/2013/218529.htm.

67. "Nitithon Lamleua plans to lead NSPRT to occupy US Embassy," *Prachatai*, December 15, 2013, www.prachatai.com/journal/2013/12//50439.

68. "Suthep clarifies PDRC's intentions in letter to Obama; Noppadon counters his claims," *The Nation*, January 26, 2014.

69. "Group calls for an end to political violence hundreds to go to 'peace rally' in Bangkok as rural support grows," *The Nation*, January 4, 2014, www.nationmultimedia.com/politics/Group-calls-for-an-end-to-political-violence-30223463.html; www.facebook.com/YaBastaThailand.

70. For example, see Yutsaphon Koetwibun, "Ubon: 'Saeng thian haeng santiphap yut khwam runraeng laeo pai leuaktang'" [Ubon: 'Candle light of peace, stop violence and go to vote'], Prachatai, January 6, 2014, www.prachatai.com/journal/2014/01/50967.

71. "Thalaengkan krueakhai '2 ao 2 mai ao' nun kaorop chai sithi tam ro.tho.no. – yut katika" [Official statement of the network '2 yeses 2 nos' to support the application of rights in accordance with the constitution – respect the rules], *Thai Rath*, January 10, 2014, www.thairath.co.th/content/395055.

72. See Thorn Pitidol, "2 Yeses 2 Nos," *New Mandala*, January 13, 2014, http://asiapacific.anu.edu.au/newmandala/2014/01/13/2-yeses-2-nos/.

73. See Sombat Kusumawali, "Khwamjaole thang wichakan kroni '2 ao 2 mai ao'" [Academic trick of '2 yeses 2 nos' case], *Manager Online*, January 13, 2014, www.manager.co.th/Daily/ViewNews.aspx?NewsID=9570000004536.

74. See Sarayuth Roeththiphin,"Nun 2 ao 2 mai ao phrom yok 4 niu dan kotmai krajai kanthu khrong thi din yang pen tham" [Support for 2 yeses 2 nos with 4 raised fingers to spread belief that the land is governed by dhamma], Prachatai, January 17, 2014, www.prachatai.com/journal/2014/01/51220.

75. "The momentum is swinging toward reform," *The Nation*, January 30, 2014, www.nationalmedia.com/opinion/The-momentum-is-swinging-toward-reform-30225518.html.

76. ANFREL, "Report on 2007 Thai General Election" (Bangkok: ANFREL, 2008), p. 22.

77. "Suthep chuan ma picnic klang krung 2 k.ph. mai pai leuaktang" [Suthep invites for a picnic in the city centre on February 2 instead of election], *MThai News*, January 30, 2014, http://news.mthai.com/politics-news/306469.html.

78. For a detailed study, see William A. Callahan, *Pollwatching: Elections and Civil Society in Southeast Asia* (Aldershot, UK: Ashgate, 2000), pp. 3–76.

79. Saksith Saiyasombut and Siam Voices, "Thai election observers openly against February 2 poll," *Asian Correspondent*, January 31, 2014, http://asiancorrespondent.com/119105/thai-election-observers-openly-against-february-2-election/.

80. See ANFREL, "Report on Thailand's 2005 Elections" (Bangkok: ANFREL, 2005), p. 7, http://anfrel.org/download/2005_thailand.pdf. The reports on the 2007 and 2011 elections are much more balanced.

81. Ichal Supraidi, interview with Suluck Lamubol, *Prachatai*, January 6. 2014, www.prachatai.com/english/node/3812.

82. ANFREL, "In Thailand, Re-Engagement with Elections Is Crucial," Press Release, February 3, 2014, http://anfrel.org/in-thailand-re-engagement-with-elections-is-crucial/.

83. ANFREL, "Briefing on the Thai Election of 2 February 2014."

84. Armanovica, "Kingdom of Thailand," p. 6.

85. "Sun khomun tittam sathannakan khwamrunraeng thang kanmuang" [Center for information on political violence], https://sites.google.com/site/violenceindicator/.

86. Rup khomun pham ruam wan thi 1 kumphaphan 2557 wela 22 n" [Summary of the situation on February 1, 2014 at 22:00], https://sites.google.com/site/violenceindicator/srup-phaph-rwm-khx-mu-l-ray-wan/rup-khxmul-phaph-rwm-wan-thi-1-kumphaphanth-2557-wela-22-00-n.

87. For details, see Thom Pitidol, "2 Yesses 2 Nos," *New Mandala*, January 13, 2014, http://asiapacific.anu.edu.au/newmandala/2014/01/13/2-yeses-2-nos/.

88. "'O lek' phlo khum ngan yaowachon Pheu Thai 'Pu-Ok-Uan' rap both kunsu" ['Oh, the young ones' emerge to control the work of Pheu Thai 'Pu (Yingluck Shinawatra)-Ok (Phanthongthae Shinawatra)-Uan (Phumitham Wetchayachai)' assume the roles of advisers], *Manager Online*, October 24, 2013, www.manager.co.th/Politics/ViewNews.aspx?NewsID=9560000133271.

89.   "Varsities offer students as political observers," *The Nation*, December 23, 2013, www.
       nationmultimedia.com/politics/Varsities-offer-students-as-political-observers-30222715.
       html.

90.   "Students cry foul after 'being forced to stage poll rally'," *The Nation*, January 21, 2014, www.
       nationmultimedia.com/politics/students-cry-foul-after-forced-to-back-feb-2-poll-30224787.
       html; "Democracy centre denies it was behind students' march," *The Nation*, January 23, 2014,
       www.nationmultimedia.com/national/Democracy-centre-denies-it-was-behind-students-
       mar-30224871.html.

91.   Anderson, "Murder and Progress," p. 34.

PART II

Prevention Success
or Local Resilience?

Map 4.1 Malawi National Map

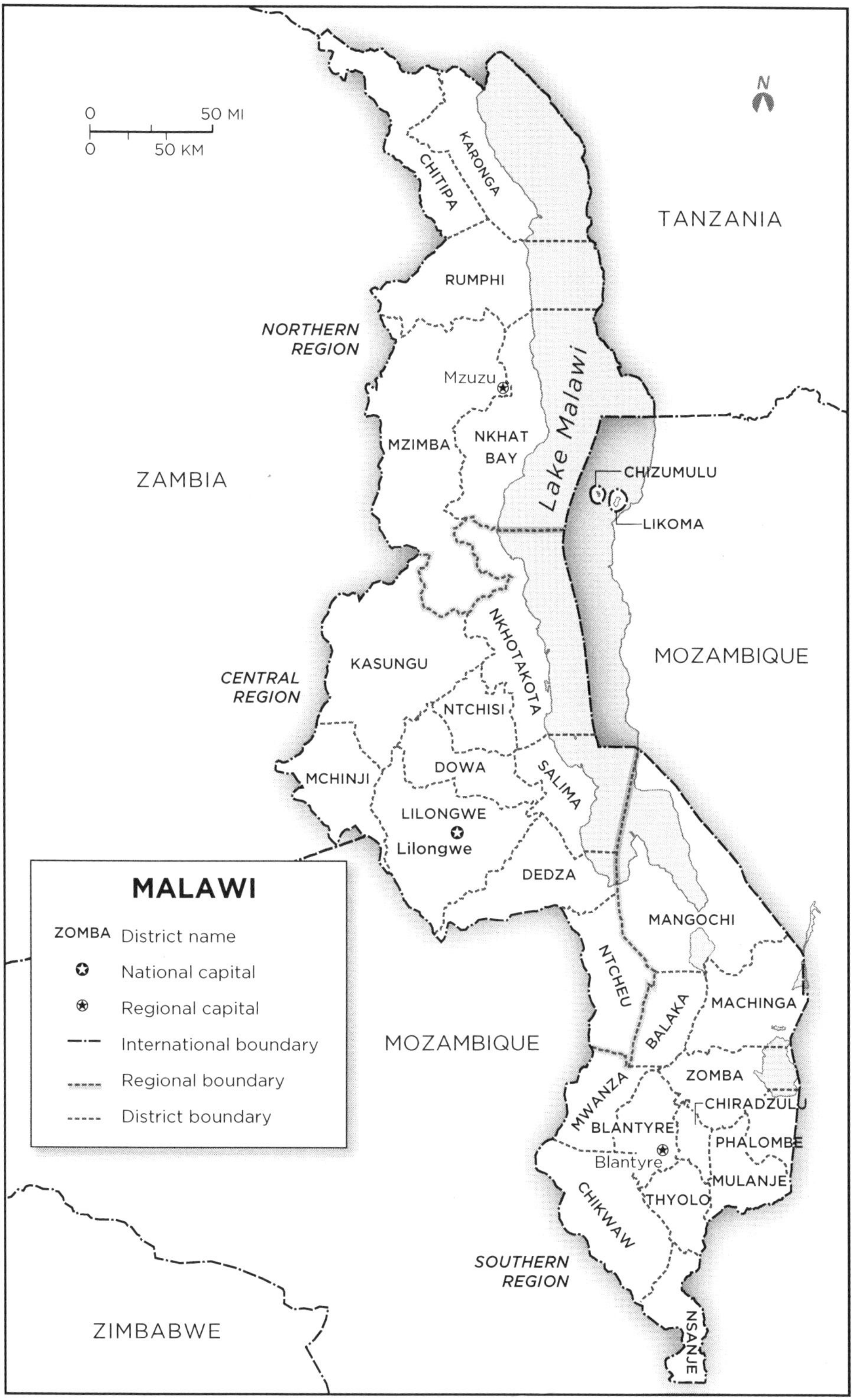

0   50 MI

0   50 KM

N

TANZANIA

CHITIPA

KARONGA

RUMPHI

NORTHERN
REGION

ZAMBIA

Mzuzu

MZIMBA

NKHAT
BAY

Lake Malawi

CHIZUMULU

LIKOMA

MOZAMBIQUE

NKHOTAKOTA

CENTRAL
REGION

KASUNGU

NTCHISI

DOWA

SALIMA

MCHINJI

LILONGWE

Lilongwe

DEDZA

MANGOCHI

MALAWI

ZOMBA   District name

✪   National capital

✹   Regional capital

–·–   International boundary

----   Regional boundary

····   District boundary

MOZAMBIQUE

NTCHEU

MACHINGA

BALAKA

ZOMBA

CHIRADZULU

MWANZA

PHALOMBE

BLANTYRE

Blantyre

MULANJE

CHIKWAW

THYOLO

SOUTHERN
REGION

ZIMBABWE

NSANJE

4

Malawi

Widespread Tension, Limited Violence

MANUELA TRAVAGLIANTI

n May 2014, Malawi held its first tripartite elections: citizens went to the polls to elect, all at once, their president, the members of its national parliament, and local councillors. Commentators were concerned that the high stakes and competitive nature of the electoral races, along with the complexity of managing the elections, could stir up tensions and lead to violence. The election proceeded calmly, however, with only a few minor incidents. Tensions were widespread throughout but in the end only three casualties were reported. The violence that did occur resulted from frustration with management of the voting process, contestation of the results, and interparty clashes.

The relatively peaceful outcome of these elections—despite risk factors such as high electoral competition and only partially consolidated state institutions—offers valuable insights into the conditions under which measures to prevent electoral violence (PEV models) can thrive. Building on interviews with key informants and focus group discussions across the country, this chapter evaluates the impact of PEV models on the behavior of politicians and of voters during key moments of the 2014 electoral process in Malawi.

In recent years, certain prevention models—peace messaging, civic education, monitoring and mapping, and preventive diplomacy—have been broadly and intensively applied across Malawi. Implementation has improved over time, especially in regard to electoral management bodies and security-sector engagement. Voter consultations and youth programming, however, have remained weak. The absence of youth programs in particular has presented a missed opportunity in light of the role youth play in perpetrating election violence.

The two most effective prevention models in Malawi have been peace messaging and preventive diplomacy, which influence the preferences of competing actors for peaceful campaigns and peaceful resolution of disputes by creating unappealing consequences for acting otherwise. In addition to pressure and mediation by Western diplomatic representatives and donor partners, a well-established and highly authoritative set of domestic nongovernmental institutions was also active in Malawi's recent elections. The success of this engagement demonstrates the value of local ownership in supporting self-sustainable peacebuilding efforts during electoral processes.

The analysis in this chapter is based on a review of secondary sources and on fieldwork interviews conducted between August 2014 and December 2014.[1] To capture variations in the outcome of electoral violence and to discuss the role of prevention in violent and peaceful contexts, interviews were carried out in both localities that experienced violence in 2014 and those that were peaceful.[2]

History of Political Violence

Malawi, known as Nyasaland during British colonization, achieved independence in 1964 after a turbulent transition during which multiple nationalist supporters were detained without trial. Two years later, it became a one-party state under the control of Hastings Kamuzu Banda and his Malawi Congress Party (MCP). Opposition, either outside or within the government, was not tolerated: Banda banned all opposition parties, detained political opponents indefinitely without charge, required party membership for access to services and jobs in the public sector, and employed the national paramilitary youth organization Malawi Young Pioneers (MYP) as an intelligence and police force.[3]

Banda's highly organized apparatus of control and repression succeeded in holding power until 1992, when political opposition to his regime formed in exile and successfully worked with the country's well-entrenched religious organizations to promote a transition to multiparty democracy. Following a two-thirds majority in the 1993 referendum to overturn one-party rule, Malawi finally embraced political liberalization. The referendum campaign, however, was marred by MCP-sponsored intimidation, violence, and arrest of opposition activists.[4]

The transition to a multiparty system, however, did not stop the political intimidation and violence, but simply changed its nature (see figure 4.1). In fact, the increased competition only fueled electoral conflict between political parties and their supporters. During the 1994 campaign, the MCP engaged in bribery, intimidation (perpetrated largely by the MYP), and outright violence to sow fear of change. Electoral violence served principally to intimidate opposition supporters and disrupt opposition rallies.[5] Voters would "be beaten if [the ruling party] heard that they belong[ed] to another party," focus group discussion revealed. Winners also engaged in retribution against those who did not vote for them. According to the research director of Young Politicians in a 2014 interview, "[In 1994] use of violence was the order of the day. People had to use any means in order to come out from the one party rule.... Perpetrators were the youths, who were being used by the political leaders. The victims were the families, people who were not active in politics."

Since then, election violence has been a recurring feature. Although fatalities appear low—at least in comparison with neighboring Zimbabwe and other countries in sub-Saharan Africa—the figures do not account for nonlethal violence such as harassment, intimidation, and destruction of property typical since 1994 and strong in people's minds.

Specifically, the 1999 elections were hotly contested between the incumbent, President Bakili Muluzi of the United Democratic Front (UDF) party, and new MCP leader Gwanda Chakuamba of the opposition party Alliance for Democracy (AFORD). Chakuamba

Figure 4.1 Authority Trends in Malawi

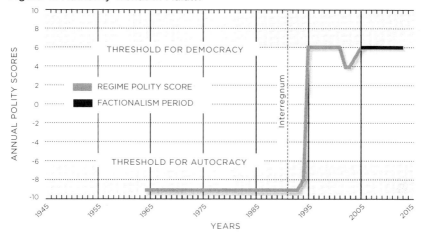

Source: Center for Systemic Peace, www.systemicpeace.org/polity/maw2.htm

threatened the UDF's territorial stronghold of the southern region, which is also the most populous area of Malawi. Sporadic violence occurred throughout the campaign, in the form of clashes between supporters and destruction of property: UDF activists attacked opposition members, for example, and AFORD supporters broke up a UDF election rally. After Muluzi was reelected, opposition leaders declared electoral fraud and organized riots.[6] Intolerance and polarization, already part of political competition and fueling hostility toward supporters of opposing parties, further intensified.[7]

Campaign violence and voter intimidation also occurred in the 2004 elections, though it was less prevalent than in 1994 and 1999. The violence was perpetrated primarily by the youth wings of the various political parties, instigated by senior politicians to intimidate political opponents.[8] More broadly, the election was plagued by irregularities and controversies starting with the registration period. Muluzi's handpicked successor, Bingu wa Mutharika, eventually won a tightly contested race involving the UDF, MCP, and the Mgwirizano coalition, that was followed by violent protest and rioting in Blantyre and Mzuzu that killed at least four people.[9] By 2004, intimidation had become so widespread that almost half of those prevented from voting in the northern region in that election said that they had been intimidated by other parties' loyalists.[10]

However, Mutharika's anticorruption reform agenda distanced him from his predecessor. In 2005, anticipating his expulsion from the party, Mutharika formed the Democratic Progressive Party (DPP) with several independent and opposition members of parliament. Mutharika and his running mate Joyce Banda then won the 2009 election. The election was marred by violence, and clashes between party supporters or disruption of political rallies was frequent throughout the electoral campaign.[11]

Intraparty conflict continued. In 2011, Mutharika appointed his brother Peter as president of the DPP. In response to being sidelined, Joyce Banda then formed the People's Party but retained her constitutional right to remain in office as vice president. Thus, when Bingu wa Mutharika died in April 2012, she took over the presidency, attracting forty MPs from the DPP to cross the floor.[12] The move was not without difficulty: Bingu Mutharika's inner circle, led by Peter Mutharika, had originally concealed the president's death and allegedly plotted a coup to secure power.

This history of repression and violence has created a general perception of politics in Malawi as what Roman Poeschke and Chijere Chirwa call a "dangerous game," reducing the willingness of citizens to actively participate in the political process (including postelection protests). Another 1998 study pointed to fear of violence by the ruling party as one reason for voter apathy in recent by-elections. Such fear, though, was not the only factor contributing to voter apathy and aversion to engaging in political demonstrations. The same 1998 study found that disengagement was also due to a loss of trust in leaders, who forgot about the electorate after coming into power. This finding has since been confirmed by other studies revealing that dissatisfaction with politics and unmet promises is connected to a lack of participation.[13] Unrealistic expectations for the political transition process and a recipient attitude toward the government has been accompanied by a lack of will or way to articulate demands by voters, producing a situation in which popular expectations are not met. Elections have thus been followed by voters' disappointment, resignation, and pessimism.[14] As a focus group participant explained during a discussion among Lunzo women in November 2015, "We are *just used* during the campaign so that we should vote for that person." This underlying attitude of fear and resignation seems to drive the "peaceful" inclination of Malawians—a factor that consistently emerged across interviews as a condition that may have discouraged postelectoral mobilization and potentially violent protest.

2014 Elections

The 2014 elections posed considerable risk of violent unrest and instability. For the first time in the country's history, Malawians went to the polls to elect the president, members of parliament, and ward counselors in the local councils (see map 4.2). The organizational complexity of these tripartite elections, with the considerable increase in the number of electoral races to be managed, posed challenges to an electoral commission that in the past had not demonstrated the ability to flawlessly manage elections.

The election—held on May 20—resulted in the victory of DPP candidate Peter Mutharika with 36.4 percent of the vote. MCP candidate Lazarus Chackwera garnered 27.8 percent, the People's Party (PP) incumbent Joyce Banda 20.2 percent, and UDF candidate Atupele Muluzi trailed in fourth with 13.7 percent. Overall voter turnout was 70.87 percent. Immediately after the vote, incumbent President Banda annulled the elections on the basis of alleged massive irregularities and ordered a stop to the tallying. When the courts rejected her order, Banda pushed for a recount. The courts allowed the Malawi Electoral Commission (MEC) to proceed with the recount within eight days of the voting, but, given these time constraints, the MEC announced the results without a recount.

Map 4.2 Malawi Presidential Election District Winners

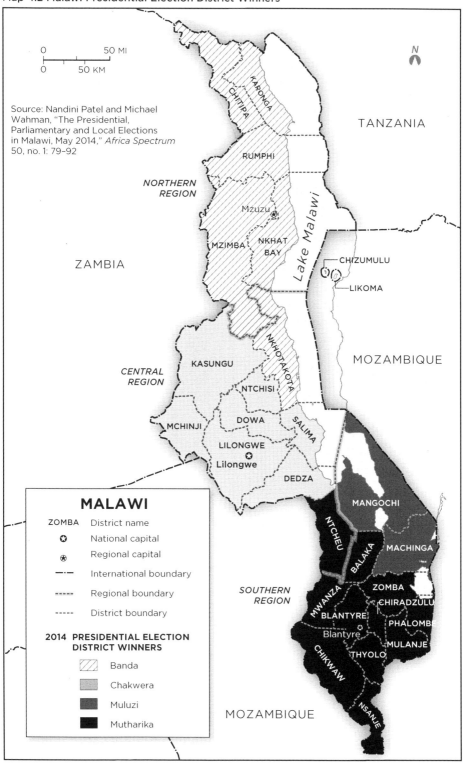

Photo 4.1 Peace message at Malawi Electoral Commission

Photo Credit: Manuela Travaglianti

Interview participants portrayed the electoral cycle as free of large-scale violence, but generally tense. Only three casualties were reported. In Goliati, Thyolo district, supporters of the DPP (the dominant party in the area) and the incumbent PP clashed during and after a rally organized by Joyce Banda, leading to two deaths (a policeman and a civilian) and various injuries, as well as property damage. In the days following the elections and the announcement of informal results, people protested in Mangochi, a district in the eastern region that was a stronghold of the UDF. These protests resulted in the death of one young protester, injuries to two policemen, and further property damage.

These events were common knowledge across the country. They were the only lethal violence, but certainly not the only incidents. Destruction of property, stoning, and verbal harassment were widespread and often underreported. Several supporters of the then ruling party had their houses set on fire.[15] An interviewee from a civil society organization in Balaka explained: "Violence is not only the fighting, it can also be verbal. There was indeed verbal violence, but it did not reach the extent of becoming worse." According to the reports of long-term observers deployed by the Malawi Electoral Support Network in the most contentious constituencies, hate speech at political rallies and political intimidation and harassment constituted the lion's share of the violent events they recorded (see figure 4.2).

Two types of violent acts were prevalent in Malawi: those motivated by competition for power and those expressing frustration with logistical failures. The factors that motivate deliberate use of violence and the conditions that lead to an escalation of tensions are analyzed for each type. Isolating these actors and conditions allows us to assess the impact of preventive peacebuilding practices and the rationale behind their failure or success.

Figure 4.2 Violence in Malawi Electoral Cycle

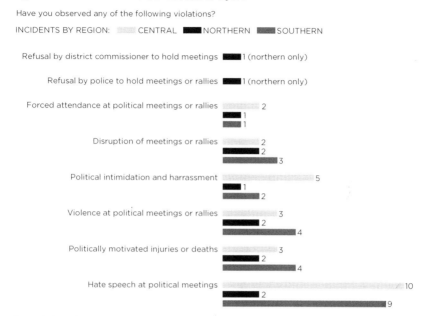

Have you observed any of the following violations?

INCIDENTS BY REGION: CENTRAL   NORTHERN   SOUTHERN

Refusal by district commissioner to hold meetings — 1 (northern only)

Refusal by police to hold meetings or rallies — 1 (northern only)

Forced attendance at political meetings or rallies — 2 / 1 / 1

Disruption of meetings or rallies — 2 / 2 / 3

Political intimidation and harrassment — 5 / 1 / 2

Violence at political meetings or rallies — 3 / 2 / 4

Politically motivated injuries or deaths — 3 / 2 / 4

Hate speech at political meetings — 10 / 2 / 9

Source: Malawi Electoral Support Network, "Malawi Tripartite Elections: Consolidating Democracy Through Better Elections," conference report, June 26–27, 2014

Competition for Power

Competition for power was the principal motivation behind electoral violence. In their run for power, strong political candidates would use all strategies at their disposal to gain votes. Before elections, this would translate into intimidation, negative messages, and verbal attacks against political opponents. This practice, in contrast with issue-based campaigning, would fire up party supporters and increase tensions. A woman in a focus group discussion in Blantyre in November 2014 summed up this connection between hate speech and violence clearly: "Insulting each other causes violence. If I am Atupele's supporter, and I hear someone talking bad about him, I cannot be happy with it and I may think of revenging." Indeed, some interpreted the decision of PP incumbent Banda to hold a rally in a DPP stronghold such as Goliati, accompanied by the use of negative comments against former DPP president Bingu wa Mutharika, as a dangerous provocation.[16]

After the elections, politicians who lost—and perhaps suspected rigging—would potentially dispute results that were unexpected (or simply not desired), and the contestation of electoral results could lead party supporters to engage in outbursts of protest. The clearest example was in Mangochi, a district where the UDF won 63 percent of

the presidential votes but trailed fourth at the national level. Not all localities supporting parties that lost at the national level, though, experienced demonstrations or violent escalations of protest. People would "murmur" but not protest. Political parties that
anticipated losing the elections did not publicly call for demonstrations, though rumors
of organized protests did surface. One interviewee in Blantyre said, for example, "I understand that there were some underground meetings among some political parties to incite
violence of some sort. But it appears that among those political parties, they did not agree
on one thing. As a result, there was nothing like a general announcement for propagating
violence. That is why we remained as calm as we were, from the time the results were
released, up to date." Similarly, the interviewed MCP spokesperson seemed inclined to
engage in some form of demonstration, but the party leader eventually did not approve.

In all circumstances of violence, the perpetrators were apparently party supporters,
and youth were consistently indicated as the main instruments of violence across the
country. Each political party that had been in government since 1994 exploited youth
wings to unleash terror on their opponents.[17] The UDF had the Young Democrats, the
DPP had the Youth Cadets, and the PP had the Young Patriots. In some cases youth (or
party supporters more broadly) reacted to insults and harassment, but most often their
actions were deliberate. A participant in a focus group discussion mentioned that voters
might be stoned on their way to party rallies. As another declared, "we the youth are
regarded as bad people but the adults are the one who start it." Youth organization members would receive money in exchange for intimidating voters or brawling the streets,
and were therefore more tools than actual instigators of violence. As one discussion
participant said, "In short, I can say that the youth are used like materials. The leaders
use us and we just go because its money, hence we do violence." Two youths in Mangochi
explained this process concisely in a focus group discussion:

> Interviewer: Why do the youths agree to do that?
> Participant 1: Mostly it's money.
> Participant 2: Because they do not have anything to do.
> Interviewer: So it [is] because they don't have something to do?
> Participant 1: Yes, if somebody say do something I will give you K100, can't refuse.

In sum, were politicians not to offer incentives, violence between party supporters
would largely be spontaneous and unsustained. However, were youth not willing to engage in violence, politicians could not easily implement violent strategies. Both factors
therefore appear to be necessary for the occurrence and escalation of violence.

Popular Protest

In addition to violence organized to influence the vote, frustrations about poor management of the voting process and disappointment with the results were also causes of tension
and violence. Should these frustrations arise amid suspicions of deliberate sabotage—as
in Blantyre, where people speculated that the MEC delayed voting in DPP-friendly
areas under the influence of the incumbent PP government—disappointment could cross

the threshold to violence. Accordingly, such violence can be prevented by ensuring that the overall process, from registering voters to counting results, is implemented smoothly and transparently.

Contextual Vulnerabilities

Preventive efforts against violence are often undertaken amid risk and uncertainty. The 2014 Malawi elections presented a highly factionalized political arena, strong regional patterns of voting, an electoral system encouraging stiff competition and producing potentially disproportional results, and unclear expectations about the electoral outcome.

Factionalized Democracy

According to the Regime Polity scores, Malawi is a democracy—but not a fully democratic system. The recruitment of the executive is in a transitional period that includes limited competition and intimidation of the opposition, especially its leaders. Nonetheless, institutionalized constraints do limit the power of chief executives' decision-making.

A significant stability risk is the presence of multiple identities—defined in the Polity dataset as relatively stable and enduring groups that compete for political influence at the national level. Such groups can be parties, regional entities, or ethnic groups that favor group members to the detriment of common or cross-cutting agendas. As a result, exclusive identity cleavages and factions are "played out contentiously within the political participation and competitiveness arenas of the central polity."[18] The Polity coding of factionalism coincides with the split of Mutharika's DPP from Muluzi's UDF, and then of Banda's PP from the DPP party. This context foreshadowed a potentially contentious electoral cycle in 2014. Furthermore, except for the People's Party, all major political parties (UDF, DPP, and MCP) were embroiled in leadership succession struggles that demonstrated a lack of internal democracy and resembled personal following more than an institutional process.

Regional identities are also strong and politically salient, and in 2014 regional voting patterns reemerged vigorously.[19] In particular, the DPP party was strong in the south, UDF in the east, MCP in the central region, and PP had some support both in the north and south. Regional voting left the impression that people would not likely be surprised by the results within their given area, but it was nonetheless possible that the same voters would look with suspicion on aggregate results at the national level.

Electoral System and Power Distribution

Malawi uses a first-past-the-post (FPTP) system based on simple majority to elect the president, members of parliament, and local councilors by universal adult suffrage.[20] This system is locally considered a good method because determining the winner is relatively simple. At the same time, it has exacerbated the competitiveness of the electoral race. According to one interviewee, many perceived the zero-sum nature of competition as contributing to a state in which "those who fear being victims then become aggressive," creating the attitude of "Let us do all [that] it takes to win because otherwise we will be victims."

The other major shortcoming is that it can produce minority governments with limited popular legitimacy that are unable to govern unless opposition parties decide to cooperate. FPTP also potentially produces disproportionate results, in that the percentage of votes won by a party can differ considerably from the proportion of seats it wins. Furthermore, unlike in the proportional representation system, FPTP elections tend to focus on the candidate's rather than the party's identity.[21] Recognizing these shortcomings, several prominent civil society organizations announced after the 2014 elections that, to enhance government stability, they would lobby for the introduction of an absolute majority requirement in the presidential election.[22]

Despite the shortcomings of the FPTP system, however, the lack of a clear majority also prompted parties to seek alliances after the elections, or at least to include members of opposition or independent parties within the government. For instance, after Peter Mutharika was inaugurated as Malawi's fifth president in June 2014, several independent members of parliament crossed the floor to join the ruling party. Floor-crossing, generally to join the ruling party, is indeed common in Malawian politics, and is practiced to maximize election prospects, to join the government, or to increase development in an MP's home constituency.[23]

Although many condemn floor-crossing and party volatility as representing a lack of political ideologies, such practices can also enable politicians to obtain power without resorting to violence. For example, in 2014 UDF leader Atupele Muluzi was appointed minister of energy and mining. This appointment was likely not the determinant of the UDF's decision to refrain from sustained postelectoral violence to protest the results, focus group discussion concluded, but nonetheless seems to have dissipated tensions among the population. The appointment was perceived as a commitment to unity (rather than a sign of opportunistic behavior) and a way to bring political benefits to Muluzi's community. As people interviewed in Blantyre explained,

> We had UDF and DPP members. We were living like a cat and a mouse. But after Peter won and took Atupele to work together with him, most of us saw that this is a good person. Had it been that he had just left him aside, things could not be fine with him. Because of this, we also decided to work together with them. If there was hatred in the past, it will end.

Similarly,

> Interviewer: After the elections, do those who have won and those who have lost work together?
> Participant: Yes they work together. The opposition is also the government because they all…rule for the country. They work together in Parliament.
> Interviewer: Does this affect their supporters?
> Participant: It does.
> Interviewer: How?
> Participant: When they see that their leaders have accepted, and there is no strife in their hearts, it brings peace.

Uncertainty About Outcome

The 2014 tripartite elections presented a highly competitive race between four main presidential candidates: the incumbent Joyce Banda (PP), Peter Mutharika (DPP), Lazarus
Chackwera of the renewed MCP, and Atupele Muluzi (UDF), the son of former president
Bakili Muluzi. The 2014 elections were widely seen as the most competitive since 1994,
and isolating a clear favorite was difficult.[24]

The most reliable preelection poll showed Mutharika leading the presidential race,
followed by Chackwera, Banda, and Muluzi, in that order.[25] However these predictions
were not the only ones circulating before the election; other polls, which suffered from
questionable sampling methods, distributed opposite predictions.[26] These polls were often
accompanied by contrasting opinions by the "prophets"—preachers to whom the population often looks for advice.[27] Therefore, as the resident coordinator for the United Nations
Development Program (UNDP) declared in a preelection op-ed, "the stakes of the May
2014 tripartite elections in Malawi [were] high, the pre-election projections uncertain, and
the rigging fears rampant."[28]

Media

The media were another contextual factor that had the potential either to prevent or exacerbate the spread of electoral violence, depending on the quality of the reporting. The mere
presence of a widespread media network is in fact not enough. The opposite can be true
when media outlets lack professionalism and adequate training. Publication of the unreli-
able opinion polls cited earlier is an example: the surveys were not regulated or rigorously
assessed and therefore could be easily manipulated.

As journalist Anthony Kasunda noted in an author interview, if some people are already
disturbed to learn about violent events targeting supporters of their preferred party, the
same feelings can only be exacerbated when these events are reported in sensationalistic
and inflammatory terms. Further, a premature announcement of results, or the announcement of unofficial results, can (in addition to influencing the vote itself) prompt protests
by susceptible supporters, as occurred in Mangochi.[29] Informal results that mirror those
of the EC and voting tabulation, however, can also strengthen confidence in the official
announcements and thus undermine the credibility of postelectoral protests—as in 2014.

According to the European Union (EU) Electoral Observation Mission report, media
outlets in Malawi are characterized by poor financial and logistical resources, which limits
the capacity of institutional bodies to promote professional values and ethics for journalists. Still, training for journalists has increased, and a few independent radio stations have
established a reputation for being professional, reliable, and neutral—to the point that
an independent station (Zodiak radio), and not the public broadcast corporation, was
chosen to partner with the MEC in distributing civic education messages and electoral
information. These signs of improvement also demonstrate that the suppression of media
in Malawi before 2012 has since improved. In fact, the Reporters Without Borders World
Press Freedom Index saw a remarkable jump for Malawi, from 146 of 179 countries in
2012 to 73 of 180 by 2014.[30]

Prevention in 2014

In this tense electoral context, several measures designed to limit or prevent election violence were implemented. Preventive diplomacy, peace messaging, civic and voter education, and election monitoring and mapping were particularly widespread in the 2014 elections (see table 4.1). Despite some shortcomings, the security sector also engaged adequately. Voter consultations and youth programming were limited and inconsistent. All prevention efforts improved in either quality or scope over previous elections. The effectiveness of these models in preventing electoral violence is discussed later.

Table 4.1 Civic and Voter Education Activities in Malawi

MONTH	MEC*	CSO‡
April	60%	91%
May	68%	89%

*Malawi Electoral Commission (MEC) ‡ Civic Society Organization (CSO)
Source: Malawi Electoral Support Network, "Malawi Tripartite Elections: Consolidating Democracy Through Better Elections," conference report, June 26–27, 2014

Security-Sector Engagement

The Malawian police, beyond ensuring public order during the electoral cycle, also provided both personnel at voting registration centers and polling stations, and—along with the Malawi Defense Force and the Multiparty Liaison Committees—security as polling materials were transported and stored.[31] The impression of electoral security that emerges from interviews is of capable and well-trained forces characterized by partisanship. Despite the lack of neutrality, the presence of police during campaigning and on election day likely mitigated the escalation of electoral clashes.

Until 2012, the Malawi Police Service (MPS) was known for its weak institutional capacity, poor government resourcing, inadequate external oversight, and variable policy and strategic direction.[32] Indeed, perceptions regarding the security situation in the country, and of the MPS itself, deteriorated in the wake of the police's violent response to 2011 antigovernment demonstrations in which twenty protesters lost their lives and more than forty were injured. The Afrobarometer survey data for 2012 reveals that one in three Malawians trusted the police not at all or very little, and that more than four in ten believed that most if not all police were corrupt.[33] Lack of strategy and training of police forces for handling demonstrations and controlling mobs also played an important role. The Presidential Commission of Inquiry on the demonstrations found a lack of professionalism, proficiency, and operational effectiveness, and identified both a lack of human capacity and glaring gaps in security and operational planning.[34]

To cope with these issues, police training intensified in the months leading up to the 2014 elections, encouraged by President Banda, who appointed a new and reform-minded inspector-general of police who pledged to improve police response to crime and insecurity, to increase police accountability, and to guarantee public order more effectively while protecting civil rights. The United Kingdom (UK) also initiated a Policing Improvement Program in Malawi, which was followed by EU support to create an Independent Police Complaints Commission, and by U.S. support for police training facilities in Botswana.

Only a few Malawian interviewees indicated knowledge of these training efforts. Interviews with members of the international community, however, confirmed that the additional training was indeed relevant to preventing violence during the elections, even though the implementation was at times imperfect. As an example, in the district of Mangochi—where violent demonstrations took place when electoral results were first announced—people lamented during focus group discussions that the police reacted violently to their demonstrations:

> The ones who started it all were the police by restraining the people who were complaining. Instead of asking them why they were doing that, they were using force with tear gas and even guns shooting up. It was this thing that provoked the people to start the violence and destroying the road and stoning the police.

On the other hand, as both interviews and focus group discussion revealed, additional training for the police was reported in this locality, suggesting that security-sector reform was pursued in most vulnerable areas—even though resources might have been insufficient to properly deploy and maintain security forces. In the case of the campaign clashes in Goliati, Thyolo district, the police were able to quell protests before they escalated.[35] Whether the training was not fully effective in preparing officers for a violent escalation or instead prevented the kind of higher-level violence seen during the 2011 protests is difficult to determine.

Professionalism and neutrality were not consistently recognized, and respondents often mentioned that the police favored the government. This perception was particularly strong in localities that witnessed postelection demonstrations. A bias toward the ruling party is not new within the Malawian police: although the Malawi army has always been professional (and remains apart from government repression), the police favored Hastings Kamuzu Banda and have since followed the government of the day.[36]

Overall, a clear regulatory framework is in place for provision of security and integrated security-sector governance. Security forces in Malawi, however, are neither fully capable and professional nor neutral (fuzzy set score: 0.75).

Election Management and Administration

Election management and administration in 2014 encountered a series of shortfalls. Failure to carry out certain key operations on election day sparked suspicion and tension. At the same time, the MEC's ability to handle complaints and its collaboration with conflict-resolution institutions at the national level did help mitigate electoral conflicts.

The MEC has not seen unqualified success. Although the commission that presided over the 1994 elections was lauded for its performance, the 1999 and 2004 elections were not efficiently administered—to the extent that international observation missions expressed lack of confidence in the results of the 2004 presidential election.[37]

In 2014, the MEC was composed of a chair, nominated by the Judicial Service Commission and appointed by the president, and nine commissioners, appointed by President Banda in 2012 in consultation with parliament, for a renewable four-year period. International technical assistance was lighter than in earlier elections, with only five UNDP technical advisers, as opposed to twenty in 2009, but nevertheless fully engaged.[38] Donors provided additional support, such as a review of electoral laws and staff and stakeholder training.[39]

The 2014 elections posed additional operational complexities in light of the higher number of competitive races. The commission did not successfully complete organizational and logistical preparations in time for election day, and showed a lack of structural capacity in conducting several key operations of the electoral process—in particular, the distribution of election material to polling stations. Serious delays in voter registration were also observed.[40] Although 94 percent of prospective voters were registered, delays in the inspection of the voter roll were significant, and ultimately no consensus was reached on the final figure of citizens of voting age.[41] According to the EU Electoral Observation Mission, the overall integrity of voter registries was intact, but delays and logistical failures led to suspicion and frustration among the population. Additional challenges came from inadequate internal communication and exchange of information.[42] These shortcomings were echoed in statements from focus group respondents and key informants, who often expressed dissatisfaction—they noted that while the MEC did have clear guidelines or processes in place for vote tabulation, voter and party registration, and party code of conduct, the implementation of these processes was often lacking.

The percentage of the Malawian population expressing a high level of trust in the Electoral Commission has consistently been around 40 percent since 1999.[43] However, in 2014 people voiced concerns that manually counted votes did not tally with those counted electronically, and speculated whether vote-rigging might have occurred. These rumors—which were particularly prevalent in areas with higher support for the opposition—increased tensions and eventually caused turmoil in some regions of the country, such as the district of Mangochi.

Confusion and suspicion about the aggregation of the electoral results through the electronic system were also widespread, and appear to be motivated largely by limited knowledge of the electoral system. In fact, the MEC tally center functioned in a transparent way and was open to the press. The MEC appeared to act impartially throughout the election period. Election experts commended the open and continuous efforts in media communication with both other stakeholders and the public, as well as the management of complaints. Following up on the recommendations of the EU Electoral Observation Mission in 2009, the period for submitting election petitions was extended from forty-eight hours to seven days after the announcement of the election results.[44] Complaints were addressed immediately, a process that was facilitated by the UNDP technical assistance mission. The National Electoral Consultative Forum (NECOF) provided an additional way for the MEC to communicate with stakeholders, political parties, the army, the police, traditional leaders, faith-based organizations, and civil society organizations to resolve electoral conflicts at the national level.[45]

However, despite the options available to express grievances and complaints, voters felt excluded and generally unable to submit claims. For example, in Petulo Village in Balaka district, one respondent said, "I don't know why MEC does not give a chance to us as voters.... Some of them [politicians] go to the courts, some to MEC, and MEC only listens to the complaints that have been made by the politicians. But we as the voters, we do not have that opportunity." It is unclear whether these perceptions indicate the absence of a voter complaint mechanisms or simply a lack of awareness or information about existing mechanisms.

Stakeholders indicated reasonable confidence in the integrity of the commission; most voters, though, were concerned that the MEC did not have the independence to effectively manage the electoral process—mainly because its composition was determined by political parties. Eventually, despite rumors of disagreements among the commissioners regarding a recount, the MEC abided by the decision of the courts. Whether this was the genuine product of commissioner attitudes or influenced by external pressure is difficult to assess.

In conclusion, Malawi's electoral management body established clear and fair election guidelines for vote tabulation, voter and party registration, polling-location monitoring, party code of conduct, party financing, results verification, and interparty dispute resolution. However, the implementation of these activities, and the overall management of the electoral process, suffered serious shortcomings (fuzzy set score: 0.5).[46] According to independent election experts surveyed by the Effective Institutions Platform (EIP), Malawi did well (and above the African average) in regard to electoral laws, but poorly in regard to campaign financing and election management.

Preventive Diplomacy

The diplomatic engagement of the international community during the 2014 electoral cycle was substantial. Voters across the country generally were not aware of the efforts of the international community in their country's politics, but these actions have been influential in the peaceful resolution of electoral disputes.

The international community provided direct support to civil society and faith-based organizations, such as the National Incentive for Civic Education (NICE) and the Public Affairs Committee (PAC), as well as to local conflict-prevention mechanisms.[47] One of the principal programs for technical assistance put in place during the election was managed by the UNDP, and included a technical committee whose goal was to strengthen the MEC's technical and operational capacity by providing mentoring and training to the commissioners and staff. A steering committee was responsible for the oversight and strategic leadership of electoral assistance projects, and was also engaged in preventive diplomacy. This steering committee was chaired by the minister of finance and the UNDP resident coordinator, and included the MEC's chairperson, and the development partners' heads of missions or cooperation.[48] The committee met about once a month as a forum for addressing electoral conflicts as they arose, and so was able to exercise effective pressure toward peaceful resolution of disputes.

The international community also engaged in diplomatic efforts through public statements and personal communications. The message was consistent across the most active actors—the U.S. embassy, the UK High Commission, the EU delegation, and the UNDP. Malawian politicians were strongly encouraged to pursue legal avenues if they wished to contest election results, and to refrain from inciting violence.

The UN also intervened with a statement from Secretary-General Ban Ki-moon three days after the elections:

> He calls on all candidates, political parties, and state institutions to remain calm and to support fully the Malawi Electoral Commission in completing its work. The Secretary-General reiterates his call to the candidates and their supporters to respect the ongoing tallying process, follow existing legal procedures to resolve any electoral challenges or complaints, and uphold the spirit of the Lilongwe Peace Declaration of 10 May. He also urges all political leaders to call on their supporters to refrain from any violence or disruption of the electoral process, whose successful completion is essential for the consolidation of democracy in the country.[49]

In sum, during the 2014 elections in Malawi an international presence with access and leverage engaged diplomatically, offering both consistent pressure and support over an extended period, targeting national and local leaders (fuzzy set score: 1.0).

Peace Messaging

Peace-messaging campaigns were widespread in Malawi during the 2014 electoral cycle and encouraged political actors—politicians in particular—to refrain from violent messages. The impact of these campaigns relied on the authority of the organizations sponsoring them.

This analysis distinguishes between peace-messaging campaigns targeting voters and those targeting politicians. This distinction is linked directly to the typology of violence observed in Malawi. Politicians intimidated voters and disturbed opposition activities before elections; voters engaged in violence if mobilized by politicians or if frustrated by the outcome of the process. For peace messages to be effective, they must therefore target the leaders, urging them to refrain from employing violence before elections and from inciting protest and fighting to contest the results; party supporters, encouraging them not to use violence regardless of the requests of their leaders; and voters in general, encouraging them to tolerate diversity of political opinions and the electoral defeat of their preferred party.

Peace messages to politicians were aimed at discouraging negative campaigns, insults targeting opposition candidates, and mobilization of supporters to engage in violent demonstrations; more generally, the messages encouraged politicians to resolve disputes peacefully. In Malawi, such peace messages were widespread and distributed by several sources. The strongest and most authoritative voice was the PAC. A faith-based organization established in 1992, PAC held meetings with key stakeholders throughout the electoral process and built a team of mediators to tackle national disputes. The committee engaged with the main twelve presidential candidates to support the Lilongwe Peace Declaration, signed in a symbolic ceremony in the capital's Civo Stadium on the

National Day of Prayers for Peaceful Elections, May 10. The declaration was disseminated through the largest national newspapers, the *Nation* and the *Daily Times*.[50]

The declaration committed candidates to "take a definite stand against the possibility of electoral violence, impunity and injustice," and to "speak out against acts of election-related violence" before and immediately after the tripartite elections. PAC and other actors— including UN Secretary-General Ban Ki-moon—often recalled the declaration in the after-math of voting and before the official announcement of results. The respect and authority that people attributed to PAC and to religious organizations in general provided the incentive to abide by the declaration—not doing so was expected to cause an important loss of legitimacy in the eyes of voters.

Providing political parties with incentives to act peacefully during the elections also reduced verbal violence during the campaign, which would potentially mobilize supporters against one another. As the Blantyre Synod program coordinator for governance explained in an interview, "If the political leaders are able to use proper language and proper messaging, obviously, that would be passed on to their followers and it will have an effect."

Peace messages to voters were distributed across the country by several sources, including civil society organizations involved in civic education (such as the NICE), religious leaders and faith-based organizations, traditional authorities (chiefs), and political leaders themselves. The messages encouraged peaceful behavior during registration and nonviolent responses to the electoral defeat of a party or candidate. Radio broadcasts were also commonly mentioned in focus groups as providers of peace messages. As with messages from civil society organizations, peace messages over radio were provided in the context of civic education activities.

When we asked people to rank the influence of the sources of the peace messages, the overall perception was that messages from religious leaders were particularly powerful in the Malawian religious society. Traditional leaders, who are considered "owners of the people" in Malawi, similarly wielded great power and authority. Perception of corruption in public office is lowest for religious leaders, only 15 percent, versus 30 percent for traditional leaders and 39 percent for the presidency.[51]

Messages by political leaders were also widespread, in particular from the opposition UDF and PP parties. People generally tended to listen more to religious and traditional leaders, the latter being perceived as interested in the well-being of the community as a whole. However, party supporters were particularly responsive to messages from their preferred party's leaders. A woman in Blantyre summed it up neatly:

> We are just the followers. If the president that I wanted to win has not won, and he is not accepting the fact that he has lost, as his supporter, I will not also accept this. But if he has accepted that he has lost, it means his supporters will also follow suit.

Overall, peace-messaging campaigns were characterized by their widespread societal and geographic reach throughout the electoral cycle in encouraging vulnerable segments of the electorate to refrain from violence and practice tolerance. Messages targeted potential instigators, the leaders, and perpetrators of violence, mostly party supporters (fuzzy set score: 1.0).

Civic and Voter Education

Implementation of civic education programs in Malawi has improved consistently over electoral cycles; in 2014 civic and voter education was widespread across the whole country. The National Initiative for Civic Education and religious organizations, such as the Catholic Commission for Justice and Peace (CCJP) and the PAC, together with the MEC had a vital role in conducting education activities. The MEC published its Civic and Voter Education Strategy and detailed a code of conduct for civil society organizations responsible for implementing civic and voter education.

Civic education was approached through various outreach mechanisms. In almost all areas, there was at least one recognized source—a civil society organization, political or religious leader, the MEC, or the radio (Zodiak in particular). The Malawi Electoral Support Network estimated that civic education by the MEC had a 68 percent outreach in May, and that the outreach of all civil society organizations combined was an average of 90 percent between March and May.[52] These actors took several approaches to appeal to communities, including dance and drama, posters, and radio messages, as shown in figure 4.3.

Among civil society organizations, and with EU financial assistance, NICE has played a crucial role in delivering education to citizens since the 1999 elections. Not only are permanent NICE structures at the regional and district levels in place, but more than nine thousand NICE volunteers also engage with traditional leaders, school headmasters, and faith-based groups, using posters, leaflets, public meetings, theater, and audio-visual material to promote awareness of the elections nationwide. The primary messages disseminated to the public are information on voting procedures and the role and importance of local councils, thus providing the opportunity for voters to make a more informed choice.

Figure 4.3 Civic Education in Malawi

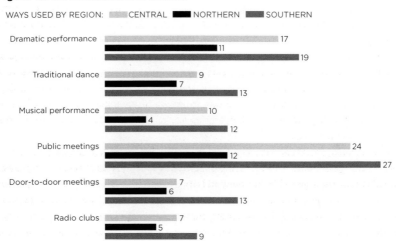

WAYS USED BY REGION: ▨ CENTRAL ▮ NORTHERN ▨ SOUTHERN

- Dramatic performance: 17 / 11 / 19
- Traditional dance: 9 / 7 / 13
- Musical performance: 10 / 4 / 12
- Public meetings: 24 / 12 / 27
- Door-to-door meetings: 7 / 6 / 13
- Radio clubs: 7 / 5 / 9

Source: Malawi Electoral Support Network, "Malawi Tripartite Elections: Consolidating Democracy Through Better Elections," conference report, June 26–27, 2014

The 2014 elections also saw an increase in education on issue-based voting, volunteers working with candidates to identify issues and problems affecting their communities, and with voters to encourage them to rate politicians and vote based on issues rather than gifts, candidates' regional origins, or intimidation.[53]

EU electoral observers assessed that these civic education activities were of good quality, in particular the activities conducted by NICE. However, the impact of such activities was hampered by insufficient financial resources and a lack access to remote areas.[54] Although 107 civil society organizations were accredited by the MEC to conduct civic and voter education, only twelve successfully obtained funding. Furthermore, the effectiveness of civic education also depended on the organizations carrying it out. Standardized messages had been developed and were intended for consistent use by all implementing partners, but were not always disseminated. The ability to carry out the message effectively varied across organizations based on available resources. And though education campaigns took place throughout the country, focus group discussions suggest that the campaigns were not as extensive as expected. The programs were also implemented quite late, only after voter registration, limiting their potential impact.

In sum, education efforts organized by state and nonstate actors objectively informed citizens about their roles and responsibilities, election procedures, and electoral outcomes. Despite the shortcomings, the programming targeted broad segments of society, including vulnerable communities, through various outreach mechanisms (fuzzy set score: 1.0).

Election Monitoring and Mapping

The 2014 tripartite elections were monitored by a variety of organizations. The EU Electoral Mission was deployed in the country from April 12 to June 19, using eighty-five observers from twenty-eight EU member states plus Norway across the country.[55] The EU mission was not the only one on the ground: international election observers were deployed by the African Union, which contributed ten long-term observers on April 14 and forty short-term observers for election week; by the Commonwealth, which sent eleven short-term observers and four staff members from the Secretariat; by the Southern Africa Development Community (SADC), which brought a total of 147 observers; and by the SADC Electoral Commission Forum.[56] In addition, diplomatic observers from the United States, the UK, Germany, and Japan were deployed on election day. Although the international presence was strong, local organizations criticized these missions as inadequate because they arrived late and sometimes departed before the results were determined.[57]

International observers were complemented by a larger group of domestic monitors. The main organizations deploying observers were the National Initiative for Civic Education and the Malawi Election Support Network, itself a platform of twenty-seven civil society organizations. For the 2014 elections, there was an unprecedented level of cooperation between the MEC and civil society organizations. In 2009, domestic election monitors were deployed to nearly all polling stations in the country. In 2014, all polling stations were covered: NICE deployed 4,200 monitors and MESN 1,400.[58] Beginning in February 2014, MESN deployed eighty-four long-term observers to political hot spots—areas where the level of competition was high and that had experienced violence and fraud in the past.[59] Religious organizations such as the CCJP and the PAC also deployed local monitors. Representatives from the various political parties were also stationed at the polling centers and had free access to the tally center in Blantyre.

Domestic monitoring organizations did not limit their observation to the voting process but also engaged in mapping and documenting electoral conflicts and irregularities. The LTOs from MESN produced reports and statements that were shared with all players and stakeholders in the political arena. Their STOs also used mobile phones to electronically submit critical incident data throughout election day. These activities were implemented within the framework of the Malawi Election Information Centre, the Election Situation Room, and the Citizen Journalism Initiative.[60] Through these initiatives, more than 4,500 local observers and one hundred mobile supervisors were deployed in the field, conducting real-time observation of all polling stations in the country. The task force in the situation room was composed of MESN, MEC, the police, civil society organizations, and political parties. PAC also monitored violence using eighty-two senior clergy volunteers.[61]

In addition to monitoring events on the ground, both before and during elections, comprehensive media monitoring was undertaken by the Institute for War and Peace, financed by USAID and UK Aid. The peculiarity of this monitoring exercise, which covered the entire official campaign (March 22 to May 18, 2014), was that it extended monitoring beyond the traditional media of print, radio and television to include news websites and social media (such as Facebook groups and Twitter).[62] The U.S. Embassy also monitored both traditional and modern social media, with the aim of identifying and acting upon early signs of potential organized unrest.

Finally, MESN also engaged in a parallel vote tabulation (PVT) exercise in eight hundred randomly sampled polling stations nationwide, conducted in close cooperation with the MEC. The data produced mirrored the official results for presidential elections later released by the MEC—all official results fell within the PVT estimated range. In 2009, the MEC rejected PVT given a lack of understanding of the methodology and a fear that it would unduly influence electoral results. However, following the engagement of relevant stakeholders from the media, political parties, donors, and academics, the MEC in 2013 allowed the implementation of PVT for subsequent elections. Results were good in 2014.[63]

In sum, credible and neutral state and nonstate actors systematically observed and evaluated the electoral proceedings (noting the source, location, type, perpetrator, and victim of election violence) throughout Malawi, and produced accurate, timely, and actionable early warnings (fuzzy set score: 1.0).

Voter Consultations

Voter consultations took place only sporadically during the electoral campaign, sponsored by organizations such as the U.S.-based National Democratic Institute. However, voters at focus groups reported consistently that they were not consulted and lamented their inability to express concerns with their elected leaders and to hold them accountable if promises are not fulfilled.

The focus group discussions are not representative of the Malawian population, but the consistent observation that voter consultations were absent suggests that even if these programs did exist they lacked inclusiveness, reach, systematic application, and accountability mechanisms (fuzzy set score: 0.25).

Youth Programming

Malawian youth are a vibrant part of every party or political grouping. Each party has a core of youth supporters who are seen as the basis of strong vocal support, popularly termed morale. However, during the 2014 election campaigns, politicians abused the passion and engagement of youth and used their party's youth wings to create distur- bances and attack opposition rallies, property, and supporters. Youths tended to engage in violence because they were provided with financial incentives, unemployment and poverty making such incentives particularly appealing.

Although this situation was well known, and the need for programs to keep youths peacefully engaged during the elections was recognized as a necessity, such programs did not appear to be widely implemented. Youth reportedly engaged in what was called peer education to reduce violence; loans and empowerment programs were made available to engage youths constructively in business and politics. However, voters in the central region noted the absence of effective programs during the elections (and of employment opportunities more generally), other than sporting activities.

This suggests that although state and nonstate actors did carry out multiple youth programs (targeting education, electoral mobilization, and employment opportunities), the programs were not fully implemented across the country or in at-risk communities (fuzzy set score: 0.25).

Assessing Prevention

At first glance, Malawi seems to confirm this project's hypothesis: in the presence of strong prevention, levels of violence were low. Compared with previous elections, all PEV models in 2014 were more developed; however, despite more limited conflict-prevention mechanisms in place in the past, the country never experienced electoral violence on a large scale in its democratic history. Therefore, it is necessary to assess whether positive electoral behavior is the product of PEV models or of other contextual factors.

Security-Sector Engagement

Assessing the impact of security-sector engagement on electoral violence involves con- sidering the ability of security agencies to ensure safety for voters during the campaign and voting, as well as the ability to quell protest. The Malawi Police Service has been long known for its weak institutional capacity and variable policy and strategic direction. The violent response to 2011 antigovernment demonstrations had the twofold effect of frightening and alienating Malawians. However, both elites and voters interviewed after the 2014 election noted that the presence of police during the campaign and the voting enhanced security. Some even stated that the strongest peace messages came from the security forces, given that the mere presence of the police discouraged violence.

The absence of episodes comparable to those in 2011 may indicate that the police were capable of peacefully discouraging protests and of generally avoiding violent escalation. But without knowing the risk factors in all areas, it is difficult to fully assess whether the absence of violence is an indicator of police ability, or simply of the lack of triggers for election violence. However, focusing on the two localities where violence did erupt offers several insights. In the campaign clashes in Goliati, Thyolo district, the police were able to quell protests hours before they escalated to a lethal level.[64] In the postelectoral protests in Mangochi, the police reportedly reacted violently to protesters despite being fully trained in that locality. These observations suggest that the security sector was not absent from vulnerable localities, and that the police did not substantially aggravate tensions on the ground (as had been true in the past, and despite perceived partisan preferences for the incumbent). In fact, according to the overall perceptions that emerged from field interviews, the presence of police was relevant to ensuring the maintenance of peace.[65]

Electoral Management Bodies

The administration of the election was in the middle range in terms of quality and scope because of the MEC's inability to successfully handle the logistics of registration and voting. Delays on election day led voters to protest in frustration, as in Blantyre. Had the Electoral Commission functioned according to best practices, this violence could have been avoided.

Furthermore, lack of confidence in the MEC—for both these management failures in registration and voting (especially in areas favoring the opposition) and for the political affiliations of the commissioners—exacerbated suspicion about results that did not favor locally preferred candidates. Again, had the electoral management body displayed neutrality in managing the electoral process, motivations to protest violently might have been minimized.[66]

However, regardless of trust in the Electoral Commission, voters may still respond violently to news that their preferred candidate has lost, especially if the results at the local level seem to contradict those at the national level. For example, after the demonstration in Mangochi—the stronghold of defeated UDF candidate Atupele Muluzi—people explained that the motivating factor for this violence was simply frustration: "People expected that Atupele is going to win, but... people were frustrated, because Peter was not conducting campaign here. But when they were announcing [the results] Peter was on top of the others."

On a positive note, the successful engagement of the MEC within the NECOF allowed key stakeholders (political parties, the army, the police, traditional leaders, faith-based organizations, and civil society organizations) to address electoral conflicts. However, this engagement was accompanied by that of other institutions at the local level that were independent from the Electoral Commission. The multiparty liaison committees (MPCPs) were inclusive bodies composed of district-level representatives of political parties, local government, traditional chiefs, the police, civil society organizations, and the youth wings of parties and had the explicit mandate to manage electoral conflict in the district.[67] Even though these institutions were less known to voters, they nonetheless provided a fruitful framework for dialogue and peaceful conflict resolution that addressed a number of election issues. Since the formation of these committees in 2003, incidents of election-related violence declined despite political tensions remaining high at the national level.[68]

Malawi's national courts have also consistently been used to adjudicate intraparty disputes over candidate selection. The courts act as a safety valve, dissipating tension and preventing violence.[69]

It follows that a better-functioning electoral management body would have certainly prevented incidental violence during and after voting; its impact on the resolution of electoral disputes was strongly enhanced by well-functioning independent conflict-resolution institutions at both the local (the MPLCs) and national level (the courts).

Education and Messaging

Interviewees and focus group participants noted that civic education campaigns in 2014 contributed to peaceful elections. Voters who were informed of their rights and the functioning of the electoral process were better able to pursue peaceful methods of complaint. However, although civic education increased voters' awareness of the electoral process—and potentially boosted voter turnout and reduced null and void votes—the impact of voter empowerment on political violence and malpractice is questionable. Voters felt generally unable to submit complaints. Either civic and voter education was not successful in conveying this information to voters or the simple provision of information was not enough to empower voters against violence.

Civic education was therefore not enough to prevent violence. The benefit of knowing how to present complaints peacefully can be undone by the presence of large logistical failures (such as delays on voting days) or by the absence of functioning channels through which to process complaints from the most vulnerable segments of the population. The successful impact of civic and voter education is thus partly conditional on the presence of a well-functioning electoral management body.

On the other hand, civic education could also mitigate violence indirectly by promoting issue-based campaigning, which limits negative campaigns against opponents and thereby reduces tensions between supporters of different groups. Civic education primarily encouraged voters to cast their vote based on issues, and candidates received similar incentives through voter consultations and peace messages from local and international organizations. The plausibility of this mechanism is summed up in the words of a woman in Lunzu market in Blantyre:

> I think it was the leaders who were starting violence. The way they would speak would provoke the other party. They would insult others, instead of just mentioning what they will do after they have been voted into power. So the followers of the one who is being insulted would cause violence. But if the leaders would come with good messages to their people, I don't [think] there can be violence.

Negative campaigning was certainly present in the electoral discourse, but issue-based campaigning also emerged. It is not clear from the collected data whether the absence of civic education and peace messaging would have led to more negative campaigning.

Furthermore, civic and voter education was present across almost the entire country, and peace messaging targeted all main political leaders, so no variation in these factors can be exploited to observe a counterfactual. Moreover, the implementation of additional voter consultations could have forced the electoral discourse toward issues, but this might also have brought on patronage and regionalism.[70] The impact of voter consultation therefore remains unclear.

Furthermore, the impact of civic and voter education and peace messaging on voters could easily be trumped by deliberate calls for violence. This is true unless these PEV models also limit the behavior of politicians who would call for violence. Therefore, in addition to depending on the quality of electoral management, the civic education and peace messaging are also influenced by the constraints of these models on political actors. In Malawi, faith-based organizations in particular—exercised their moral and (indirect) political authority by persuading political parties to refrain from encouraging violence. Peace messages to leaders were thus generally successful in discouraging politicians from stirring up violence, which effect trickled down to party supporters.

However, it is possible that not all political parties were equally subject to the same incentives of the peace-messaging campaign—many informants said that if the DPP had lost the elections, Peter Mutharika would have been more inclined to fight the results, leading to higher levels of violence.

Preventive Diplomacy

Diplomatic intervention during the election was substantial, and according to many it meaningfully encouraged defeated candidates to fight the electoral outcome in the courts rather than in the streets. However, the political leaders with whom the international community interacted were likely more receptive to such pressure. For example, the MCP spokesperson seemed more willing to engage in some form of demonstration than the party's leader, who peacefully conceded the election. Given this situation, though pressure for peaceful resolution of electoral disputes would not have occurred in the absence of preventive diplomacy, the same level of implementation might well not have delivered a generally peaceful election had conditions on the ground been different.

Monitoring and Mapping

Monitoring and mapping is one of the strongest prevention models in terms of scope and quality. But did it make a difference? In Malawi's 2014 election, well-implemented monitoring and mapping effectively reduced electoral violence in two ways: by increasing the credibility of and confidence in the electoral results, and by raising awareness of potential conflicts.

The legitimacy of the election or the electoral outcome is an important potentially stabilizing factor. However, although the presence of a large contingent of both international and local electoral observers certainly enhanced the legitimacy of the elections in the eyes of elites, the impact of election monitoring on election legitimacy is indistinguishable from the impact of PVT efforts, the results of the Afrobarometer preelection opinion poll, and the informal results released by various media.[71] These programs presented the same results as the MEC, increasing the legitimacy of the electoral outcome. Combined, however, these monitoring efforts undoubtedly increased confidence in the MEC results.

In addition to directly influencing the population, monitoring and mapping also decreased the credibility of claims advanced by opposition candidates regarding the validity of the election, and strengthened the pressure on them to accept the results. This might have significantly calmed postelectoral protest. However, this positive impact is again conditional on the overall management of the election—that is, on whether the results are believed to be legitimate. People are more likely to protest if they believe that the election is not fair.[72] As one respondent put it, "Had it been that MEC released results different [from those expected based on preelection polls and the postelection PVT], I think we could have been telling another story by now." This occurred in 2004, when "violence happened because the election was not fair and everybody knew it."

In addition, reporting on specific incidents of violence also appears to have had an overall positive impact, if not in preventing violence then at least in keeping it from escalating. The coordinator of MESN, which deployed long-term observers in high-risk locations and produced regular monitoring reports, described the value of accountability in limiting violence. Long-term observation, he said, "is not there to prevent; it is there to record. Prevention comes… after violence has taken place; we come in with advocacy to name and shame, because we say we know who has started this because our observers are on the ground and we tell them particularly we know the perpetrator."

By documenting hot spots and by identifying perpetrators and victims, mapping efforts also make it easier for violence-prevention agents to act immediately to resolve the conflict and quell the violence. Monitoring and mapping seem to have intensified the peace campaigns and alerts issued during the electoral period. For instance, the program coordinator of a faith-based civic education initiative saw immediate value in the monitoring: "Yes it [the PEV model] was effective because when violence is about to erupt, people would be called to a round party, through a multiparty liaison committee to discuss about the same and prevent the occurrence of violence. It assisted in one way to prevent the occurrence of violence."

Obviously, awareness can prevent violence only if security forces are capable of an appropriate response and conflict-resolution mechanisms are able to cope with tensions. In 2014, local conflict mediation and resolution institutions were already in place throughout Malawi, and operated independently from the monitoring and mapping framework. Because they were, the monitoring and mapping did increase awareness of electoral conflicts and violence, and so facilitated the deployment of necessary actions to resolve them.

Youth Programming

Of the two weakest PEV models in Malawi, youth programming likely had the most potential to have a relevant impact. Malawi's youth have been used by politicians to perpetrate violence during the electoral cycle since 1993, mostly in the form of clashes among party supporters, intimidation of voters, and destruction of property. Beyond simply partisan zeal, unemployment and poverty make youths particularly inclined to take on these sorts of violent engagements in the hope of monetary reward.

That said, respondents to focus group discussions often mentioned that youths participated voluntarily in political activities, and (most importantly) that their engagement was also sometimes important in pacifying tense situations. Voters in some localities marred by electoral violence explained that youths "are used to calm people and some other times to incite violence in a particular way."

Therefore, the nature of specific youth programs is critical to evaluating their impact accurately. The implementation and geographic spread of PEV youth programs was generally poor. However, according to interviews in localities that experienced violence, youth programs nonetheless did operate in those regions. Programs were implemented, but they could not resolve the underlying issues of poverty and unemployment. Still, the presence of programs aimed at involving youth in the political process (rather than just diverting their attention into some temporary activity, such as sports) is potentially associated with additional productive engagement in political life and therefore with peaceful leadership roles in the community.

That youth programs were implemented in locations where violence took place indicates that such programs were unsuccessful in preventing violence, but that they nonetheless might have been relevant in keeping violence at lower levels than it would otherwise have been. These considerations are helpful in designing meaningful programs for engaging youth during elections in a sustainable way.

Conclusion

The Malawian ruling party's slogan in 1992 and 1993 when canvassing against the multiparty system was "Multi-party is war."[73] The country's electoral history shows that electoral competition breeds conflict between political parties (and their supporters) competing for power. The 2014 contest also shows that widespread conflict does not necessarily result in lethal violence, and can in fact be channeled through peaceful conflict resolution.

This chapter offers two important findings. First, violence can be prevented—and certain conflict-prevention methods are particularly well suited to achieve this. Peace messaging, preventive diplomacy, and monitoring and mapping appear to have reduced both the occurrence and the escalation of violence in Malawi. However, the positive impact of these PEV models was possible thanks to the presence of authoritative local nongovernment actors that increased the cost of noncompliance with commitments to peace. Furthermore, the effect of these models depended on the ability of security forces to intervene, and on the functioning of local conflict-management institutions to address local conflicts as they emerged.

Second, the impact of prevention models depends heavily on the structural context in which PEV models operate. In Malawi, the consistency of the official results with those recorded by independent organizations demonstrated the fairness of the electoral outcome and reduced incentives to contest the results. Additionally, the transparency of the tallying process and the efforts of independent and active media increased awareness of these results and reduced the legitimacy of postelectoral protests. The general aversion of many Malawians to political upheaval further reduced the likelihood of sustained protests. Most important, the tendency of politicians to deviate from original party affiliations and join the winner's coalition—also a way of making minority governments work—increased access to power for losing candidates, and in turn reduced the contentious zero-sum nature of political competition.

The interaction between these favorable context conditions and the strong implementation of the outlined PEV models by authoritative and functioning local implementing actors and mediators contributed significantly to Malawi's low levels of electoral violence in 2014. At the same time, a better-functioning electoral management body might have avoided voter frustration and dissipated suspicions of unfair results, and a more focused and sustained engagement of youth might have finally reduced the availability of strongmen for politicians willing to foment violence while competing for power.

Notes

1. Thirty-five semistructured interviews were conducted with members of both the international community and local civil society and with local media in the three major cities of Lilongwe, Blantyre, and Zomba in August and October of 2014. A team of eleven researchers from the Malawi-based Invest in Knowledge Initiative completed an additional twenty-eight structured interviews with local leaders and members of civil society and political parties, and conducted twenty-eight focus group discussions across towns and villages in all four regions of the country.

2. Respondents were selected purposively or using snowball sampling. The composition of the focus groups represented urban and rural areas and captured women's and men's views both separately and together. Focus group discussion participants were recruited through community access points (generally the local chief), but also following an alternative methodology based on interviewing small groups gathering in public places (such as the market). This practice of "community conversations" was considered particularly appropriate for discussing potentially sensitive questions. Both forms of group interview are referred to simply as focus group discussions for simplicity.

3. Catherine Musuva, "Malawi," in *Compendium of Elections in Southern Africa, 1989–2009: 20 Years of Multiparty Democracy*, ed. Denis Kadima and Susan Booysen (Johannesburg: Electoral Institute of Southern Africa, 2009). Banda brutally dispatched political rivals even before the country achieved independence. See Richard Carver, *Where Silence Rules: The Suppression of Dissent in Malawi* (New York: Human Rights Watch, 1990).

4. Daniel N. Posner, "Malawi's New Dawn," *Journal of Democracy* 6, no. 1 (1995): 131–45.

5. Commonwealth Secretariat, "The Parliamentary and Presidential Elections in Malawi," *Commonwealth Observer Group Report*, May 17, 1994. According to this report, political intimidation was generally carried out by party supporters, and even made use of the Nyau cult—traditional masked dancers thought to perform sorcery—to strike fear into people's hearts and to intimidate or even kill opposition supporters of the MCP party in the central region.

6. John A. Wiseman, "Presidential and Parliamentary Elections in Malawi, 1999," *Electoral Studies* 19, no. 4 (2000): 637–46.

7. According to one study, support for parties other than the UDF in the south was often perceived as a betrayal or rejection of the ethno-regionalist identity. See Roman Poeschke and Chijere Chirwa, *The Challenge of Democracy in Malawi: Socio-Anthropological Conditions* (Lilongwe: GTZ, 1998).

8. Musuva, "Malawi."

9. Chris Maroleng, "Malawi General Election 2004: Democracy in the Firing Line," *African Security Studies* 13, no. 2 (2004): 77–81.

10. Malawi Electoral Commission and National Incentive for Civic Education (MEC and NICE), *Study into the Reasons for Non-Voting During the 2004 Presidential and Parliamentary Elections in Malawi* (Lilongwe: MEC and NICE, August 2008).

11.   Nandini Patel and Arne Tostensen, *Parliamentary-Executive Relations in Malawi 1994-2004* (Lilongwe: Chr. Michelsen Institute, 2006); Musuva, "Malawi."

12.   Daniel J. Young, "An Initial Look into Party Switching in Africa Evidence from Malawi," *Party Politics* 20, no. 1 (2014): 105–15.

13.   Peter Mvula and John M. Kadzandira, *Baseline Study on Civic Education and Voter Apathy* (Lilongwe: University of Malawi, Centre for Social Research, 1998). Although disappointment and fear explain why people tended not to participate in politics, the Malawian electorate should not be considered completely apathetic. In fact, only one in three was uninterested in politics in 1998 and 2000. See Gero Erdmann, Nandini Patel, and Sylvia Schweitzer, *Political Attitudes in Malawi: Results from Two Opinion Surveys, 1998 and 2000* (Lilongwe: National Initiative for Civic Education, 2004). Among nonvoters in 2004, only 33 percent did not want to vote (MEC and NICE, *Study into the Reasons*).

14.   Poeschke and Chirwa, "Challenge of Democracy."

15.   FRC, "Malawi: Civil Unrest," DREF final report (Geneva: International Federation of Red Cross & Red Crescent Societies, June 16, 2014).

16.   James Mwangali, "When Non-Issue Based Campaign Starts Bearing Bitter Fruits: A Case of Goliati Violence Saga," *Malawi Voice*, March 17, 2014.

17.   E. Kanyongolo, "Back to the Courts: Legal Battles and Electoral Disputes," *Democracy in Progress: Malawi's 2009 Parliamentary and Presidential Elections* (Balaka: Montfort Media, 2010).

18.   Monty G. Marshall, Ted Robert Gurr, and Keith Jaggers, "Polity IV Project: Political Regime Characteristics and Transitions, 1800–2013 Dataset Users' Manual" (Vienna, VA: Center for Systemic Peace, May 6, 2014).

19.   Nandini Patel and Michael Wahman, "The Presidential, Parliamentary and Local Elections in Malawi, May 2014," *Africa Spectrum* 50, no. 1 (2014): 79–92.

20.   Presidential, parliamentary and local council terms are for a period of five years, with a limit of two consecutive terms in the presidential office. The president appoints the cabinet of ministers. The parliament has 193 members elected from single-member constituencies. In 2012, the Malawi parliament unanimously amended the constitution to allow for the conduct of local government elections together with the general elections in a single day in May 2014. See EU Electoral Mission, "Republic of Malawi: Presidential and Parliamentary Elections 20 May 2004, Final Report" (Lilongwe: European Union Election Observation Mission, 2014), http://eeas.europa.eu/eueom/missions/2014/malawi/pdf/eueom-malawi 2014-final-report_en.pdf.

21.   Sean Dunne, presentation, National Conference on Electoral Reforms in Malawi, December 12, 2014.

22.   Public Affairs Committee, GO Gender Co-ordination Network, and Centre for Human Rights and Rehabilitation; EU Electoral Mission, "Republic of Malawi."

23.   Young, "An Initial Look"; Nandini and Wahman, "Presidential, Parliamentary and Local Elections."

24.   Blessings Chinsinga, "The May 20 2014 Malawi Elections: A Democratic Success Story?" (Brooklyn, NY: Social Science Research Council, July 3, 2014).

25.   Carolyn Logan, Michael Bratton, and Boniface Dulani, "Malawi's 2014 Elections: Amid Concerns About Fairness, Outcome Is Too Close to Call," ADI no. 1, *Afrobarometer.org*, 2014, http://afrobarometer.org/sites/default/files/publications/Dispatch/ab_r6_dispatchno1.pdf.

26.   According to Research Tech Consultants, Joyce Banda was expected to win with more than 40 percent of the vote, and the *Nyasa Times* expected the DPP to come last.

27.   Some of the prophets are well known and regularly interviewed by local papers. See, for example, "Prophets contradict on 2014 elections winner," *Face of Malawi*, January 29, 2014, www.faceofmalawi.com/2014/01/prophets contradict-on-2014-elections-winner.

28.   Mia Seppo, "Message from UN Resident Coordinator," *Nkhani Zanthu* (UN in Malawi newsletter) no. 1 (July 2014): 5, www.ilo.org/wcmsp5/groups/public/---africa/---ro-addis_ababa/ documents/genericdocument/wcms_251020.pdf.

29.   The Malawi Broadcast Corporation has been announcing unofficial results ahead of the

MEC since 1993. MEC, "Building Capacity for Multiparty Liaison Committees" (Blantyre: Malawi Electoral Commission/Forum for Dialogue and Peace, April 2006).

30. Baldwin Chiyamwaka, "Media in the 2014 Elections: Did They Inform or Misinform?" in *The 2014 Malawi Tripartite Election: Is Democracy Maturing?* ed. Nandini Patel and Michael Wahman (Lilongwe: National Initiative for Civic Education, 2016).

31. Malawi Electoral Support Network (MESN), "Report on Tripartite Elections: Consolidating Democracy Through Better Elections," report presented at the Post-National Elections Conference, Golden Peacock Hotel, Lilongwe, June 26–27, 2014.

32. P. Biesheuvel and Andrew McLean, "Report of SJG Assessment Mission on DFID Malawi's Support to Policing" (November 2012), cited in UK Aid, "Malawi Policing Improvement Programme" (London: UK Aid, Department for International Development, June 2013).

33. Apart from a period in 2005, these percentages are constant over time. In fact, in 1999 lack of trust in the police was almost 50 percent (*Afrobarometer*, Malawi Round 5 codebook, 2012, www.afrobarometer.org/countries/malawi-0).

34. "Report of the Findings and Recommendations of the Presidential Commission of Inquiry into the Demonstrations, Death, Injuries, Riots, Looting, Arson, Public Disorder and Loss of Property that took place on 20th and 21st July 2011" cited in "Final report on July killings out in May," *Nyasa Times*, March 28, 2012, www.nyasatimes.com/2012/03/28/final-report-on-july-20-killings-out-in-may/.

35. "Inspector General of Police Loti Dzonzi admits of poor relationship between Malawi Policy Service and the media," *Oracle*, February 27, 2014, www.orakonews.com/inspector-general-of-police-loti-dzonzi-admits-of-poor-relationship-between-malawi-police-service-and-the-media/.

36. Heiko Meinhardt and Nandini Patel, "Malawi's Process of Democratic Transition: An Analysis of Political Developments Between 1990 and 2003," *Democratic Transition and Consolidation in Africa* (Lilongwe: Konrad-Adenauer-Stiftung, 2003).

37. EU Electoral Mission, "Republic of Malawi."

38. Seppo, "Message from UN Resident Coordinator"; United Nations Development Program, "Malawi Electoral Cycle Support 2013–2016" (New York: UNDP, June 2013).

39. MEC, "Report on Tripartite Elections."

40. EU Electoral Mission, "Republic of Malawi."

41. MESN, "Consolidating Democracy."

42. EU Electoral Mission, "Republic of Malawi."

43. *Afrobarometer*, Malawi, Round 1-5.

44. EU Electoral Mission, "Republic of Malawi."

45. Robert Silungwe, interview, November 10, 2014.

46. Pippa Norris, Ferran Martínez i Coma, and Max Grömping, "The Year in Elections, 2014: The World's Flawed and Failed Contexts," February 2015; Grömping and Martínez i Coma, "Election Integrity in Africa," July 2015.

47. Many conflict-resolution programs were supported at both the national and the local level, such as the multiparty liaison committees (MPLC), which first implemented in local government elections in 2000 and drew their jurisdiction from the Malawi Electoral Commission, and the National Elections Consultative Forum, introduced in 2003.

48. UNDP, "Malawi Electoral Cycle."

49. Statement attributed to the spokesman for the secretary-general on the elections in Malawi, New York, May 24, 2014.

50. PAC, "Social Cohesion Project. Simulation and Training Report," June 2014.

51. Boniface Dulani and Joseph J. Chunga, "When Is Incumbency No Longer an Advantage? Explaining President Joyce's Defeat in the May 20, 2014 Tri-Partite Elections," in *Democracy Maturing? The 2014 Malawi Tripartite Election*, eds. Nandini Patel and Michael Wahman (Lilongwe: National Initiative for Civic Education, forthcoming); *Afrobarometer*, Malawi Round 6 codebook, 2014, www.afrobarometer.org/data/malawi-round-6-codebook-2014.

52. MESN, "Consolidating Democracy."
53. Although handouts are common practice during the campaign, participants mentioned in the focus group discussions that they took the opportunity of the rallies to receive these handouts but then voted following their true preferences.
54. EU Electoral Mission, "Republic of Malawi."
55. In contrast with 2004—when the EU deployed a team of both long-term observers and short-term observers—only STOs were deployed in 2014.
56. EU Electoral Mission, "Final Report Malawi."
57. MESN, "Consolidating Democracy."
58. EU Electoral Mission, "Republic of Malawi."
59. MESN, "Democracy, Elections, Governance" (Limbe: Malawi Electoral Support Network, August 2014), www.mesnmw.org/wp-content/uploads/2014/12/Election-Report-2014.pdf.
60. These initiatives were funded by Open Society Initiative for Southern Africa and the international NGO HIVOS.
61. UNDP, "Social Cohesion Project," Project Code 00073899, 2014 Annual Report, http://open.undp.org/#project/00073899.
62. MESN, "Consolidating Democracy."
63. Ibid.
64. "Inspector-General of Police Loti Dzonzi."
65. "Those messages are not enough. They become enough if we go and find somebody is in uniform and has carried a gun, is when we…is when the message is enough and you can't do anything because there is police."
66. Although the work of the MEC was far from perfect, it showed substantial improvement compared with the election ten years earlier. According to the EU Electoral Mission report of 2004, "voter registration was unsatisfactory and the tabulation of results seriously lacked transparency to the extent that it is not possible to have full confidence in the accuracy of the results of the elections." The MEC "failed to address complaints filed by political parties, provide sufficient instructions to polling officials or allow observers or party representatives to attend its meetings. This resulted in widespread lack of confidence in the MEC by election stakeholders." The 2014 findings on popular confidence in the MEC therefore must be put in perspective: while confidence was not at very high levels in 2014, it nevertheless was meaningfully higher than in the past.
67. The MPLCs were established in 2000 with the support of the German Development Assistance Agency, and were subsequently supported by the UNDP.
68. Doc Mwale, "'Multi-Party Is War': Reflections on Local Mediation in Malawi's Electoral Conflicts" (Pretoria: University of Pretoria, 2013).
69. Siri Gloppen, Edge Kanyongolo, Nixon Khembo, Nandini Patel, Lise Rakner, Lars Svåsand, Arne Tostensen, and Mette Bakken, "The Institutional Context of the 2004 General Elections in Malawi," CMI Report no. 21 (Bergen: Chr. Michelsen Institute, 2006).
70. According to a nationally representative survey carried out in 2013 by the Institute of Public Opinion and Research, the two most important factors influencing voting decisions in Malawi were "Candidate's personality or leadership qualities" and "Candidate's ability to deliver jobs or development to your area" (Dulani and Chunga, "When Is Incumbency?").
71. Voters did not seem to be very aware of the presence and impact of electoral observers. Pilot focus group discussions encountered difficulties explaining to voters the meaning of questions about the observers, and generally returned confused or non-meaningful answers. For this reason, questions about electoral monitoring and mapping were removed from the focus group questionnaires and asked only during interviews with key informants.
72. Ursula E. Daxecker, "The Cost of Exposing Cheating International Election Monitoring, Fraud, and Post-Election Violence in Africa," Journal of Peace Research 49, no. 4 (2012): 503–16.
73. Mwale, "Multi-Party Is War."

Map 5.1 Moldova National Map

MOLDOVA

ORHEI	County name
✪	National capital
✸	County capital
—·—·	International boundary
-----	County boundary*
=====	Gagauzia boundary (AREA NOT COTERMINOUS)

*NOTE: CHISINAU IS BOTH A COUNTY AND A MUNICIPALITY.

EDINET
Edinet
SOROCA
Soroca
BALTI
Balti
ROMANIA
ORHEI
Orhei
Nistru River
TRANSNISTRIA
UKRAINE
UNGHENI
Ungheni
CHISINAU
Dubasari
DUBASARI
CHISINAU
Chisinau
TRANSNISTRIA
Hincesti
LAPUSNA
TIGHINA
Causeni
Comrat
GAGAUZIA
CAHUL
UKRAINE
Cahul
Black Sea
Danube River

0   30 MI
0   30 KM
N

5

Moldova

Tense Calm, Regional Instability

DOMINIK TOLKSDORF

The November 2014 parliamentary election in Moldova took place amid deep political polarization.[1] Debates on the country's geopolitical orientation were especially fierce: the parties in government since 2009 promote a rapprochement with the European Union (EU), whereas some opposition parties favor close relations with the Russian Federation. The violence in neighboring Ukraine throughout 2014 raised fears in the Moldovan government that provocateurs could organize an antigovernment *maidan* in Moldova to instigate unrest.[2] The Moldovan police conducted several special operations before the election and arrested individuals who had allegedly planned electoral violence. The most controversial development was the exclusion of the opposition party Patria as a contestant a few days before the vote for allegedly receiving funds from Russia in violation of the electoral code, which heightened the risk of violence.

National security services and both local and international election monitors were in place and highly visible. Other instruments to prevent electoral violence, however— including voter consultations, youth programming, and peace messaging—were conspicuously weak or absent. The election administration was not able to prevent the government from interfering in the electoral process, which was intended to disadvantage the opposition parties. Because of such flaws in the process, the elections were not entirely fair. Regardless, and despite the increased risk of violence, election day remained peaceful. This can in part be attributed to successful monitoring efforts, civic and voter education, and the engagement of the security sector (despite the bias in its operations). The oppositional Socialist Party surprisingly became the strongest party in parliament and had thus no interest in postelectoral violence. Ultimately, two pro-EU parties in February 2015 formed a minority coalition that was approved in parliament with the help of the Communist Party. Political instability continued throughout 2015, the new prime minister, Chiril Gaburici, resigning in June, his successor Valeriu Streleț receiving a vote of no-confidence in October, and a massive banking scandal leading to some of the biggest street protests in the country's history.

Moldova's peaceful 2014 election provides an illuminating comparison with the other cases in this study. The likelihood of electoral violence in Moldova may appear much lower than in Bangladesh or Thailand, for example. However, because multiple destabilizing incidents prior to the election, including tensions within Moldova, regional uncertainty, as well as the recent precedent of electoral violence in 2009, the potential for electoral violence in 2014 was real. Why did it not occur, and what role did preventive peacebuilding play in this? This chapter analyzes the vulnerabilities for violence in Moldova before the election as well as the strength or weakness of prevention throughout the campaign, examining how strong instruments contributed to the prevention of election violence (PEV) and which instruments should be strengthened in future elections.

Background

Any analysis of Moldova's 2014 election must be seen against the background of electoral violence in April 2009. The earlier election was won by the ruling Party of Communists of the Republic of Moldova (PCRM), but accusations by opposition parties that the election had been rigged led to violence. In snap elections in July 2009, the pro-EU parties won a slight majority in parliament that they have since retained. The legacy of the 2009 elections increased the risk of violence in 2014 election because it introduced a precedent through which opposition parties feel empowered to oust the incumbent government. Several additional risk factors, including differing views on national identity within society, conflicts over the distribution of power within the state, frustrations over the incomplete democratic consolidation, and disagreement over Moldova's geopolitical orientation, contributed to a tense environment and raised the likelihood of violence in 2014. Polarization has significantly increased since 2013 and presented the possible pretext for the mobilization of frustrated citizens in the context of close elections.[3]

Exception to the Rule

Electoral violence is the exception rather than the rule in Moldova since 1991. The 2009 election took place in a heated atmosphere between the ruling PCRM and the pro-EU opposition parties. The PCRM had dominated Moldovan politics since 2001 and held absolute majorities in parliament. A first blow to its political dominance had come in 2007, when the opposition Liberal Party won the mayoral elections in Chișinău. Fearing that it could lose its parliamentary majority in the April 2009 elections, the PCRM conducted an aggressive election campaign with fierce attacks on the opposition and police intimidation of local activists. According to the preliminary results announced by the Central Election Commission (CEC), the PCRM had won 49.5 percent of the vote. The party had been expected to win a plurality, but a near majority was unanticipated. As a result, the opposition claimed that the elections had been rigged and called on their supporters to protest the result.[4] Although most of the demonstrations remained peaceful, a few hundred protesters did attack and loot the presidential palace and parliament building.[5] In the police crackdown that followed, hundreds of demonstrators were arrested and dozens were beaten and tortured. Several deaths are attributed to the 2009 violence.[6]

Following a ballot recount, which did not significantly change the election result, the PCRM held sixty seats in parliament and thus remained one vote short of electing a new president.[7] Because parliament failed to elect a new president in two attempts, the incumbent—Vladimir Voronin of the PCRM—was constitutionally required to dissolve parliament and call early elections. In the snap elections of July 2009, the PCRM vote fell to forty-eight seats in parliament. A new government was formed from four opposition parties under the name Alliance for European Integration. Because the new coalition was eight votes short of being able to elect a president, peaceful elections were once again held in November 2010, leading to a renewed coalition of the pro-EU parties—the Liberal Democratic Party of the Republic of Moldova (PLDM), the Democratic Party of the Republic of Moldova (PDM), and the Liberal Party (PL)—that now held fifty-nine seats in parliament.[8]

Power had thus been transferred by election from the government to the opposition. Doubts remain, however, whether the transition would have occurred without the violent incident in April 2009, a contentious issue until today.[9] The incident introduced a precedent for change of government that could inspire future opposition parties to oust the incumbent.

Polarization

Since independence in 1991, debates within Moldova on its national identity have contributed to rifts within society. Society is roughly divided into three communities with distinct political preferences: the first argues that Moldova has been a nation since the fourteenth century, considers Moldovan a different language than Romanian, and fears unification with Romania. A second believes in a Moldovan political nation separate from Romania and that Moldova should remain an independent state, but posits that the language spoken in Moldova is Romanian. A third community considers itself Romanian, holds that Moldova and the Moldovan language are an artificial creation of the Soviet Union designed to fragment the Romanian nation, and does not rule out a unification with Romania.[10] This third scenario is feared by several minority groups, particularly ethnic Russians and Ukrainians.[11] Frequent debates over national identity contribute to an unstable political environment within Moldova and are a contextual vulnerability for violence during election periods.

Conflicts over the distribution of regional political power within the country are another source of tension. Such conflicts have existed since Moldova's secession from the Soviet Union and its foundation as an independent state. Under a nationalist government in the early 1990s, some groups (particularly the ethnic Russian population) feared that the new state would eventually unite with Romania. In 1991, the local authorities in Transnistria, a region with a large ethnic Russian population, proclaimed its independence as the Pridnestrovian Moldavian Republic, which led to an armed conflict with the authorities in Chișinău. Backed by Russia, Transnistria became a de facto state. Efforts to resolve the conflict with Chișinău, including a proposal to federalize Moldova, have failed.[12] Other regions within Moldova promote decentralization and frequently criticize the government in Chișinău for its reluctance to grant more autonomy to local authorities and to strengthen the political and socioeconomic rights of minority groups. These include Gagauzia, a region in southern Moldova with a large Turkic-speaking population. The Moldovan Constitution of 1994 granted some autonomy rights to the region to prevent Gagauzia's secession, including legislative powers in education, culture, local development, finances, and taxation. But tensions between the central authorities and the region have not subsided, and the Gagauz elite frequently criticize the central government's lack of financial support to the region, its nonobservance of Gagauzia's autonomy rights in national legislation, and the region's inadequate political representation at the central level. In addition, the government's rapprochement with the EU has been seen critically by Gagauz stakeholders, who often support close links with the Russian Federation.[13]

Tensions between Gagauzia and Chişinău significantly increased in February 2014 when the Gagauz authorities organized two referenda that the central government declared illegal. The referenda revealed that a large majority of the Gagauz population would prefer Moldova to join the Customs Union rather than the EU and that Gagauzia should exercise its right to self-determination if Moldova were to "lose its independence" (a reference to future EU membership).[14] Tensions between the central government in Chişinău on the one hand and local authorities in Gagauzia and Transnistria on the other continued throughout 2014 and were influenced by the crisis in neighboring Ukraine.[15] According to Stanislav Secrieru, the Russian government tried to take advantage of the tensions by penetrating local authorities and by using Gagauzia and Transnistria as springboards to orchestrate public disorder and destabilize Moldova.[16] In fear of electoral violence, the Moldovan security services conducted several special operations in Gagauzia.

Another risk factor is the incomplete democratic consolidation, which frequently leads to frustrations within large segments of society. Between 2001 and 2009, when the PCRM held absolute majorities in the parliament, Moldova was often considered a semi-authoritarian system.[17] The 2009 protests were largely motivated by calls for democracy and rule of law, objectives that were promoted by the parties that gained power in July 2009. However, the state's move toward a fully consolidated democracy has been slow since then. It has become more pluralistic, but state capture, systemic corruption, and political interference in the judiciary and the media sector remain prevalent and undermine democracy.[18] Economic elites (sometimes referred to as oligarchs) frequently exert influence over political institutions and have engaged in a fierce competition for control over policymaking and state institutions.[19] Systemic corruption is considered one of the most urgent problems, and political parties, the parliament, and the judicial branch are considered particularly vulnerable.[20]

A key hurdle in tackling corruption is the weak rule of law. According to the constitution, the judiciary is independent from the legislative and executive branches. However, Moldova inherited the Soviet tradition of judicial subordination to executive power, and, because this system has not yet been reformed, the implementation of justice is often considered selective.[21] Particularly worrisome elements are the courts and the prosecutors' offices, which are both regularly used as instruments in political fights.

A good example that illustrates the scope of informal networks in Moldovan politics is the revelation in 2013 about close connections between top officials in the judiciary and influential persons in the business and political world. It contributed to the increasing lack of trust in the executive and judicial institutions and has undermined the confidence in the liberal-democratic system that has gradually developed since 2009.[22]

The media, often considered the fourth estate in consolidated democracies, is also not free of political intrusion. Although a pluralistic media scene is in place, many outlets remain vulnerable to political influence through editorial policies and internal censorship. Mass media companies are largely controlled by a few businessmen who frequently use them to manipulate public opinion during election campaigns.[23] The director of Moldova's Independent Press Association therefore argues that media in 2014 was as biased as in 2009, when it was still largely controlled by the PCRM.[24]

In sum, various weaknesses in Moldova's evolving liberal-democratic system contribute to broad frustrations within society that can be mobilized by political actors intent on using violence. Many of the 2009 protesters were driven by frustrations over the abuse of power within the government and the lack of democratic standards in Moldova. In 2014, widespread frustrations over state capture, corruption, weak rule of law institutions, and the abuse of power within the government could have led to violent mass demonstrations in the context of the elections.

Fears

The growing frustrations among opposition parties combined with anxiety over the close elections and an uncertainty about the election outcome created a combustible mix (see table 5.1). The 2014 elections were expected to be a close race between the pro-EU parties and the opposition (see map 5.2). Between September to November 2014, the predicted results of the pro-EU parties remained largely stable, support for the center-right PLDM (around 20 percent) and PL (9 to 10 percent) stagnating and support for the PDM increasing (from around 11 percent to 17 percent). Among the opposition parties, changes were most dramatic for PCRM, whose support fell from around 35 percent to 23 percent. The beneficiaries of this development were the Patria, or Homeland, Party (between 10 to 12 percent of support) and the Party of Socialists of the Republic of Moldova, or PSRM (between 8 and 15 percent)—two parties that openly promoted close relations with the Kremlin.[25] Given growing uncertainty about the election outcome, a turn to violence as a tactical measure among incumbents or challengers could not be ruled out. The government suspected that groups with links to the opposition parties might plan electoral violence and conducted several special operations against them. On the other hand, Renato Usatîi, a top Patria candidate, suspected that the ruling parties were preparing scenarios for the annulment of the elections in the event that they did not win. Many election experts, an interviewee explained, claim that supporters of Moldova's pro-EU orientation would have likely initiated demonstrations had the opposition won the election.

Map 5.2 Moldovan Parliamentary Election Results by District

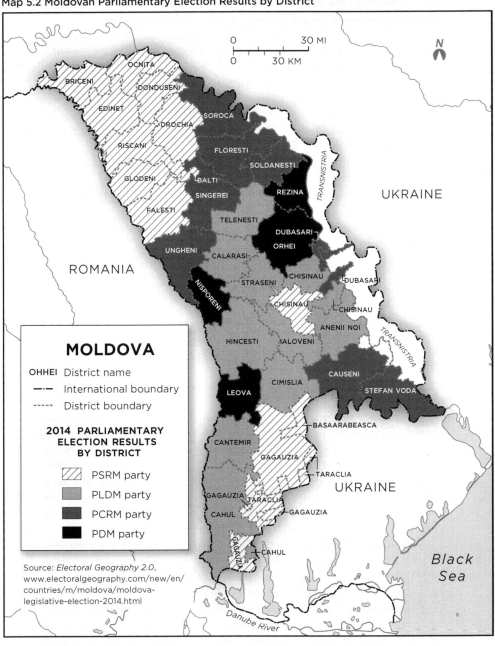

MOLDOVA

OHHEI District name

—·— International boundary

- - - - District boundary

2014 PARLIAMENTARY ELECTION RESULTS BY DISTRICT

- PSRM party
- PLDM party
- PCRM party
- PDM party

Source: *Electoral Geography 2.0,*
www.electoralgeography.com/new/en/
countries/m/moldova/moldova-
legislative-election-2014.html

ROMANIA

UKRAINE

TRANSNISTRIA

Black Sea

Danube River

OCNITA
BRICENI
DONDUSENI
EDINET
DROCHIA
SOROCA
RISCANI
FLORESTI
SOLDANESTI
GLODENI
BALTI
REZINA
SINGEREI
FALESTI
TELENESTI
DUBASARI
ORHEI
UNGHENI
CALARASI
CHISINAU
DUBASARI
STRASENI
NISPORENI
CHISINAU
CHISINAU
ANENII NOI
HINCESTI
IALOVENI
CAUSENI
LEOVA
CIMISLIA
STEFAN VODA
BASAARABEASCA
CANTEMIR
GAGAUZIA
TARACLIA
GAGAUZIA
TARACLIA
CAHUL
GAGAUZIA
GAGAUZIA
CAHUL

Table 5.1 Moldova 2014 Parliamentary Election Poll (percentages)

| "If parliamentary elections were held next Sunday, which party would you vote for?" | | | | | | |
DATE	PCRM	PLDM	PDM	PL	PATRIA	PSRM	UNDECIDED
11/11-20	23.2	18.1	16.2	8.4	9.0	15.6	13.2
11/11-21	23.6	20.9	17.8	8.9	11.2	6.4	27.1
11/8-19	24.5	21.5	17.8	10.6	10.9	6.6	20.0
10/26-11/13	20.6	20.6	17.6	10.3	11.8	10.3	32.0
11/1-10	27.2	22.8	16.6	9.4	12.3	5.0	22.1
10/11-20	26.5	18.7	13.7	9.5	9.8	9.1	17.6
9/5-22	31.9	25.4	14.6	8.6	9.1	3.8	26.7
9/2-20	36.7	19.4	8.8	8.6	13.0	8.0	22.3
9/1-12	33.6	20.1	11.3	10.0	5.1	9.6	31.0
7/22-8/10	36.1	21.7	11.1	10.4	10.3	5.6	41.5
5/26-6/20	36.6	23.9	13.8	10.1	1.8	1.8	28.5
3/28-4/13	39.1	23.3	12.9	12.6	n/a	1.8	37.9

Source: eDemocracy, www.e-democracy.md/en/elections/parliamentary/2014/public-opinion-polls

Instabilities

Within this vulnerable context, after 2013 the potential for violence steadily increased in response to frustrations over scandals within the government, growing disagreements over the country's geopolitical orientation, and fears of a public protest in Moldova.

The Alliance for European Integration coalition that had ruled Moldova since July 2009 collapsed in March 2013 following a controversy that put leading politicians of the coalition at odds.[26] In the following weeks, deep confrontations, particularly between Prime Minister Vlad Filat and Vladimir Plahotniuc, an influential businessman and vice president of the PDM, came to light in political mudslinging that ended with a vote of no-confidence for Filat. However, under the threat of early elections with a potential victory of the opposition, a new coalition of the PLDM, PDM, and the Liberal Reformists Party (a breakaway fraction of seven members of the Liberal Party) was formed in May 2013. Similar to the previous government, the uniting element was the objective to strengthen ties with the EU. The scandal of 2013 revealed the rifts between the coalition partners and the level of corruption, malpractice, and abuse of power in the government.

Power struggles between the political parties over the electoral system also increased frustrations about Moldovan politics among many voters. Despite the governmental crisis, in April 2013 the Alliance for European Integration adopted amendments to the electoral code that altered the electoral system from a proportional to a mixed system.[27] The change was intended to benefit the coalition parties and to disadvantage the oppositional PCRM.[28] However, the system was changed again shortly afterward when the PDLM and the PCRM tactically cooperated to adopt new legislation that restored the proportional system. To prevent smaller left-wing parties that had split from the PCRM from entering parliament, the PDLM and the PCRM raised the electoral threshold from 4 percent to 6 percent. The parties changed the system by using parliamentary majorities rather than initiating a broad and inclusive debate. The episode illustrates how the parties in parliament manipulated the election law to disadvantage political opponents—a development that frustrated many voters and undermined their trust in the democratic system.

Since 2013, growing disagreements over Moldova's geopolitical orientation further intensified tensions between the political parties, partly fueled by outside powers, particularly Russia and the EU. Both neighbors have, to different degrees, respectively interfered in local politics to ensure that Moldova seeks membership in the Customs Union or to intensify relations with the EU.[29] In recent years, Moldova has adopted several EU-promoted reforms, illustrating a rapprochement process regarded with suspicion by the Russian government.[30] The Kremlin since 2013 has imposed embargos on various Moldovan products and threatened gas cuts and the expulsion of Moldovan guest workers from Russia to persuade the Moldovan authorities not to intensify relations with the EU.[31]

Tensions between Russia and the EU over spheres of influence in their "shared neighborhood" peaked following the 2013 EU Eastern Partnership summit in Vilnius. Many Moldovans feared that the Kremlin would send "green men" to destabilize Moldova, a reference to Russia's tactics in Crimea. Given the situation in Ukraine and the broad dissatisfaction within Moldova, analysts also feared that some opposition politicians, with the support of the Kremlin, could organize an antigovernment *maidan* in Chișinău.[32]

Disagreements between local parties over Moldova's geopolitical orientation increased both the East-West polarization within the country and the potential for violence. The PCRM, which held power until 2009, has been keen to maintain Moldova's neutrality status, as enshrined in the constitution, and therefore ruled out NATO membership. In contrast, the parties in government since 2009—PLDM, PDM, and PL—have proactively sought EU membership.[33] The opposition PSRM and Patria Party opposed EU membership and supported close cooperation with the Russian Federation. An association agreement with the EU ratified by parliament in July 2014 therefore led to protests in Moldova.[34]

Several contextual vulnerabilities for violence, then, were present before the 2014 election. Structural risk factors included ongoing debates over the national identity, which contributed to rifts within the population. Prevalent disagreements over the distribution of power and geopolitical orientation further contributed to tensions and polarization. This volatile political climate was put to the test by political scandals in 2013 that led to increasing disenchantment with politics, undermined trust in the liberal-democratic system, and strengthened the opposition parties. Before the 2014 election, the unstable political environment in Moldova might have presented the pretext for the mobilization of frustrated citizens. Close elections and uncertainty about the election outcome could have served as triggers within this combustible environment.

Flawed Process

Despite the risk of violence, a large part of the electorate seemed apathetic about the elections and the campaigns remained mostly peaceful.[35] The electoral process was only partially fair because the run-up to election day was shaped by several controversial decisions by the authorities, some of which were intended to secure a victory for the ruling parties in the election.[36]

Photo 5.1 Election campaign posters in Chișinău

Photo Credit: Dominik Tolksdorf

Photo 5.2 Pro-Russia election advertising in Chișinău

Photo Credit: Dominik Tolksdorf

The exclusion of the opposition Patria Party offered the greatest potential for instigating violence. On November 26, the General Police Inspectorate delivered evidence to the CEC that Patria, under its candidate Renato Usatii, had received foreign funds (presumably from Russia), in violation of the electoral code.[37] Based on these findings, the CEC, under pressure to make a quick decision, requested the Court of Appeals to annul the party's registration.[38] In a swift decision, the Court of Appeals did so the following day, a decision that the Constitutional Court upheld on November 29. Shortly before the election, Patria had been polling at double digits, largely because of Usatîi's popularity.[39] Because party lists closed a week before the election, Usatîi could not register as a candidate for another party. The procedure was criticized from many sides. The exclusion of parties shortly before an election does not comply with democratic standards, and the OSCE Election Observation Mission in Moldova noted in a report that "the late timing of this case and the circumstances surrounding it raised questions."[40] Patria's exclusion was seen by many observers, interviews reveal, as a manipulation of the election process by the government and a typical example of selective justice in Moldova.

As in April 2009, when allegations of electoral fraud had triggered violence, the exclusion of one opposition party could have been the pretext for violence in November 2014. The Moldovan authorities feared that Patria's exclusion might indeed lead to protests and violence. In the end, though, the party did not have enough of a structure in place to mobilize its supporters.[41] The chances of mass demonstrations and violence would have been greater had one of the larger opposition parties (with more developed party structures) been excluded instead.[42]

Despite the various controversies, no physical violence was reported during the preelection period.[43] The OSCE mission did report that "a number of candidates had accused each other of bribing and intimidating voters, and of planning post-election unrest."[44] The civil society organization (CSO) Promo-Lex also reported several cases of voter intimidation. For example, the director of the company Rezina-gaz in Rezina district had allegedly shown employees a list of PDM candidates for which they were called upon to vote and required employees to submit a request to join the PDM. Similarly, the director of the company Registru had allegedly urged his employees to vote for the PDM.[45]

The postelection period was also peaceful despite surprising results. The PSRM became the strongest party (garnering 20.51 percent of the vote), followed by the PLDM (20.15 percent), PCRM (17.48 percent), PDM (15.80 percent), and the LP (9.67 percent).[46] It is widely believed, one interviewee reported, that the PSRM had no interest in postelectoral violence because its leadership was satisfied with the election results. In December 2014, the Constitutional Court—rejecting the requests by PSRM and PCRM to either annul the results or hold a rerun of the election—approved the election results.[47] Overall, election violence was absent during the 2014 cycle (fuzzy set score: 0).

Prevention in 2014

In light of the risk in Moldova in the lead-up to the November 2014 election, strong and effective prevention tools ensured the peaceful conduct of the poll. However, not all prevention tools were present. Security-sector engagement, civic and voter education, and monitoring were priority instruments; the implementation of preventive diplomacy, voter consultations, and youth programming remained weak. Because of political interference in the electoral process, the quality of election management and administration remained questionable. Peace messaging was not used.

Security-Sector Engagement

A well-trained and equipped security sector provides an important guarantee for election security, as long as it prioritizes the protection of the electorate over elite interests and displays professional conduct. Thus, by being nonpartisan, accountable, and professional, security actors can minimize or deter election violence.

Moldova's law enforcement agencies were highly visible throughout the 2014 preelection period through public warnings and special operations against groups allegedly planning electoral violence. Security-sector engagement was thus a prioritized PEV tool. On a negative note, police actions were not impartial.

The conflict in neighboring Ukraine generated fears throughout 2014 that provocateurs might instigate unrest in Moldova, the November election presenting a particularly vulnerable opportunity. The Russian government had allegedly supported movements that could orchestrate public disorder in Moldova, a suspicion that the law enforcement agencies took seriously.[48] Moldova's Intelligence and Security Service (SIS) closely monitored regions, such as Gagauzia or the region around Bălți with its large ethnic Russian population, where it suspected tensions and regularly declared its preparedness to combat security threats posed by "paramilitary groups and/or individual followers of extremist ideologies."[49]

In June 2014, the police searched several houses in Gagauzia and purportedly uncovered a group that delivered specialized training in managing firearms, street fighting techniques, seizing buildings, and building barricades and check points in military camps in Russia. According to police reporting, as many as one hundred people had been trained to undertake such subversive activities in Moldova. As a result of the investigations, the courts opened criminal cases against eight Gagauzians, two of whom were sentenced for crimes against the state. Several heads of local police and intelligence services were also suspended from office.[50]

The Moldovan security services, concerned that affiliates of the Russian military might directly instigate violence in Moldova, took measures to secure its borders, particularly the unofficial one into Transnistria. Approximately thirty Russian citizens later identified as military personnel or political consultants were denied entry, for example.[51] In November, law enforcement agencies deported two Russian and four Ukrainian citizens suspected of illegal involvement in the election campaigns (providing subversive materials) and of planning activities to destabilize the society.[52] The SIS also alleged the existence of groups seeking to undermine national security and "generate destabilization of the social equilibrium, and warned the population to be vigilant.[53] The presidential spokesman warned that some persons and parties had tried to destabilize the situation by disseminating "messages that distort realities" and reassured the public that Moldova's police would guarantee public order and security for the election.[54]

Law enforcement agency prevention efforts peaked on November 26 when forces conducted special operations in Chișinău, Bălți, Ialoveni, and Soroca. Raids targeted groups that were purportedly preparing demonstrations and violent provocations; five people were detained; and firearms, ammunition, and grenades were confiscated. According to police reports, around fifteen alleged members of the group Antifa (antifascists) were

Photo 5.3 Pro-Europe election advertising in Comrat (Gagauzia)

Photo Credit: Dominik Tolksdorf

involved in recruiting and arming new activists and raising financial resources for activities intended to overthrow the government. In a so-called campaign of oppression, police forces also raided the houses of Patria members suspected of subversive intentions and of organizing a so-dubbed Bloody Maidan in Chişinău.[55]

The security sector throughout 2014 was actively engaged in investigating groups said to be planning to instigate public disorder. The conduct of special operations provided the government the opportunity to show both its ability to deal with internal security threats and the effectiveness of the reforms it had adopted since 2009.[56] During the 2009 election, Moldova's security services had not been well-prepared for public unrest and committed various abuses during the crackdown. After that, the Ministry of the Interior began to train carabinieri forces and other special units in crowd control.[57] Some commentators, however, doubted the capacity of these forces to defend or quickly regain control over administrative and governmental buildings in the event of public unrest.[58]

Critics also claimed that the security sector favored PDM and PDLM politicians. Indeed, throughout 2014, the police openly supported Moldova's orientation toward the EU and specifically suspected that the "promoters of the Eurasian vector" would be the ones to instigate violence.[59] This raises doubts about the security sector's impartiality in domestic disputes between the political parties. The special operations throughout 2014 were contested, and critics claimed that the government overemphasized security threats in Moldova and used the police to intimidate the opposition parties.[60] Western diplomats also expressed doubts about the necessity of the operations and the authenticity of the confiscated items.

In sum, despite certain deficiencies, the security sector has a clear regulatory framework under which to provide election security and was well-governed during the 2014 election. It largely acted in a professional and capable manner and was accountable to civil authorities (fuzzy set score: 0.75).

Election Management and Administration

A well-administered electoral process will reduce the risk of violence by alleviating frustrations and suspicions. An independent election management body (EMB) that provides clear election guidelines and enforces them in a consistent and nonpartisan way will deter or mitigate election violence, such as by providing incentives for legitimate dispute resolution and by implementing a protocol for transparent registration, voting, and result verification. In the 2014 election, the CEC only partly fulfilled these criteria. According to the OSCE monitoring mission, the electoral process was "generally well administered, with the exception of the functioning of the new electronic system for the processing of voters on elections day."[61] The CEC worked "in a professional and transparent manner" and enjoyed the confidence of most stakeholders. This assessment overshadows the several flaws and significant political interference in the electoral process. That the CEC was unable to prevent the interference led to frustration among the opposition parties and fostered tensions rather than mitigating them.

The CEC played a controversial role in the run-up to the April 2009 elections when it ordered two parties to pull TV advertisements that criticized the ruling PCRM. It fueled further controversy by taking forty-eight hours after the election to present precinct results. Opposition politicians did not trust the results and mobilized their supporters for protests. The CEC was thus partly responsible for the subsequent violence. It has, however, according to interviewees, since been reformed and has revised its organizational structure. Organizations such as Transparency International have praised the development of professional skills within the CEC and the increased transparency in its activities.[62] Innovations included establishing its Centre for Continuous Electoral Training and introducing a centralized voter registration system that helps guard against multiple voting and reports results to the CEC once votes have been counted in electoral bureaus. Clear regulations on political party and campaign finances are yet to be established, however.[63] As a result, according to interviews with CEC officials, in 2014 the CEC had only limited capacity to effectively monitor campaign finances and their origin and to verify contestants' financial reports. After the election, the CSO Promo-Lex estimated that almost 15 million lei of campaign funds remained undeclared.[64] The CEC is thus not an effective watchdog of campaign finances, which is an important aspect of its responsibilities.

Nevertheless, the CEC efficiently prepared the elections, including registration of political parties, electoral blocs, and independent candidates.[65] According to the OSCE, election day "proceeded in an orderly manner (but) considerable technical deficiencies were noted throughout the voting and the counting processes."[66] Indeed, the state automated information system elections stopped functioning because of a temporary breakdown of the CEC's server network, which meant that voter's data had to be processed manually. The Eastern

Partnership Civil Society Forum argued that this intermittent system failure "meant that in very many cases there was no immediate safeguard against multiple voting," which undermined the credibility of the electoral process.[67] The OSCE was more cautious in its criticism, arguing that the CEC had failed to conduct full-scale testing of the reliability of the system or to train computer operators before election day.[68]

The 2014 election also showed that the CEC is vulnerable—partly the result of the party affiliations of its members—to political meddling.[69] For example, it set the ceiling for campaign spending at 55 million lei for political parties, a twofold increase.[70] The decision to lower the ceiling for independent candidates, which was done without a clear rationale, advantaged the established parties. Political interference in the electoral process also occurred when the Ministry of Foreign Affairs (MFA) decided to open ninety-five polling stations abroad for diaspora voters, only five of which were in the Russian Federation. This allotment appears unfair given that Russia has the largest number of Moldovan guest workers.[71] The CEC recommended a higher number of polling stations in Russia, but was ignored by the MFA. The decision contributed to perceptions that the government sought to discourage voting in the Russian Federation.[72] The PSRM unsuccessfully submitted three appeals against the government's decision, claiming that the government had intentionally restricted the right to vote.[73]

This controversy illustrates the lack of effective electoral dispute resolution mechanisms before and after the election. According to the OSCE, electoral complaints were "generally handled satisfactorily" and the CEC took decisions on complaints "in an open manner."[74] However, the OSCE also reported that two cases "raised concerns over the perceived selective use of the justice system" and "the lack of effective legal remedies for the affected contestants."[75] First, the rapid exclusion of Patria Party left the party without an opportunity to seek legal remedy before the election. In a second case, the authorities failed to deregister the Communist Reformist Party of Moldova (PCR), which had been founded in May 2014 and was registered by the Ministry of Justice. The PCRM challenged the registration on the grounds that the acronym of the PCR is close to the PCRM acronym and that the PCR's symbols (hammer and wheat-ears) too similar to the PCRM emblems. On November 4, the Court of Appeals issued a decision requiring the Ministry of Justice to suspend the PCR registration, but the ministry claimed it needed further clarification and did nothing. The Supreme Court upheld the decision only forty-five days after the election. The PCR ran and garnered votes, but was (at 4.95 percent) about 1 percent short of parliamentary eligibility. According to election experts, the PCR had confused many voters who had intended to vote for the PCRM.[76] After the election, the PCRM unsuccessfully requested the Constitutional Court to annul the results on the basis of the PCR's participation.

In sum, the CEC established and enforced guidelines for some election-related issues and was able to manage the electoral process for the most part successfully. On a negative note, the CEC lacked capacity to ensure a fair electoral process because important aspects remained largely unregulated and dispute resolution efforts were inconsistent. Moreover, interference by government institutions raised suspicions and led to increasing frustrations among the opposition parties that could have resulted in violence (fuzzy set score: 0.5).

Preventive Diplomacy

The involvement of international actors in preventive diplomacy can mitigate violence, for example, by resolving disputes among local leaders or by using incentive-based foreign assistance. In 2014, a few embassies sporadically called on the electorate not to instigate violence, but preventive diplomacy could hardly be considered a prioritized prevention tool. The opposite was true. Discord among powerful foreign actors in Moldova regarding the country's foreign policy direction in fact contributed to political polarization and thus increased tensions instead of reducing them. Russia and the EU regularly use incentives and sanctions to influence politics in the country. In the wake of the growing conflict between Russia and the West, sparked by the Ukraine crisis, Russia in particular openly supported opposition parties in Moldova. This limited the potential for coordinated international mediation.

Western governments feared that a conflict similar to that in Ukraine was possible in Moldova. Some embassies encouraged the electorate to refrain from violence and to take advantage of their democratic right to vote. The U.S. Embassy, for example, was explicit in its hope "that the people of Moldova can peacefully express their democratic will in line with international standards and democratic principles."[77] At the same time, some openly criticized the procedures that led to Patria's exclusion and thus the electoral process as well. Not surprisingly, most critical in this respect was the Russian Ministry of Foreign Affairs, which argued that Patria's exclusion "puts in question the democratic nature of the…polls" and questioned whether the deregistration process met "the norms and principles of European democracy." Two days before the election, the Russian MFA wondered whether "Moldovan voters will be given the opportunity to make an independent, fully democratic choice, free from pressure."[78] Afterward, the Russian Embassy in Chișinău criticized the irregularities, including the exclusion of Patria Party and the disregard of the voting rights of Moldovan citizens in Russia.[79]

The U.S. Embassy had also warned that it was "deeply concerned about ensuring respect for rule of law and a fair and democratic electoral process."[80] After the election, the U.S. ambassador said, "we share ODIHR's concern with the decision of Moldova's CEC to remove one party from the ballot only a few days before the elections."[81] The EU did not release any official statements, though its officials in Chișinău reportedly voiced their concern. After the election, however, they merely noted the OSCE statement on the election.[82] The EU thus shied away from openly criticizing the pro-EU government, missing the opportunity to use its leverage in Moldova to pressure the government to respect democratic standards. This reluctance raised frustration among the opposition parties, which accused the EU of not being an impartial actor in Moldova.

Russia and the EU routinely try to influence the domestic geopolitical orientation debate. Their interference was visible before the election in support of various Moldovan policymakers. The Kremlin openly supported the PSRM, and party billboards showed a meeting between PSRM chairman Igor Dodon and Russian President Vladimir Putin in November 2014. After the meeting, Russia's Federal Migration Service announced that unregistered Moldovan guest workers in the Russian Federation who wanted to vote in Moldova would be allowed to return to Russia afterward. The announcement was clear interference by the Russian government. Shortly after the election, the Russian ambassador met with PSRM leaders and congratulated them on the results. Western European politicians criticized the Kremlin's attempts but also visited Moldova during the campaign and declared their support for EU orientation.[83] Shortly before the election, for example, German Chancellor Angela Merkel mentioned Moldova's EU prospect in a letter to Prime Minister Iurie Leancă of the PDLM.[84] In November 2014, the EU delegation in Moldova indirectly supported the campaign of the PDLM when it donated police cars to the Moldovan authorities in a public ceremony also attended by Leancă.[85] Finally, EU officials also brokered an informal DPM-PLDM nonaggression pact before the campaigns to keep the coalition of pro-EU parties intact.[86]

An important precondition for effective preventive diplomacy is impartiality—a feature that did not characterize influential foreign powers in Moldova in 2014.[87] Russia's open support for opposition parties made it a particularly partisan actor. Russia and the EU's disagreement on Moldova's geopolitical orientation and Russia's negative sanctions fostered polarization and tensions rather than mitigating them. Discord among the international actors also significantly limited their potential to offer coordinated short-term crisis management and effective mediation (fuzzy set score: 0.25).

Peace Messaging

An effective peace-messaging campaign can reduce conflict by promoting nonviolence throughout the election cycle and across the country. Although the risk for electoral violence increased in November 2014, peace messaging was not used as a prevention tool. Political parties organized various events such as pop concerts that were not necessarily related to peace messaging but rather intended as campaign events. In November, the Moldovan Intelligence and Security Service appealed to opinion makers and electoral contestants "to avoid and renounce statements and activities that would generate insecurity," but these statements were warnings rather than proactive peace-messaging efforts (fuzzy set score: 0).[88]

Civic and Voter Education

Effective civic and voter education program can theoretically mitigate the risk of violence by educating voters on democratic procedures and responsibilities, empowering vulnerable communities, and enhancing the legitimacy and transparency of the electoral process. In 2014, the CEC and civil society undertook several voter information and education efforts. At the same time, international donors that had conducted such programs in the past reduced their activities. Civic and voter education was nonetheless a priority prevention tool in 2014.

According to the Moldovan electoral code, the CEC is to cooperate with mass media and public associations in conducting civic and voter education activities and raising public awareness about electoral procedures.[89] According to the International Foundation for Electoral Systems (IFES), the CEC has improved both its capacity for voter education activities and its strategy and techniques for educating and motivating citizens to participate in elections, such as by using modern communication technologies and taking a leading role in coordinating donors to develop and deliver voter education.[90] In 2014, the CEC took on this responsibility, producing voter education and information material on the importance of voting, election procedures and absentee voting, and outreach activities such as visits to universities, open door events, and engagement with the media. The CEC also assisted the public television broadcaster Moldova 1 and Promo-Lex in producing additional voter information and education spots, which were aired in Moldovan and Russian.[91] Minority groups, such as the Roma community, were not targeted, which partly explains their low participation and the absence of Roma representatives in elected bodies.[92]

In past years, interviews reveal, Moldovan governments were often unwilling to invest in civic and voter education programs (also for financial reasons), relying on external donors to do so. International donors commonly led education projects in cooperation with the CEC and local CSOs. The United Nations Development Program (UNDP), for example, worked with the CEC between 2007 and 2011 to promote voter participation and to increase the transparency of the electoral process. UNDP also financially supported implementation of voter education campaigns and civic education programs for voters in the diaspora, interviewees reported. The Council of Europe and the International Organization of Migration also implemented voter education programs.

A variety of international nonprofit organizations and political foundations have for years promoted civic education activities.[93] Germany's Friedrich Ebert Foundation (FES), for example, frequently partners with local nongovernmental organizations (NGOs) to organize seminars and public debates across the country to discuss citizen participation in decision-making, citizen access to information of public interest, and effective participative democracy tools. In a project funded by the U.S. Agency on International Development (USAID) on elections in Moldova, it contributed to a new voter education concept (Lume-Lume) between 2010 and 2013. Given a stable political situation in Moldova, an election expert explained, USAID in 2012 decided to reduce its activities. This example illustrates a trend in international donor activities in Moldova—a trend that is likely to change because of the new conflict between Russia and the West in Eastern Europe.

Programs by state and nonstate actors to inform citizens about their roles and responsibilities and election procedures, to engage and empower citizens, and to overcome voter apathy through outreach activities are therefore in place. These efforts, however, could more effectively seek to engage minority groups. Partly thanks to international assistance, the CEC has improved its capacity for voter education activities, and most voters are better informed about democratic norms, voting rights, and elections procedures. OSCE officials agree that civic and voter education has reached a high level, particularly when Moldova is compared with other countries in the post-Soviet space (fuzzy set score: 0.75).

Monitoring and Mapping

The systematic monitoring and mapping of election violence by neutral and credible actors reduces violence by deterring potential perpetrators of violence, identifying areas of risk, and facilitating a timely and effective security response. In 2014, mapping was largely absent in the lead-up to the election. At the same time, international actors and local CSOs did conduct comprehensive election monitoring, which was a priority PEV tool in 2014.

In 2014, twelve CSOs formed the Civic Coalition for Free and Fair Elections to contribute to a free, fair, transparent, and democratic organization of the parliamentary elections. As part of the coalition, Promo-Lex conducted a long-term monitoring of the election campaigns that included forty-one observers who prepared regular reports on electoral preparations. A key area of analysis was candidates' estimation of their financial resources, including income and spending as well as their reporting on these subjects in accordance with national legislation. Promo-Lex tried to be strictly neutral and fair to all electoral contestants and regularly pointed out shortcomings, including irregularities in campaigns finances.[94] On election day, it deployed two thousand observers to conduct parallel vote tabulation in polling stations across the country.

As in previous elections, the OSCE deployed a large election observation mission (EOM) to assess the election's compliance with OSCE commitments for democratic elections as well as with national legislation. The decision to deploy an EOM was based on a report by a September 2014 OSCE Needs Assessment Mission that expressed concerns over possible manipulations of the electoral process.[95] The EOM consisted of around thirty long-term election observers that had been deployed throughout the country to monitor candidate registration, campaign activities, CEC work, election-related legislation, media environment, and election-related dispute resolution. An additional two hundred short-term observers supported the EOM on election day by monitoring the voting, counting, and tabulating results. In its regular reports, the EOM identified several shortcomings in the electoral preparations (such as technical problems in voter registration). On election day, the EOM joined efforts to monitor the election procedures with delegates of the OSCE Parliamentary Assembly (OSCE PA), the Parliamentary Assembly of the Council of Europe (PACE), and the European Parliament. The CIS Parliamentary Assembly had also deployed a small observation mission.

The lack of mapping efforts was surprising given the unstable regional situation and the polarized atmosphere before the election. Although Promo-Lex and the EOM observed the security situation, they did not provide continuous data on election-related incidents and early warning systems that would have helped identify areas of risk. On a positive note, they did systematically observe and evaluate the quality of the electoral proceedings. All relevant local stakeholders considered both actors to be credible and neutral. Despite the scant mapping, monitoring was deemed a strong PEV model (fuzzy set score: 0.75).

Voter Consultations

Voter consultations can reduce potential violence by creating the perception that parties acknowledge voter grievances and by allowing media and the electorate to hold politicians accountable to their political programs. Before the 2014 election, some international projects were in place to promote voter consultations, but local efforts to interact with the electorate were scant and lacked both inclusiveness and voter recognition.

International organizations have pointed out the weakness of voter consultations in Moldova for years. The EU and the Council of Europe deemed it necessary to involve voters more deeply in the electoral process "as a pre-condition for full participation in public and political life."[96] Mistrust is widespread among large parts of the electorate toward the political elites, as is a perception that politicians and parties are rarely held accountable to their campaign promises.[97] Interviews reveal a prevalent belief that most politicians try to maximize their political power rather than serve the public interest.[98] Lack of effective government and the political party communication with citizens further contributes to dissatisfaction among the populace. The advantages of EU integration is a good example.[99] The parties in parliament in 2013 adopted changes to the electoral system without public discussion. In 2014, many voters also remained frustrated about the lack of political responsiveness to the high levels of poverty, corruption, and unemployment.

In 2014, Moldovan parties mainly conducted their campaigns via the media, billboards and posters, and free concerts—essentially "bread and circus" tactics.[100] Parties and politicians rarely entered into meaningful discussion with voters and, according to many observers, then only immediately before the election. Members of minority groups were largely ignored. The voter turnout of 55.86 percent in the 2014 elections was the lowest percentage since Moldova's independence and indicates a growing disillusionment about politics.

In past years, some international NGOs have initiated projects to promote voter consultations. The National Democratic Institute for International Affairs (NDI) has initiated civic forums to allow residents in small towns to identify pressing issues, such as road conditions, to parties.[101] Relatedly, the Friedrich Ebert Foundation launched a series of public debates in rural communities throughout Moldova to increase civic activism and electoral participation.

In sum, most local parties are not willing to engage in voter consultations on an ongoing basis. As a result, voters in 2014 had few opportunities to express their grievances, concerns, and interests (fuzzy set score: 0.25).

Youth Programming

Youth programs can reduce election violence by turning the primary perpetrators of violence into economic and political stakeholders. Several international donors conducted projects to strengthen youth participation, but the Moldovan government and political parties showed almost no interest in youth programming in 2014.

Most young people rarely come in contact with politicians outside the preelection period. Although all parties have youth wings, according to Promo-Lex director Ion Manole, young candidates have no real influence within the parties, and party leaderships use youth wings solely to mobilize young voters.[102] The number of young politicians in parliament is low: only fourteen of the 101 MPs are thirty-five or younger.[103] Interest in politics among young people was significant after the pro-EU parties formed a government coalition in 2009, but interest in politics has generally decreased and disappointment over the slow pace of reforms has increased. Voter turnout is therefore lowest among young voters. This trend is reinforced by the lack of opportunities to become involved in political processes. Renato Usatîi, who was admired by many young citizens for his extravagant lifestyle and his critical stance toward Moldova's political elites, planned to establish a youth organization similar to Nashi, a patriotic youth movement in Russia that has close ties to President Putin. Because such an organization would be likely to promote close relations with Russia, Usatîi's plans alarmed the pro-EU parties.

Whereas efforts by state actors are scarce, interviewees report, several international donors have been active in youth programming. The NDI, for example, supported youth initiatives to solve community problems and aimed to increase the turnout of young voters. The Friedrich Ebert Foundation established an academy for youth leaders.[104] Some initiatives also attempted to target youth leaders from minority groups. The OSCE Mission to Moldova launched a project, Youth Centre Piligrim-Demo, that focuses on training courses on civic and political leadership for young people from Gagauzia and other regions.

In sum, youth are not well integrated into the political process, can hardly be considered stakeholders, and remain vulnerable for recruitment by political actors to incite violence. International donors have few programs in place to offset this potential (fuzzy set score: 0.25).

Assessing Prevention

Several prevention models were strengthened in 2014: the security sector was better prepared to respond to public unrest; the electoral management body improved its technical capacities; and civic and voter education efforts were enhanced. Voter consultations and youth programming remained as weak as in 2009, however, and peace messaging was conspicuously absent. Last, because of the growing East-West divide, preventive diplomacy has become less likely to be effective.

In light of the contextual vulnerabilities and potential triggers, the risk of violence surrounding the 2014 election was real. The absence of violence can be attributed to the effective implementation of three PEV models. The poor implementation of the other five assessed in this study somewhat increased the risk of electoral violence. The track record of prevention in Moldova is therefore mixed.

- **Security-sector engagement.** Security-sector engagement prevented violence. Alarmed by warning signs, Moldova's law enforcement agencies were highly visible. The security services observed potential conflict regions and took preventive measures by uncovering groups allegedly planning electoral violence. Because security-sector activities generally are not and cannot be transparent, and because police bias was open, the truth of these claims remains questionable. However, the robust engagement of the security forces had a deterrent effect, attested to by the absence of unrest.
- **Civic and voter education.** Civic and voter education was well implemented and effective. By taking Moldova's vulnerabilities into account, civic and voter education measures swayed frustrated citizens to use their voting

rights to demonstrate their grievances and political preferences rather than to instigate violence. PSRM, which had not been represented in the previous parliament and in 2014 was a protest party, became the strongest party in the new parliament. Many voters were therefore clearly disenchanted with the previous government and used their voting rights to protest—illustrating that civic and voter education was indeed effective. From a long-term perspective, civic and voter education measures have contributed to the development of a political culture in which disappointed citizens use democratic avenues to demonstrate their dissatisfaction and to vote parties into and out of office.[105]

- **Mapping and monitoring.** Local and international efforts to monitor the electoral process were comprehensive and helped minimize violence. Local monitoring was organized by a coalition of committed CSOs that examined specific areas of the electoral process. This constellation permitted an effective division of labor. The international community, within the framework of the OSCE, helped ensure a fair and transparent electoral process by investing in a large monitoring mission. Postelectoral violence arising from suspicions of rigged elections, such as that in 2009, was prevented by the widespread presence of monitors who reported on election-related incidents and potential irregularities in vote tabulation. The presence of many international observers also ensured that the Moldovan government would have been criticized by foreign partners had the election results been rigged. By ensuring that vote counting was transparent, monitoring had a positive impact. On a negative note, monitoring efforts could not prevent government interference.

- **Election administration and management.** How the elections were administrated increased frustrations among the electoral contestants instead of mitigating them. Government interference undermined the trust in the CEC as an impartial institution and left the impression that the government had tried to put the opposition parties at a disadvantage. The interference led to an only partially fair electoral process and increased frustrations. The lamentable quality of election management thus contributed to the existing vulnerabilities. In this context, the opposition's mobilization of supporters to protest the perceived unfair elections could not be ruled out.

- **Preventive diplomacy.** Preventive diplomacy was not strongly implemented and the meddling of outside powers, particularly the Russian government, in the campaigns increased tensions. Some embassies called on voters to refrain from violence but had no coordinated position. Such actors were not perceived as unbiased, reducing their potential for effective mediation.

- **Voter consultations.** Voter consultations were largely absent, which also increased the potential for violence. Among the important triggers for the 2009 unrest were broad frustrations about the abuse of power by the government and the lack of democratic standards. Broad frustrations were also present in 2014 and a large part of the population did not feel that their interests were properly represented in parliament. Apart from a few short-term measures shortly before the election, political parties rarely took initiative to address these grievances.

- **Youth programming**. Youth programming was also poorly implemented and political parties rarely took the interests and concerns of youth into account. In the context of a dire economic situation and the large absence of initiatives by the Moldovan authorities and parties to better integrate youths into political processes, young voters remained vulnerable to political actors that planned to mobilize them for protest activities. The Patria Party, in particular, tried to take advantage of this situation. Fortunately, the party's exclusion did not lead to major protests by frustrated youths, illustrating a certain level of resilience. This resilience, though, should not be taken for granted. Stronger local efforts in youth programming could reduce the risk of future violence.

- **Interaction effects**. The absence of electoral violence in 2014 is partly due to the implementation of effective PEV models, which often had important interaction effects. Close cooperation between the CEC and Promo-Lex helped strengthen the civic education measures both actors carried out. Promo-Lex also reviewed CEC activities and thus served as its watchdog. Promo-Lex and the OSCE closely cooperated to increase the number of people involved in monitoring, which in turn strengthened the evaluation mechanism and increased the likelihood of election results being accepted.

The positive impact of individual PEV models, though, could be further strengthened by better combining them with other instruments. To increase trust in the police among young voters, stronger links could be established between youth programs and the security sector. This could be highly relevant given that youth more frequently demonstrate their frustration in clashes with the police during demonstrations. Positive effects are also likely if civic and voter education measures, voter consultations, and youth programming were to be expanded and better coordinated. They could all contribute to raising the perception among voters that politicians take their interests seriously. These three models also illustrate how the weakness of one model can have a negative effect on the prevention effect of another. For example, a weak implementation of voter consultations and youth programming might lead voters to conclude that their participation in elections is in vain, which would in turn undermine civic and voter education efforts aimed to remind citizens of their democratic rights and responsibilities (including voting). To avoid voter apathy, the CEC should call on the electoral contestants to increase their consultations with voters beyond elections and urge the government to engage in youth programming.

Conclusion

Despite the tense climate and some incidents that could have easily triggered unrest, the 2014 election remained peaceful because security-sector engagement, monitoring, and civic and voter education were all successfully implemented. The government invested especially in security-sector engagement and civil society groups organized strong monitoring efforts, but other prevention models were poorly implemented and did not contribute to the prevention of violence. These models, particularly those that increased frustrations rather than mitigated them, should be strengthened.

The 2014 election was characterized by government interference in the electoral process. Both the security sector and election management body should remain impartial to be effective prevention actors. Security-sector engagement was in particular a double-edged sword: security services prevented electoral violence through robust engagement but were also biased. Critics claim that security threats were overstated to enable the security forces to conduct special operations to intimidate the opposition parties. Police involvement certainly increased frustrations among the opposition and could have provoked protests. If such protests had turned violent, the special forces would have—somewhat ironically—provoked violence. The government's interference in election administration could also have led to violent protests.

In future elections, international actors should pressure the government to avoid such interference. This, however, presupposes that the international community itself is impartial—a precondition not met in 2014. Because international actors contributed to the polarizing debates on Moldova's geopolitical direction and were thus not unbiased, foreign missions were ill-suited for preventive diplomacy. The relatively high degree of impartiality in monitoring and civic education efforts, by contrast, explains why these models were more effective in preventing violence.

The absence of voter consultations and youth programming did not result in violence in 2014, but strengthening both models could prevent violence in future elections. This seems particularly important in the wake of a growing conflict between Russia and the West, one that significantly affects Moldova. In the context of growing frustrations over the lack of democratic progress and the 2009 developments, youths are a vulnerable group for violence. To strengthen their resilience against all forms of polarization, youth programming should be reinforced.

The best way to reduce the potential for electoral violence in the long term is to remedy structural vulnerabilities, particularly deficits in the political system and polarization in society. Comprehensive efforts to reform the judiciary, the prosecutor's office, and the state's capacity to more effectively fight corruption could address the existing shortcomings in the rule of law sector and increase voter trust in Moldova's electoral process.

Notes

1. The analysis is based on the author's research in Moldova in November and December 2014 and between October 2014 and April 2015 in Berlin, Brussels, and Washington, DC. The research includes interviews with Moldovan public servants, representatives of civil society organizations and political foundations, diplomats, officials of international organizations, researchers, and journalists. The author would like to thank both the interviewees and the project team's members.
2. Popular protest on a central square, similar to the protests in Kiev between November 2013 and February 2014. The term *maidan*, a word of Persian origin, means square or open space.

3.   According to the Bureau of Diplomatic Security, the overall threat of political violence in Moldova in 2014 was medium. See "Moldova 2014 Crime and Safety Report" (Washington, DC: U.S. Department of State, May 19, 2014), p. 2.

4.   The Organization for Security and Cooperation in Europe (OSCE) election observation mission in Moldova gave a fairly positive assessment of the electoral process, but noted the influence of the PCRM over the electorate through the state-controlled media and the "blurring of the distinction between the duties of State officials and their campaign activities." See OSCE, "Moldova, Parliamentary Elections, 5 April 2009," Final Report (Warsaw: OSCE Office for Democratic Institutions and Human Rights, June 16, 2009), www.osce.org/odihr/elections/moldova/37568. According to Henry Hale, the postelection protests were not spontaneously organized via social networks but had been planned and advertised by the opposition parties before the election in anticipation of fraud (from the Liberal Party). See Henry Hale, *Explaining Moldova's 'Twitter Revolution that Wasn't'* (Washington, DC: Ponars Eurasia, 2013), p. 12.

5.   The opposition parties accused the PCRM of using provocateurs to infiltrate the peaceful protests and instigate the violence in order to discredit the opposition and create an outcry for stability rather than change in Moldova.

6.   The OSCE reported three fatalities in connection with the demonstrations and the detentions (see "Moldova, Parliamentary Elections, 5 April 2009," p. 2). According to Theodor Tudoroiu, the police arrested nearly seven hundred demonstrators, many of whom suffered numerous beatings and two died in police custody. See "Structural Factors vs. Regime Change: Moldova's difficult Quest for Democracy," *Democratization* 18, no. 1 (2011): 242.

7.   Moldova is a fully parliamentary system with a 101-member unicameral parliament whose members are elected through proportional representation with closed lists in a single nationwide constituency. The Moldovan parliament elects a president with a three-fifths majority (sixty-one votes).

8.   A president was finally elected in March 2012—Nicolae Timofti, the candidate of the Alliance for European Integration—with the help of three PCRM defectors, who voted for him. During the voting session, several thousand PCRM supporters demonstrated in Chișinău.

9.   The doubts are also attributable to thorough investigations of the events never being conducted. In April 2009, then President Voronin appointed a commission to investigate the incident but representatives of the opposition parties were not invited to participate. The OSCE/ODIHR Election Observation Mission attempted to verify some of the allegations of electoral fraud and indicated that some claims of fraudulent voting might have been credible, but was unable to provide a conclusive assessment. See Bob Deen, "Deadlock and Division in Moldova: The 2009 Political Crisis and the Role of the OSCE," *Security and Human Rights* 4 (2009): 333.

10. See Deen, "Deadlock and Division," p. 328; Nicu Popescu, "Moldova's Fragile Pluralism," *Russian Politics and Law* 50, no. 4 (2012): 46.

11. According to Moldova's 2004 census, the largest minority groups are Ukrainians (8.4 percent), Russians (5.9 percent), Gagauzians (4.4 percent), Romanians (2.2 percent), Bulgarians (1.9 percent), and other nationalities (1.0 percent, including Roma). See Republic of Moldova, "Population Census 2004: Demographic, national, language and cultural characteristics," *National Bureau of Statistics*, www.statistica.md/pageview.php?l=en&idc=295&id=2234. Members of minority groups, interviews indicate, often see themselves as second-class citizens.

12. The authorities in Transnistria have in the past years increasingly claimed its right to accede to the Russian Federation.

13. As in many other parts of Moldova, Russian is lingua franca in Gagauzia. Russian television channels are popular in Gagauzia and most guest workers from the region work in the Russian Federation.

14. The referenda were acclaimed by the authorities of the neighboring district of Taraclia, a region with a majority ethnic Bulgarian population that requests more autonomy.

15. State officials argue that the government has spent overproportionally high amounts of assistance funds for Gagauzia, but observers from the region claim that the government largely ignores Gagauzia's interests and remains reluctant to invest in confidence-building measures. As an example, Chişinău did not respond to the Gagauz requests to send more Romanian-language teachers to the region.

16. Stanislav Secrieru, *How to Offset Russian Shadow Power? The Case of Moldova* (Warsaw: Polish Institute of International Affairs, 2014), p. 1.

17. See Vladislav Kulminski and Martin Sieg, *Moldova at a Crossroads: Why an Association Agreement with the EU Matters More than Ever* (Berlin: Deutsche Gesellschaft für Auswärtige Politik, 2014), p. 4.

18. See USAID Moldova, "An Analysis of the State of Democracy and Governance in Moldova" (Washington, DC: U.S. Agency for International Development, 2012), p. 5. Freedom House considers Moldova a "partly free democracy." See *Freedom in the World 2015* (Washington, DC: Freedom House, 2015), p. 24.

19. See Theodor Tudoroiu, "Democracy and State Capture in Moldova," *Democratization* 22, no. 4 (2014): 655–56.

20. See Celinda Lake, Daniel Gotoff, and Kristy Pultorak, "Public Perceptions of Politics and Government: Findings from a June–July 2014 Survey" (Washington, DC: National Democratic Institute, 2014), p. 11; Maria Ciubotaru, Nadine Gogu, Mariana Kalughin, Ianina Spinei, and Cristina Ţărnă, "National Integrity System Assessment: Moldova 2014" (Chişinău: Transparency International Moldova, July 2014).

21. USAID Moldova, "An Analysis," p. 15.

22. The EU, Council of Europe, and United States have for years expressed concern about shortcomings in the rule of law in Moldova. Previous governments have adopted legislation to overcome these problems, but often lacked political will to turn their laws into reality. An EU report of 2014, for example, referred to "the destructive impact of corruption at all levels and the need for sustained political will to tackle them." See European Commission, "Implementation of the European Neighbourhood Policy in the Republic of Moldova: Progress in 2013 and Recommendations for Action," Joint Staff Working Document (Brussels: European Commission, March 27, 2014), p. 3.

23. For example, Vlad Plahotniuc, vice chairman of the PDM, is believed to control six television channels. The Audiovisual Co-ordination Council (CCA), Moldova's media oversight body, fails to ensure a competitive market. As journalists have confirmed, most media outlets are practically subjugated to party interests and many journalists have become "mercenaries."

24. See "Synthesis and Foreign Policy Debates," *FES Newsletter* 7, no. 101 (September 2014): 8, www.fes-moldova.org/media/publications/2014/Newsletter_APE_FES_2014_7_ENG.pdf.

25. See "If parliamentary elections were held next Sunday, which party would you vote for?" *eDemocracy*, 2014, www.e-democracy.md/en/elections/parliamentary/2014/public-opin-ion-polls/. The Patria Party was led by Renato Usatîi, a Moldovan businessman who had been operating in Russia for years and who entered Moldovan politics in early 2014. Alluring to mostly poor and frustrated voters, Usatîi announced in the election campaigns decisive actions to fight oligarchs and corruption in Moldova.

26. In January 2013, a journalist revealed an illegal hunting excursion during which a participant was accidentally shot and killed. The incident was initially hidden from the public because several businessmen and judicial officials had participated in the hunt, including Prosecutor General Valeriu Zubco. When Zubco, a PDM nominee, had to resign from office, the coalition members clashed over his replacement. In February 2013, Prime Minister Vlad Filat (PLDM) accused the PDM of corruption and capturing judicial offices.

27. In the mixed system, fifty-one MPs were to be elected through proportional representation and fifty deputies in uninominal constituencies.

28. In 2014, the Council of Europe's Venice Commission warned that "when changing fundamental aspects of an election law, care must be taken to avoid not only manipulation to

the advantage of the party in power, but even the mere semblance of manipulation" and criticized that the new legislation had not been discussed inclusively with all electoral stakeholders. Council of Europe, "Joint Opinion on the Draft Law Amending the Electoral Legislation of the Republic of Moldova," Opinion no. 749/2014 (Warsaw: OSCE, March 24, 2014), pp. 3/4, www.osce.org/odihr/elections/116887.

29. However, Russian and EU interference differs significantly: the EU usually works with incentives vis-à-vis the Moldovan authorities, but the Kremlin often uses coercive diplomacy by applying negative pressure to promote its interests.

30. For example, the EU granted Moldovan citizens with biometric passports visa free travel to the Schengen area.

31. Russia also openly supports the authorities in Transnistria that in 2014 requested the region's accession to the Russian Federation. To strengthen the standing of pro-Russia parties in Gagauzia, the Russian Federation in the fall of 2014 lifted the embargo on wines produced in Gagauzia, whereas an embargo remained in force for all other Moldovan wines.

32. See Piotr Oleksy, "A pro-Russian Maidan in Chișinău?" *New Eastern Europe*, November 28, 2014, www.neweasterneurope.eu/articles-and-commentary/1404-a-pro-russian-maidan-in-chisinau.

33. In broad terms, the pro-EU parties believe that European integration will stimulate economic growth, attract foreign investments, reduce poverty, increase energy security, and improve anti-corruption policies.

34. Support for European integration has decreased somewhat, from around 75 percent in 2007 to around 44 percent in 2014. See Institute for Public Policy, "Barometrul Opiniei Publice: noiembrie 2014," Press Release, November 18, 2014, www.ipp.md/public/files/Barometru/Rezumat_de_presa_BOP_11_2014_final.pdf. EU integration is particularly opposed by most of the minority groups in Moldova.

35. Main campaign topics were Moldova's geopolitical orientation and several socioeconomic issues, including economic development, tackling corruption, and reducing poverty.

36. This assessment is shared by the director of Promo-Lex, Ion Manole (email correspondence, February 18, 2015). Interestingly, the lack of fairness was anticipated by many citizens before the election. According to an opinion poll of April 2014, only 26 percent of the respondents considered elections in Moldova to free and fair; 62 percent rejected this notion (Institute for Public Policy, "Barometer of Public Opinion: Republic of Moldova, April 2014," www.ipp.md/libview.php?l=en&idc=156&id=681).

37. Election experts such as Arcadie Barbarosie doubt that the evidence against Patria Party was valid. Usatîi would have brought his own money in cash from Russia and would have also declared it at the Moldovan border. The electoral code leaves the definition of "foreign funds" unclear. The deregistration of Patria Party was therefore illegal, a 2015 telephone interview revealed.

38. On the grounds that the CEC was not given enough time to examine the police's evidence, CEC Vice President Ștefan Urâtu did not approve the CEC decision to request Patria's deregistration. See EuropaLibera, "Un membru CEC explica de ce a votat IMPOTRIVA excluderii partidului Patria," November 27, 2014, http://protv.md/stiri/actualitate/europalibera-un-membru-cec-explica-de-ce-a-votat-impotriva-excluderii---790411.html.

39. See eDemocracy, "If parliamentary elections were held next Sunday, which party would you vote for?" November 2014, www.e-democracy.md/en/elections/parliamentary/2014/public-opinion-polls/.

40. OSCE, "Republic of Moldova, Parliamentary Elections, 30 November 2014: Statement of Preliminary Findings and Conclusions" (Chișinău: OSCE, December 2014), p. 2, www.osce.org/odihr/elections/moldova/128476.

41. Following Patria's exclusion, Usatîi immediately left for Russia, arguing that the government oppressed and intimidated Patria activists and that he feared to be arrested by the Moldovan authorities.

42. According to observers, all major parties have the capacity to mobilize thugs qualified to

instigate (potentially violent) demonstrations if leadership deems it necessary. An exclusion of the bigger opposition parties PCRM or PSRM would have certainly led to large protests and potential violence.

43. Some commentators argued that a murder shortly after elections day was a result of political party rivalry. On December 9, 2014, the PDLM politician Ion Butmalai, a deputy of the outgoing parliament, was found dead. The police's assumption that he committed suicide was questioned by some observers because Butmalai had previously condemned illicit activities of PDM Vice President Plahotniuc and announced plans to call the Prosecutor General's Office to bring high-ranked state officials to court for committed crimes. Some observers therefore assume that Butmalai's murder was a revenge killing. See "Cahul Raion Prosecutors Office starts Litigation on the Death of Parliamentarian Ion Butmalai," *INFOTAG*, December 10, 2014, www.infotag.md/populis-en/196944/.

44. OSCE, "Preliminary Findings," p. 7.

45. Promo-Lex, "Report No. 2: Monitoring Parliamentary Elections of 30 November 2014" (Chișinău: Promo-Lex Association, October 16, 2014), p. 11. In addition, some infractions do not qualify as electoral violence. For example, some PDM representatives allegedly tried to bribe voters and organized transportation of voters to the polling stations. See Promo-Lex, "Report Election Day: Monitoring Parliamentary Elections on 30 November 2014" (Chișinău: Promo-Lex Association, December 4, 2014). After the elections, the PSRM argued that many voters had been bribed by pro-EU parties.

46. All other parties did not pass the 6 percent threshold to enter parliament. Observers claimed that many voters did not vote for the pro-EU parties out of real conviction but out of fear that the foreign policy direction would be reversed.

47. It can be assumed that the PSRM leadership was rather satisfied with the election result and had no interest in postelection violence. Because the three pro-EU parties, which still hold fifty-five of the mandates in the new parliament, could not agree on a coalition, PLDM and PDM formed a minority government that was approved with the support of some MPs from the PCRM. The PSRM expected the minority government to collapse and was hoping to win the majority of the votes in snap elections.

48. See Secrieru, *How to Offset*, p. 1. Other observers warned of hybrid threats in which militant groups would establish a network of small cells throughout Moldova that could be mobilized for protests, provocations and unrest. See Resource Center for Human Rights, *Hybrid Threats: Implications for Moldova 2014* (Chișinău: Resource Center for Human Rights, 2014).

49. See Intelligence and Security Service, "SIS took notice of the 'secret meeting' in Bălți from June 5th, 2014," June 10, 2014, www.sis.md/en/comunicare/noutati/sis-took-notice-secret-meeting-balti-june-5th-2014.

50. Secrieru, *How to Offset*, p. 1. The Gagauz authorities denied their involvement in the case and argued that the central government used artificial security threats to disrespect Gagauzia's autonomy rights.

51. Ibid.

52. "Police Make Searches and Detain Some Antifa Activists," *INFOTAG*, November 26, 2014, www.infotag.md/populis-en/196307/; Intelligence and Security Service, "Press release," November 18, 2014, www.sis.md/en/comunicare/noutati/press-release-0.

53. Intelligence and Security Service, "Statement," November 21, 2014, www.sis.md/en/comunicare/noutati/statement.

54. Tele Radio Moldova, "Intelligence and Security Service Warns the Electoral Competitors not to Make Declarations that Might Cause Instability," November 24, 2014, www.trm.md/en/politic/sis-atentioneaza-concurentii-electorali-sa-nu-faca-declaratii-care-ar-putea-genera-instabilitate/.

55. See Cornel Ciurea, *Comparative Analysis of Options for Assurance of National Security of the Republic of Moldova in the Context of Russian Aggression in Ukraine* (Chișinău: Foreign Policy Association, 2015), p. 12.

56. In the weeks before the election, the special forces of the Ministry of Interior provided

a show of force in Chișinău to illustrate their preparedness to counter security threats. Several measures had been adopted since 2009 to reform the police. For example, to reduce political interference in police work, legislation in 2012 transformed the police into an independent agency (the General Police Inspectorate) no longer directed by the Ministry of the Interior. The national chief inspector can no longer be discharged on political grounds but only for serious misconduct. The General Police Inspectorate is responsible for all operational policing, and the Ministry of Foreign Affairs only for developing, implementing, and coordinating police policies.

57. However, some observers consider the carabinieri forces as overly militarized and in urgent need of reform. Victor Munteanu, *Recommendations for the MAI Reform in 2014* (Chișinău: Foreign Policy Association, 2014). Interestingly, only 1 percent of opinion poll respondents stated that they "feel free to make street protests against the decisions taken by the country's leadership"; 17 percent said that there is "no freedom" to do so. See Institute for Public Policy, "Barometer of Public Opinion, April 2014," p. 38.

58. Dumitru Minzarari, "Moldovan Armed Forces Train for Hybrid Warfare the Wrong Way," *Eurasian Daily Monitor* 11, no. 194 (2014). A government official interviewed in Chișinău shared this view.

59. By calling "the European course of our country" as "irreversible" (see Intelligence and Security Service, "SIS took notice of the 'secret meeting' in Bălți from June 5th, 2014"), the SIS took a clear position on Moldova's foreign policy orientation.

60. According to Ciurea, Moldova was in November and December 2014 in "collective hysteria" with campaigns similar to "witch hunts" (*Comparative Analysis*, p. 12).

61. OSCE, "Preliminary Findings," p. 1.

62. Transparency International, "National Integrity System Assessment," p. 119; see also Steven Grey, "A Successful Five-Year Partnership in Moldova," *IFES Moldova Newsletter* no. 5 (May 2013), p. 2 [copy in author's possession].

63. In 2012, the CEC established a working group that developed a number of proposals to amend legislation with the objective to increase transparency of processes related to party and electoral campaign finances. See Central Election Commission and International Foundation for Electoral Systems, *Amendments to Laws Relating to Political Finance in Moldova* (Chișinău: Republic of Moldova Central Election Commission and IFES, 2012). Under pressure from international organizations, the majority of the Moldovan MPs in 2014 adopted the proposals in a first reading but did not further discuss them later. Interviews with CEC officials reveal an assumption that all political parties benefit from illegal finance through domestic donors.

64. Most of the unreported revenues and expenses covered the organization of public events and were detected by the PDM (9.5 million lei) and the PLDM (2.9 million lei), which both went beyond the 5 percent deviation from the set threshold (Promo-Lex, "At Least 14 Million Lei Undeclared During the Campaign," December 18, 2014).

65. See OSCE, "Election Observation Mission, Interim Report: 24 October–11 November 2014" (Warsaw: OSCE Office for Democratic Institutions and Human Rights, November 14, 2014), p. 1.

66. OSCE, "Moldova, Parliamentary Elections, 30 November 2014," Final Report (Warsaw: OSCE Office for Democratic Institutions and Human Rights, March 10, 2015), p. 3.

67. "Report by an Eastern Partnership Civil Society Forum Monitoring Team on the Parliamentary Election in the Republic of Moldova on November 30, 2014" (Brussels: Eastern Partnership Civil Society Forum, November 30, 2014), p. 2. After the elections, the PCRM asserted instances of multiple voting.

68. OSCE, "Moldova, Parliamentary Elections, 30 November 2014," p. 8.

69. Eight members of the CEC are appointed by parliament and proportionally represent the parties, and one member is appointed by the president. All CEC members are required to have ten years of legal experience, but according to observers, too few mechanisms are in place to ensure their integrity. See Transparency International, "National Integrity System Assessment," p. 119.

70. Promo-Lex, "Report No. 2," p. 13.
71. As a comparison, twenty-five polling stations were opened in Italy, eleven in Romania, and six in the United States. According to estimates, the countries with the largest number of Moldovan guest workers are the Russian Federation (64 percent), Italy (18 percent), Germany and France (4 percent each). See Institute for Public Policy, "Barometer of Public Opinion, November 2014," p. 4.
72. See OSCE, "Preliminary Findings," p. 2. Some CEC officials acknowledged in interviews that the determination was a purely political decision that had also surprised the CEC. In November 2014, delegations of the Parliamentary Assembly of the Council of Europe and of the Parliamentary Assembly of the Commonwealth of Independent States raised concerns about the "unbalanced distribution of the 95 polling stations abroad" but these statements had no effect on the government's decision (see Council of Europe, "Statement by Pre-electoral Delegation Visiting the Republic of Moldova," November 7, 2014, www.assembly.coe.int/nw/xml/News/News-View-EN.asp?newsid=5281&lang=2&cat=31).
73. According to some media outlets, numerous Moldovan guest workers in Moscow were excluded from voting because the polling station had only three thousand ballot papers. See Karl-Peter Schwarz, "Moldauische Wähler in Russland behindert," *Frankfurter Allgemeine Zeitung*, November 30, 2014, www.faz.net/aktuell/politik/ausland/europa/russland-behin-dert-moldauer-bei-parlamentswahlen-in-moldau-13295288.html.
74. OSCE, "Moldova Parliamentary Elections, 30 November 2014," pp. 3, 19.
75. Ibid., p. 21.
76. Arcadie Barbarosie, as he revealed in an interview, also believes that the PCR has intentionally been founded by the PDM to weaken the PCRM.
77. Embassy of the United States, "Press release," November 27, 2014, http://moldova.usembassy.gov/112714.html.
78. Ministry of Foreign Affairs of the Russian Federation, "Comment by the Information and Press Department of the Russian Ministry of Foreign Affairs on Disqualification of the Patria Party from the Elections in Moldova," November 28, 2014, www.mid.ru/brp_4.nsf/0/2CB3CA2F87BC6CADC3257D9E0065D56B.
79. Embassy of the Russian Federation to the Republic of Moldova, "Комментарий Департамента информации и печати МИД России об итогах парламентских выборов в Молдавии" [Comment Information and Press Department of the Russian Foreign Ministry on the results of parliamentary elections in Moldova], Press Release, December 3, 2014, www.mid.ru/brp_4.nsf/newsline/6BEC856896F8857FC3257DA300465670.
80. U.S. Embassy, "Press release, November 27, 2014."
81. U.S. Embassy, "Press release, December 1, 2014."
82. European Union External Action Service, "Joint Statement on the Parliamentary Elections in the Republic of Moldova," December 1, 2014, http://europa.eu/rapid/press-release_STATEMENT-14-2270_en.htm.
83. See Rolf Kleine, "Interview with German foreign minister Frank-Walter Steinmeier," *BILD*, November 29, 2014, www.auswaertiges-amt.de/DE/Infoservice/Presse/Interviews/2014/141129-BM_Bild.html.
84. See "Moldova's Election: Slouching Towards Europe," *Economist*, December 6, 2014, www.economist.com/news/europe/21635508-pro-russia-parties-lose-close-vote-corrupt-land-slouching-towards-europe. In addition, Moldova's association agreement with the EU was ratified by the European Parliament and the national parliaments of Estonia, Hungary and Sweden shortly before the election.
85. OSCE, "Interim Report," p. 5.
86. Vladimir Socor, "Inside Moldova's Governing Coalition After the Elections," *Eurasia Daily Monitor* 11, no. 217 (December 2014).
87. Organizations such as the UN did not comment on the election in Moldova.
88. Intelligence and Security Service, "Statement." On the occasion the UN International Day

of Peace on September 21, 2014, in an event in Chişinău somewhat relating to the situation in Moldova, citizens expressed their support for peace in neighboring Ukraine.

89. Administration and Cost of Elections Project, "Voter Education Moldova," www.aceproject.org/epic-ar/CDCountry?set_language=en&topic=VE&country=MD.
90. Grey, "A Successful Five-Year Partnership," p. 2.
91. OSCE, "Preliminary Findings," p. 5.
92. OSCE, "Parliamentary Elections, 30 November 2014," p. 19.
93. For example, the CSO International Research and Exchanges Board between 2004 and 2008 and with USAID funding implemented a program that aimed to use participatory democratic processes to help citizens identify community priorities (for example in community meetings) as well as to increase understanding of democratic processes among Moldovan citizens. According to its own data, IREX implemented more than 280 community-driven development projects throughout Moldova and held various capacity-building trainings. See IREX, "Community Solutions," www.irex.org/projects/community-solutions.
94. Promo-Lex, "Report No. 1: Monitoring Parliamentary Elections on 30 November 2014" (Chişinău: Promo-Lex Association, September 25, 2014), p. 3.
95. OSCE, "Moldova Parliamentary Elections, 30 November 2014: OSCE/ODIHR Needs Assessment Mission Report," September 19, 2014, p. 4, www.osce.org/odihr/elections/moldova/123800.
96. See Council of Europe, "Action Plan to Support Democratic Reforms in the Republic of Moldova: 2013-2016," document ODGProg/Inf(2013)17 final, November 15, 2013, https://wcd.coe.int/com.instranet.InstraServlet?command=com.instranet.CmdBlobGet&InstranetImage=2651638&SecMode=1&DocId=2070312&Usage=2, 7.
97. An opinion poll from April 2014 revealed that only 14 percent of the respondents believe that the will of the people rules in Moldova, and that 78 percent do not. See Institute for Public Policy, "Barometer of Public Opinion, April 2014," p. 52.
98. A structural problem that helps explain the lack of voter consultations is Moldova's proportional representation system in which MPs are not directly elected in electoral constituencies to which they are accountable. The proportional system strengthens the power of political parties and does not incentivize voter consultation efforts by individual politicians.
99. More than 70 percent of the citizens are dissatisfied with the level of information they receive from the government on important topics such as the country's economy or national security. See Celinda Lake, Daniel Gotoff, and Kristy Pultorak, "Public Perceptions of Politics and Government: Findings from a June –July 2014 Survey" presentation (Washington, DC: National Democratic Institute, November 2015), www.ndi.org/files/NDIMoldovaSurveyNov2015.pdf.
100. OSCE, "Preliminary Findings," p. 7.
101. Other NDI activities, such as regular opinion surveys, aim to support political parties in better responding to citizens' interests.
102. Similarly, many young people join NGOs to bolster their CVs and not for being actively involved in civil society. The PCRM in particular has the image of a "gerontocratic" party whose leadership is unwilling to give space to young politicians. Under long-term chairman Vladimir Voronin, the PCRM has in past years dissolved several young politicians from leading positions within the party.
103. Half of these young MPs are members of the PSRM (seven of twenty-five), followed by the PDLM (three of twenty-three), PL (two of thirteen), and PDM (two of nineteen). The PCRM has no MP under age thirty-five. The number of young MPs has slightly increased since 2010, when only twelve were thirty-five or younger.
104. In its Political Academy, the FES aims to educate and train young members of political parties, public institutions, and CSOs on topics such as good governance.
105. This finding can lead to the assumption that a country with similar contextual vulnerabilities and similarly controversial elections but a less developed political culture than Moldova is likely to encounter electoral violence.

Map 6.1 Honduras National Map

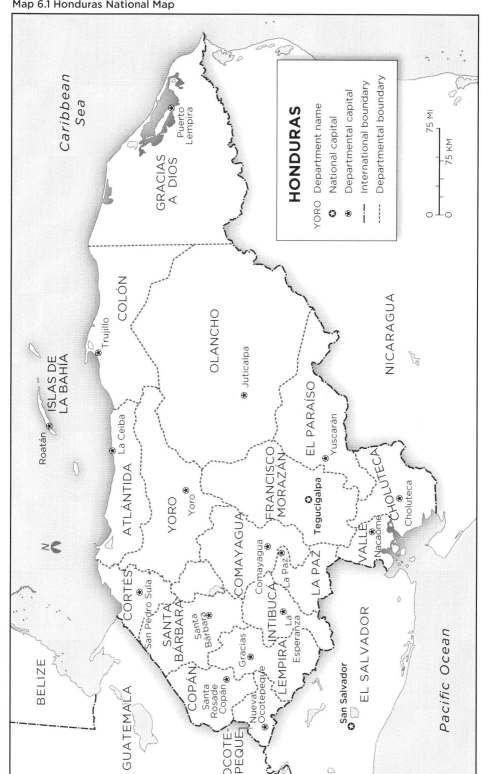

HONDURAS

YORO — Department name
✪ — National capital
✪ — Departmental capital
–·–·– — International boundary
------ — Departmental boundary

0 — 75 MI
0 — 75 KM

Caribbean Sea

GRACIAS A DIOS

Puerto Lempira ✪

COLÓN

Trujillo ✪

OLANCHO

Juticalpa ✪

ISLAS DE LA BAHÍA

Roatán ✪

NICARAGUA

ATLÁNTIDA

La Ceiba ✪

EL PARAÍSO

Yuscarán ✪

YORO

Yoro ✪

FRANCISCO MORAZÁN

Tegucigalpa ✪

COMAYAGUA

Comayagua ✪

LA PAZ

La Paz ✪

CHOLUTECA

Choluteca ✪

VALLE

Nacaome ✪

CORTÉS

San Pedro Sula ✪

SANTA BÁRBARA

Santa Bárbara ✪

INTIBUCÁ

La Esperanza ✪

LEMPIRA

Gracias ✪

COPÁN

Santa Rosade Copán ✪

OCOTE PEQUE

Nueva Ocotepeque ✪

EL SALVADOR

San Salvador ✪

BELIZE

GUATEMALA

Pacific Ocean

N

6

Honduras

Unrealized Fears, Ordinary Violence

ELIZABETH MURRAY

"Electoral violence? We don't have that here. Hondurans are a peaceful people."

This sentiment, which Hondurans invoke when asked about their experience with electoral violence, seems incongruous in the country with one of the highest homicide rates in the world. It begins to make more sense when understood through the lens of Honduras's relatively limited experience of armed conflict in recent decades—especially in comparison with its Central American neighbors—and its historical absence of mass violence on election day.

As the 2013 election cycle commenced, however, many Hondurans and international observers feared that Honduras was poised to experience widespread violence around election day.[1] Democracy was still recovering from the significant setback of the June 2009 coup that unseated democratically elected President Mel Zelaya. The political system was also undergoing an unprecedented transformation because four new parties had registered and were poised to capture a significant proportion of the vote.

Mass violence ultimately did not occur around the general elections held on November 24, 2013. One notable disruption did unfold in El Paraíso de Copan, where armed men prevented poll workers from reaching the polling station. Aside from that, however, election day itself was generally calm. In the months that followed, two disputed mayoral results would result in one fatality and one destroyed mayoral building.

The most frequent form of electoral violence, by a wide margin, was targeted homicides, which were fairly regular throughout the eighteen-month election cycle. They occurred in the context of shockingly high criminal violence: various estimates placed the 2012–2013 homicide rates between seventy-nine and ninety per hundred thousand persons per year, among the highest in the world.[2] Near total impunity, widespread organized crime, and increasingly active youth gangs are among the many contributing factors to the high homicide rate.

The highest official estimate of the targeted election-related homicides is forty-eight.[3] Other reports cite zero confirmed deaths, arguing that incomplete or absent investigations make it impossible to confirm a political motive.[4] Even at the highest estimate, these politically motivated killings are not a notable increase to the general homicide rate. Because persistent poverty and pressing security concerns dominate the national agenda, it is unlikely that a consensus will ever be reached on the scope of election-related fatalities. Because election-related deaths in the 2013 election season looked nearly identical to "everyday" homicides, analyzing Honduran electoral violence and its prevention is a complicated exercise.

Based on a review of the differing accounts of electoral violence, this chapter assumes a range of between twelve and thirty-six election-related homicides in 2012 and 2013 (primary and general election seasons), in addition to the one fatality in 2014 indisputably related to the contested mayoral results (for a total of thirteen to thirty-seven). Violence levels were still lower than many had anticipated. The higher than usual risk was mitigated in large part by the strong international pressure coupled with intense domestic and international monitoring efforts. This chapter also analyzes the presence and impact of six other prevention models: security-sector engagement, electoral management, civic education, peace messaging, voter consultations, and youth programming.

The impact of the security sector in the elections was mixed in that the police force—both poorly trained and corrupt—failed to prevent assassinations in the lead-up to the election. On the other hand, the sector did have some deterrent value when deployed en masse on election day. Similarly, the impact of the electoral management body, the Supreme Electoral Tribunal (TSE), had strengths and weaknesses. By deftly managing the registration of new parties, the TSE reduced the risk of violent protests by excluded groups. Other dimensions of the electoral management, however, raised the risk of violence.

Youth programming, though robust, did not play a significant role in reducing violence. Civic education and peace-messaging campaigns were present but not fully developed. Given the nature of the violence, these models may not have had significant impacts even had they been applied more robustly. A final preventive model, voter consultations, was applied only sporadically. Even if party consultations had been more widespread, it is unlikely that they would have had a significant impact. The current state of political parties in Honduras—weak ideology and continuous failure to craft policy addressing constituents' needs—calls into question whether parties are poised to utilize feedback from their constituents in a meaningful way.

In the lead-up to the election, several contextual factors combined to create a mid-level risk of political violence in Honduras: the fragile state of democracy, a polarized political climate, and widespread insecurity. These same vulnerabilities influenced whether the preventive models—even if applied widely and in accordance with international best practices—had the potential to affect the outcome.

History of Political Violence

Honduras has experienced moderate levels and various forms of political violence since its 1821 independence from Spain, but the absence of large-scale fatalities on election days has been relatively constant. After 1950, with the exception of the 2009 coup d'état, violence was minimal. This calm seems especially mild in comparison with neighboring Nicaragua, El Salvador, and Guatemala, where civil wars killed tens of thousands in each country.

During its state formation and in the first half of the twentieth century, Honduras saw intermittent factional civil wars and a repressive sixteen-year dictatorship. From the 1950s until the transition to democracy in 1981, Honduras was primarily governed by a series of military governments, which oversaw a period of relative stability. Despite the official declaration of democracy, the military police and intelligence were responsible for the disappearance of dozens of Hondurans during the 1980s and early 1990s. The next major political violence began after the 2009 coup d'état, when the newly installed government repressed the deposed president's supporters, journalist assassinations markedly increased, and conflict over land tenure became more pronounced along the Atlantic Coast.

The First 150 Years

Following its independence from Spain, Honduras was characterized by significant upheavals interspersed with periods of calm. In his book *Reinterpreting the Banana Republic*, the historian Dario Euraque identifies 146 separate lethal military conflicts in Honduras between 1870 and 1949. In the first decades after independence, many of these were initiated by local *caudillos*, powerful landowners with political and economic interests, who sought to expand their regional sphere of influence or to dominate the national political arena. In the early twentieth century, as the two-party system crystallized in Honduras, the battles began to be fought between political parties and within factions. The years from 1920 to 1923 were particularly tumultuous, and saw seventeen uprisings. Although unrest was frequent during the late nineteenth century and the first half of the twentieth century, none of the conflicts resulted in widespread, protracted war; the two most lethal conflicts, between 1892 and 1894 and in 1924, incurred approximately five thousand casualties each.[5]

Although elections were not yet institutionalized, they did occur. Euraque documents seventeen between 1877 and 1948, often marred by coercion, fraud, or repression of opposition voices.[6] The rule of Tiburio Andino Carias—a sixteen-year stretch that came to be known as the Cariato—paved the way for an emblematic election. Although Carias had been democratically elected to the presidency, he gradually became less tolerant of dissent and used the military to intimidate and weaken the Liberal Party, leftist movements, and organized labor. His chosen successor, National Party candidate Juan Manuel Galvez, easily won the presidency in the 1948 elections, which were held amid a call for abstention from the exiled Liberal Party.

The outcome of that 1948 election was influenced by the actual and threatened violence that Carias applied to his political adversaries. Political violence also indisputably influenced many other transfers of power in the first hundred years of Honduras's independence. The pattern of violence, though, particularly as Honduras entered the twentieth century, was not centered around mass disruptions on election day; violence may in fact well have occurred in the late nineteenth century, but it is neither well documented nor part of the Honduran cultural narrative. The pattern of a calm election day, despite intimidation in the preceding weeks and months, was established relatively early on and is a significant aspect of Hondurans' political self-conception today.[7]

Formal Military Rule, Quiet Military Violence

The military played a prominent role in governing Honduras during the second half of the twentieth century. It largely maintained stability during its formal rule but exerted a more insidious influence after handing the government over to civilians in the early 1980s. The pattern of disappearances and killings by military police and intelligence in the 1980s and 1990s was distinct from the pattern of overt civil conflict experienced during the first century of independence.

In 1963, to prevent the likely presidential win of Modest Rojas, whose leftist ideals raised alarm in light of newly communist Cuba, the Honduran military deposed President Villeda Morales of the Liberal Party. Led by Oswaldo Lopez Arellano, the period from 1963 to 1971 saw the first formal military government in the country.[8] After a brief civilian government in early 1971, the military returned to power in 1972 before officially stepping away from it in 1981. This period of military rule was better tolerated in Honduras than similar regimes in other Central American countries, in part because the military was relatively progressive, carrying out agrarian reform and implementing pro-labor policies.[9]

Honduras's transition to democracy in the early 1980s was less disruptive than those of its neighbors, perhaps because of high societal approval for the military. In light of serious civil conflict in neighboring El Salvador, Guatemala, and Nicaragua, the Honduran military, assisted by the U.S. government, was intent on preventing leftist insurgencies from taking hold inside Honduras. The secret police Battalion 3-16 arrested and tortured Salvadorans and members of the labor movement, farmers, and leftist student activists in Honduras.[10] A 1994 government investigation of the 3-16 revealed that 184 people had disappeared or been killed, many in secret torture centers.[11]

Daily life and politics for Hondurans were relatively stable under the military governments of the 1960s and 1970s. After the declared shift to democracy, the vast majority of political violence in the 1980s and early 1990s was clandestine, overt civil conflict and electoral violence both minimal during the period. The influence of the military in Honduran politics, though at times violent, did not result in electoral violence. Leftist threats in Honduras were eliminated quietly and largely outside electoral politics.

Democracy on the Decline

The first three decades of civilian rule in Honduras were characterized by regular, if somewhat flawed, elections. Power was split relatively evenly between the National Party and the Liberal Party, with each acceding to the presidency four times between 1982 and 2009; support for the Liberal Party trended downward over time, in contrast to the growing popularity of the National Party. In 2009, a military coup d'état initiated another period of political violence that included violent repression of the supporters of the deposed president, increased attacks on journalists, and violent land disputes.

On the morning of June 28, 2009, the military removed President Mel Zelaya of the Liberal Party from his residence at gunpoint and unceremoniously flew him to Costa Rica in his pajamas. This followed a constitutional crisis centered around Zelaya's proposal to conduct a nonbinding referendum on the possibility of holding a constituent assembly to create a new constitution. Although the Supreme Court declared the referendum unconstitutional, Zelaya continued publicly discussing the possibility, which raised fears that he planned to run for a second term under a new constitution (second terms are prohibited by the 1982 constitution).

Immediately after Zelaya's removal from office, the Honduran Congress produced a letter of resignation from him—which he later declared was fake—and proceeded to swear in Roberto Micheletti, the president of Congress, as the new president of the country.[12] Micheletti declared a forty-five-day state of emergency that suspended freedoms of movement, assembly, and expression.[13] Micheletti's de facto government committed a variety of human rights abuses, including at least six killings, excessive use of force, and arbitrary detention, all of which were carefully documented by the Inter-American Commission on Human Rights and Human Rights Watch.[14]

Initial negotiations in Costa Rica to return Zelaya to power were not fruitful. The crisis took a strange turn when Zelaya sneaked back into Honduras in September 2009, seeking refuge within the Brazilian Embassy before formally going into exile in the Dominican Republic. Two months later, in the hastily organized November 2009 elections, a record low turnout of 50 percent of eligible Honduran voters selected National Party candidate Porforio Lobo as their new president. Lobo assumed office without major disruption, but the results of the election were not recognized by the majority of the international community.[15]

Two other varieties of political violence also increased after the coup. Beginning in 2009, lethal attacks on journalists in Honduras rose sharply. According to the Committee to Protect Journalists, three were killed between 1992 and 2008, versus eighteen between 2009 and 2013.[16] In 2013, Freedom House cited Honduras as one of the most dangerous countries in the world for journalists.[17] In addition, conflict over land tenure sharply increased in 2009 in the Bajo Aguan region on Honduras's Atlantic Coast. After Zelaya was ousted the same year, Roberto Micheletti's government failed to implement an accord Zelaya had signed with the main peasant movement to establish dialogue on land distribution.[18] As a result, peasant groups began to organize land occupations and other forms of protest and were then subject to violent reprisals. Between 2009 and 2013, more than a hundred *campesinos* were reportedly murdered by various armed actors, including the Honduran state and private security firms of the landholding businesses.[19]

Honduras's fledgling electoral democracy experienced a serious setback with the 2009 coup, but appeared to recover quickly, organizing democratic elections less than six months after the coup. Although the immediate postcoup political violence calmed within several months, violence against journalists and peasant movements continued over the following several years. As with the patterns of violence during the early post-independence years and the era of military rule, these new manifestations of violence occurred largely outside the electoral cycle.

Limited History of Electoral Violence

This study was significantly complicated by the high levels of everyday violence and a widely accepted cultural narrative that Honduras does not experience overt electoral violence at the level of some of its neighbors. Although elections are acknowledged to have historically involved some intimidation and fraud, analysts and ordinary Hondurans point out that election day itself has typically unfolded without major disruption.[20]

Another challenge in analyzing Honduras's political context is a lack of historical data on electoral violence. No single source has tracked election-related fatalities over more than three subsequent elections. Freedom House has touched on the issue in its annual reports, which recorded one fatality in the 2001 elections and two in 2005. Electoral violence in 2009 is much harder to define, because significant violence occurred after the coup and before the elections, and definitively linking violence to the coup, the upcoming elections, or both is challenging at best. Freedom House notes that during this year "motives and identities of the perpetrators of the various attacks were often unclear." Another source, the Committee of Relatives of the Disappeared and Detained in Honduras, cites nine fatalities in the 2009 electoral cycle.[21]

The limited history of electoral violence in Honduras could plausibly mitigate the risk of future violence. Although it has never neared the scale of neighboring El Salvador, Guatemala, and Nicaragua, political violence has appeared in myriad forms throughout Honduras's history. At times, this has included manipulation and threats around the election. Very likely certain homicides are tied to the electoral process, but this has not been carefully studied and is not a focus in the Honduran political narrative. Political violence in Honduras has primarily focused on other processes, tactics, and targets—including civil unrest, coups, secret military repression, the murder of journalists, and violence around land tenure. Given the many ways to commit violence in Honduras in support of political goals—and limited chances of being apprehended or punished—resorting to violence around the elections may simply not be necessary.

With other words, in comparison with other countries examined in this book (such as Thailand or Bangladesh), Honduras has no tradition of electoral violence, which reduces the risk of violence in future elections. Hondurans may have been less likely to commit electoral violence in 2013 simply because they have not done so en masse in previous elections.

The 2013 Presidential Election

As the 2013 elections approached, much international attention focused on Honduras. Given a coup in the recent past and the wife of a deposed president (Zelaya) running for the same post, many feared that 2013 could break the Honduran pattern. Political polarization, weak democracy, and widespread insecurity presented significant contextual risks for violence. Fortunately, the fears of mass violence were not realized. Electoral violence in 2013 closely mirrored criminal violence with its high concentration of targeted homicides. The (at least) twenty-five homicides linked to electoral politics were numerically insubstantial given the overall rate.

The 2013 elections were mostly noteworthy for the transition from a two-party to a multiparty system. The overall effect of this transition on electoral violence was positive because the opportunity to form new political parties allowed frustrated actors to channel their grievances through the political system rather than resort to violence.

Before 2013, Honduras had one of the longest-standing two-party systems in Latin America. The two traditional parties have shared philosophical roots; the Liberal Party was founded in the late nineteenth century and the National Party emerged as a splinter from it in the early twentieth. Given their similar origins, the parties have never been far from each other ideologically. During the rule of General Carias (1933–1948), the National Party became more closely allied with the military, pro-business, and less tolerant of emerging social movements; the Liberal Party meanwhile represented the interests of labor, students, and the emerging middle class. This period of more pronounced ideological variation between the parties was relatively brief. During military rule, the limited philosophical differences between the two further receded into the background, perhaps aided by the threat of communism across the region and increased nationalist sentiment brought about by the brief Futbol War with El Salvador in 1971.

Throughout the transition and the first decades of democracy, the two main parties remained close to each other ideologically. Both had alliances—often simultaneously—with most stakeholder groups, and neither made a serious or sustained effort to craft policy that addressed the needs of the poor majority.[22] After the 2009 coup d'état, the Liberal Party splintered into those who wanted to form a new party around deposed President Zelaya and those who supported the Liberal Party leadership that remained in Honduras.

In accordance with the 2011 Cartagena Accords that allowed for Zelaya's return from exile, Honduras's Supreme Tribunal of Elections facilitated the registration of new political parties in 2012, including Zelaya supporters, who formed the Liberty and Refoundation Party—Partido Libertad y Refundacion, or LIBRE. This was the first time that new parties had registered since 1994.[23] LIBRE's early efforts to organize and register had a galvanizing effect on the electorate and prompted three additional parties to register, including the Anti-Corruption Party (PAC) led by popular sports commentator Salvador Nasralla.

For the first time, the primary elections, which were held in November 2012, included three parties: the Liberal Party, the National Party, and the LIBRE party.[24] On May 23, 2013, the TSE convened all nine parties to officially register candidate lists for the general elections. The election results represented a major shift in the Honduran political system because two new parties, LIBRE and PAC, captured a significant share of the vote and ended a century of Liberal Party and National Party dominance.

Honduran politics were characterized by unusually high polarization as the 2013 elections approached. At the same time, that more electoral options (*mas oferta electoral*) allowed individuals who were dissatisfied with the traditional parties to express their dissatisfaction by supporting new parties rather than committing acts of violence, partly explains why electoral violence did not reach higher levels. The creation of new parties channeled dissatisfied voters, including those frustrated with Zelaya's ouster, into legitimate new political voices. If Zelaya's supporters—who represented a significant proportion of the electorate—had not been permitted to register as a party, they would have likely carried out protests, violence, or other disruptions during the electoral cycle.

In the months leading up to the 2013 elections, several contextual factors indicated a risk of violence. These included Honduras's recent coup and status as an unconsolidated democracy, intense political polarization, broad uncertainty about the election outcome, and widespread domestic insecurity.

Unconsolidated Democracy

The risk of electoral violence is understandably greater in weaker democracies. Citizens are more likely to turn violent when they do not believe the electoral system to be fair, have no confidence that elected leaders will respond to their needs, and have no faith that elected leaders will carry out their terms. The 2013 elections took place after a significant weakening of democracy in Honduras. Although a minority of analysts and politicians immediately took the position that Manuel Zelaya's removal from power in 2009 was legal, it was widely acknowledged to be unconstitutional. The Organization of American States (OAS) immediately issued a statement calling for Zelaya's return, and when Micheletti did not allow this, Honduras was suspended from the organization.

In 2012, the Economist Intelligence Unit, which evaluates democracies according to five factors, ranked Honduras at 5.84 of 10, in the category of hybrid regimes.[25] This was a slight improvement over the 2010 score of 5.76 but both scores were worse than the 6.18 of 2008, which merited inclusion in the partial democracies category.[26] Between 2008 and 2012, Honduras worsened on three of the five categories: functioning of government, political participation, and political culture. It held relatively steady in civil liberties and improved on electoral process.

Data from the well-established and widely cited Latin America Public Opinion Project (LAPOP) further verifies that democracy in Honduras had significant weaknesses in the lead-up to the 2013 elections. Survey data from 2008, 2010, and 2012 showed public support for democracy at 59.9 percent, 62.6 percent, and 52.6 percent, respectively. The 2012 support levels earned Honduras the lowest ranking in the hemisphere, more than 30 percentage points behind Uruguay, where 86.5 percent of citizens support democracy. The LAPOP project posits that low support for democracy and low political tolerance combine to form what is termed a *democracy at risk*. In 2012, only 36.8 percent of Hondurans showed attitudes conducive to political tolerance (respect for other citizens' right to vote, conduct peaceful demonstrations, and run for public office).[27]

An enduring feature of Honduran politics is clientelism, which has not weakened since the 1982 transition to democracy.[28] The country's permanent, professional civil service is quite small, and the vast majority of ministry positions are awarded to the victor's supporters. The president has sweeping powers to place his party activists and political allies in various positions. Relatedly, a well-known, albeit publicly scorned, tradition of *parachuters* comes into play. Such individuals are on a public institution's payroll and receive a monthly salary even though they do not actually perform public service but rather remain dedicated to activities in a political party or the private sector.[29] These privileges afforded to the incoming president raise the stakes at election time and provide incentives for violence.

Polarization and Uncertain Election Outcome

Intense polarization and an uncertain election outcome heighten the risk of electoral violence. Close competition with an opponent provides the motivation to use violence to shift the odds in one's favor. Moreover, when political campaigns are acrimonious, voters may fear the prospect of being disadvantaged or excluded if the opposing candidate wins. This fear creates another incentive for violence. The 2013 Honduran elections were closely contested and highly polarized.

Following the coup, Hondurans demonstrated a broad dissatisfaction with both Zelaya and Micheletti. Sixty-three percent of those surveyed in a 2009 Gallup-CID poll preferred that a third party—neither Zelaya or Micheletti—lead the country. At the same time, citizens were highly polarized on their support for Zelaya's return: 49 percent in favor and 47 percent opposed.[30]

Per the terms of the agreement that facilitated Zelaya's return from exile in May 2011, his supporters—initially known as the Frente Nacional de Resistencia Popular (National Popular Resistance Front)—were permitted to register as a political party. This prompted the registration of other new parties as well. Zelaya's supporters registered as LIBRE and nominated Zelaya's wife Xiomara Castro as their presidential candidate; a total of four new parties registered.[31]

The rhetoric in the months leading up to the elections was unprecedentedly acrimonious. LIBRE was a split from the Liberal Party, and both the Liberals and the Nationals tended to refer to LIBRE activists and members as *radicales*, truly a dirty word in a predominantly conservative political culture that favors tradition and loyalty. On the other end of the spectrum, the newly registered Alianza Patriotica party was led by Ramon Vasquez Velasquez, who had played a prominent role in ousting Zelaya. During the campaign, Vasquez and his supporters were derogatively referred to as *golpistas* (coup-ists).

The new multiparty system also demonstrated increased differentiation along a liberal-conservative spectrum when compared with the previous two-party system. Prior to 2013, the two main parties were considered center-right, the National Party slightly more conservative than the Liberal. In his study of vote-buying, the political scientist Carlos Melendez demonstrates through a nationwide survey that political parties in the 2013 elections were more widely distributed along the liberal-conservative spectrum.[32] Although more ideological differentiation can be a first step to more mature party platforms, it also presents an increased risk of violence because voters may disagree more strongly with opposing candidates than they did in previous elections.

The LIBRE party's recent history as a protest movement was perceived as another risk for violence. LIBRE descended directly from the National Front for Popular Resistance organized after the 2009 coup to demand the return of the deposed president, Mel Zelaya. Although the movement espoused nonviolent tactics, it became closely associated with the mass street protests in the aftermath of the coup. Given the limited tradition of civic activism in the country, these actions seemed radical, even revolutionary. As the election season began, LIBRE was anticipated to be the largest instigator of violence. Two months before the vote, the competition was intense and the leading candidates—Juan Orlando Hernandez of the National Party and Xiomara Castro of the LIBRE party—nearly tied.

A CID/Gallup poll in early September 2013 showed Castro with 29 percent support and Hernandez with 27 percent.[33]

Given the recent coup and the demands of Zelaya's supporters to register as a party, the creation of new parties was a necessary step to facilitate political participation and reduce incentives for violence. The intensely acrimonious climate also presented a significant risk of violence, but tensions would have been even greater had a large proportion of the population been excluded from electoral politics.

Widespread Insecurity

Persistently high rates of homicide and other violent crime were another risk factor as the election cycle got under way. Especially within Latin America, the murder rate in Honduras—between eighty-four and ninety violent deaths per hundred thousand people annually—is unusually high. The statistic earns the country the dubious distinction of having the world's highest homicide rate.[34] Equally troubling is that this rate continued to rise even after that of most neighboring countries stabilized. Violence levels are highest on the Atlantic Coast, more than a hundred deaths per hundred thousand people annually.[35]

Another source of violence is the phenomenon of *limpieza social* (social cleansing), which refers to unofficial security forces or vigilante groups taking to the streets to kill, displace, or round up suspicious individuals, particularly unemployed youth thought to be responsible for crimes.[36]

With high homicide rates, a high proportion of robberies that included violence, and widespread *limpieza social*, Honduras in the lead-up to the 2013 elections was one of the most violent places in the world and a country in which authorities most certainly did not have a monopoly on the use of armed force. This context was a major risk factor for electoral violence. It was entirely conceivable that Hondurans, given their ready access to arms and being inured to violence, might take violent action, disrupt the elections, and overwhelm the weak security sector.

Key Dimensions

Under the current electoral system, established by 2004 electoral law, citizens elect a president every four years by simple majority. Through an open list proportional representation system, they also elect 128 deputies to the unicameral legislature for four-year terms. A simple majority vote determines the country's 298 mayors and 2,092 aldermen. Citizens living outside the country may vote only in presidential elections.

As described, society remained highly divided after the 2009 coup. Although tensions were high, the campaign lacked substantive debate, perhaps unsurprisingly given the ideological weakness of the two historically dominant parties. The Honduran National Observatory on Violence summarized the climate during the campaign period as follows:

> In spite of the fact that civil society organizations and government entities organized forums for the presidential candidates to debate their plans for government, many times these spaces were not taken advantage of to debate ideological-programmatic proposals to contain the country's problems. Rather, the campaign was characterized

by extreme ideological polarization, with candidates slinging mutual accusations, repeating slogans, and referring to past events.[37]

Although the quality of discourse was generally poor, the candidates differentiated themselves somewhat on domestic security policy. The National Party candidate, Juan Orlando Hernandez, focused on improving security through the justice system and more frequent deployments of the military police. Xiomara Castro, the LIBRE candidate, proposed security-sector reform, returning the military to the barracks, and community-based methods of policing.

On November 24, 3.3 million Hondurans—approximately 59 percent of registered voters—cast their ballots at 5,437 polling stations around the country. Election results were not formalized until December 11, but the TSE provided regular updates as votes were tabulated. When National Party candidate Juan Orlando Hernandez emerged as a clear leader, LIBRE's Xiomara Castro and Anti-Corruption Party's Salvador Nasralla protested and alleged fraud. The largest protest of the electoral results came on December 2, when more than a thousand LIBRE supporters took to the streets to demand a recount.

The official TSE election results announced on December 11 closely mirrored the quick counts carried out by NDI/Hagamos Democracia, the OAS, and the EU (see table 6.1 and map 6.2). National Party candidate Juan Orlando Hernandez won the presidency with 36.9 percent of the vote, followed by Xiomara Castro of LIBRE (28.8 percent), Mauricio Villeda of the Liberal Party (20.3 percent), and Salvador Nasralla of the Anti-Corruption Party (13.4 percent).[38] Congressional results closely mirrored the presidential vote.

Table 6.1 Election Results

PARTY	CANDIDATE	VOTES	PERCENTAGE
National Party	Juan Hernandez	1,149,302	36.89
Libre	Xiomara Castro	896,498	28.78
Liberal Party	Mauricio Villeda	692,320	20.30
Anti-corruption Party	Salvador Nasralla	418,443	13.43

The remaining four presidential candidates captured less than 1% of the vote.

Source: Tribunal Supremo Electoral, "Convocatoria Elecciones Generales 2013," www.tse.hn/web/elecciones_2013

Election Violence

Assessing election violence in Honduras's 2013 elections is challenging. Many in the country simply do not distinguish election violence from any other violence. Given extraordinarily high levels of daily violence and pervasive underdevelopment, election violence simply does not concern many citizens. Ironically, the few days immediately before the election, and election day itself, tend to see fewer homicides than usual, most likely because thousands of military and police are on the streets.

Map 6.2 Honduras Presidential Election Winners by Principality

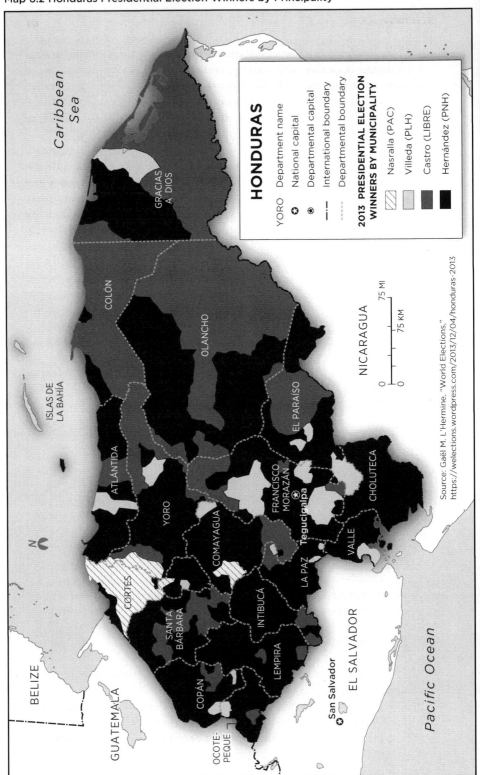

High crime and near total impunity for criminals make it impossible to definitively identify the number of election-related fatalities. The nature of election violence, however, is fairly clear: targeted threats, attacks, and assassinations in the months before and after the election, though not on election day itself. These attacks are designed to change the outcome of the elections by eliminating candidates, intimidating candidates into withdrawing, or intimidating voters.

Hondurans differ widely in their interpretations of the extent of electoral violence. A widely read report published by the National Observatory on Violence claims thirty-five fatalities in the general election and thirteen in the primary.[39] Many civil society and political party leaders, however, believe that these attacks occurred because the victim was either targeted for reasons relating to other (licit or illicit) activities, or simply in the wrong place at the wrong time. Given the strength of criminal networks in the country and their penetration of politics at the local and national level, this is not hard to believe.

The European Union acknowledged the opaque nature of the violence in its election observation report:

> The EU EOM observed that on the whole, candidates enjoyed their rights to freedom of expression, association and movement, with no greater limits placed on them than those experienced by all citizens in connection to the country's precarious security conditions. Nonetheless, the EU EOM recorded instances of violence and intimidation against candidates in 12 departments, although due to low rates of reporting incidents to the authorities and low rates of investigation, it was not possible to determine whether these cases were of a political nature.[40]

Several pages later, the report seems to more strongly acknowledge the possibility that the violence was politically motivated:

> Nonetheless, EU EOM observers noted instances of violence or intimidation against candidates in 12 departments, specifically Colón, Yoro, Cortés, Santa Bárbara, Copán, Lempira, Intibucá, Comayagua, La Paz, Francisco Morazán y El Paraíso. The EU EOM does not exclude the possibility that violence or intimidation took place in other departments, but rather, notes that only on the cited departments were cases brought to its attention together with evidence which gave them credibility. The victims of violations of campaign rights tended to be from the new political parties: the Libertad y Refundación party (Libre) was affected in nine cases; the Anti Corruption party (PAC) in six cases; Faper in three and Alianza Patriótica in two. Among the traditional parties, the cases of violence and intimidation recorded by the EU EOM affected the National and Liberal parties in two cases, and the Unificación Democrática, Democracia Cristiana and PINU in one case.[41]

The tension between the two passages mirrors the debate that has surfaced within society and the broader community of Honduras watchers.

To date, the Honduran National Observatory on Violence has issued the most concrete assessment of electoral violence during the 2013 cycle. This report describes in detail the circumstances surrounding forty-eight violent deaths and twenty-six serious but nonlethal attacks. The primary weakness of the report is that the case descriptions are based solely on interviews with witnesses, family members, and victims of nonlethal attacks. No formal evidence supports the theory that the violence was electoral.

The National Observatory report breaks down violent incidents by political party, position in relation to the elections (incumbent, challenger, family member, or political party activist), and geography (see table 6.2). The geographic distribution of the election attacks largely mirrors the overall pattern of homicide and violence, which would seem to lend itself to two possibilities: first, that some of the supposed electoral violence is in fact common crime; and, second, that the perpetrators of electoral violence are the perpetrators of criminal homicides. At the same time, the National Observatory agrees with the EU that election violence disproportionately targeted new political parties, particularly LIBRE, which seems to indicate that violence was indeed politically motivated.

Table 6.2 Violent Incidents by Party

PARTY	INCIDENTS OF LETHAL VIOLENCE	PERCENTAGE OF TOTAL LETHAL VIOLENCE	PERCENTAGE OF VOTE
National Party	24	50	36.89
Libre	12	25	28.79
Liberal Party	11	23	20.30
Anti-Corruption Party	1	2	13.48
	TOTAL: 48	TOTAL: 100%	TOTAL: 100%

Source: Blas Enrique Barahona, "Informe final de la conflictividad y violencia politica electoral: elecciones generales de 2013" (Tegucigalpa: Instituto Universitario en Democracia Paz y Seguridad, 2014), www.tzibalnaah.unah.edu.hn/handle/123456789/287

Across five regions, participants in citizen dialogues acknowledged the occurrence of electoral violence, though the perceptions varied. In Santa Barbara, disagreement was about geographic extent; some thought the violence was only in certain places, and others that it was more generalized. Participants noted that the election day itself was largely calm and that voting was without incident. Participants in Santa Rose de Copan referred to violence being worse in areas where "big men" dominate politics. Comments in San Pedro Sula, Honduras's second largest city, mirrored those in Santa Barbara: election day itself was not overtly violent (despite bribes and coercion) but the aftermath was.

Although most claims of election violence are disputed, agreement that it occurred is widespread in three geographic areas. In the municipality of El Paraiso in the Department of Copan, poll workers affiliated with the LIBRE party were locked in their hotel and threatened by unknown assailants, preventing many of them from reaching the polling places they were slated to staff.[42] El Paraiso mayor Alexander Ardon is a National Party member widely believed to be affiliated with Mexico's Sinaloa cartel. That day, more than 80 percent of voters reportedly cast in favor of National Party presidential candidate Juan Hernandez. These results are not at all in keeping with nearby or previous results, and are thought to be the result of fraud at the polling station and a massive intimidation campaign by SMS, telephone, and word of mouth.

The municipality of San Luis in the Department of Comayagua was the site of a convoluted electoral dispute. On the day of the elections, mayoral candidates Leny Flores of the Liberal Party and Ivan Zelaya of the National Party ended in an exact tie. Both candidates agreed to a coin toss to decide the result, and Flores won, though the Supreme Court subsequently ruled Zelaya the victor.[43] This ruling provoked popular protests in which Flores supporters burned down the municipal building. The dispute was settled by plebiscite on July 14, 2014.[44]

San Francisco de Opalaca also saw a dispute over electoral results. Socorro Sanchez of the National Party was elected mayor in a close election, but LIBRE activists alleged fraud and maintained a four-month blockade of the mayor's office to prevent Sanchez from taking office. In May 2014, supporters of Sanchez attacked the LIBRE protestors, severely injuring Irene Meza. As she was en route to the hospital, a group of hooded men shot at the car, killing her and wounding two others.[45]

Aside from these three incidents, no agreement has been reached on whether the targeted attacks and assassinations during the 2013 elections were electoral or criminal. The TSE's official position is that no election-related fatalities occurred. The National Observatory on Violence identifies forty-eight. The European Union is more cautious, identifying intimidation or violence against candidates in twelve departments but noting that verifying these attacks were political is not possible. It is highly probable that no consensus will be reached on the extent of the violence; the security sector and justice system have neither the capacity nor the political will to investigate.

Honduran candidates and party activists were also the victims of nonlethal attacks and the targets of numerous threats to both themselves and their family members. According to the National Observatory on Violence, most of these were either nonfatal gunshot wounds or shots that missed—intentionally or unintentionally. Threats were primarily by SMS and telephone, though one candidate was threatened by anonymous flyers distributed in his neighborhood.

Prevention in 2013

Local civil society leaders, domestic institutions, and the international community have developed and honed a variety of tools to prevent electoral violence. Depending on the nature of the perceived threat, these efforts can engage citizens at different times and at different levels in the electoral process, from candidate registration to inauguration and from voters to presidential candidates.

Security-Sector Engagement

Generally speaking, the security sector—especially the police—is characterized by low capacity, corruption, and poor governance. In 2010, the EU's Initiative for Peace Building's case study found that "impunity is the rule" in the country. The description of the

National Police was particularly stark: in addition to suffering from inadequate training and resources, it has "serious problems of corruption, is infiltrated by organized crime, and is responsible for serious violations of human rights, including extrajudicial killings, torture, arbitrary arrests, and illegal searches."[46]

The country's military is involved in a variety of domestic security issues typically left to police, including drug interdiction and antigang operations. Citizens generally mistrust the military (52 percent) and the police (71 percent).[47]

A full 63 percent reported believing that the police are complicit in crimes.[48] Even casual conversations are likely to reveal a near total dismissal of the police's ability and interest in protecting citizens. Public disgust reached new heights in 2011 when Rafael Alejandro Vargas, the son of National University Rector Julieta Castellanos, was murdered by the police in what was revealed to be a botched kidnapping. In 2013, in response to the growing number of scandals within the police and with support from the U.S. government, the Security Ministry created a new elite police force, the TIGRES (tigers), which is intended to raise police performance and eventually replace some of the scandal-ridden units.[49] Critics observed that creating this force is part of a larger trend of militarization of the police.[50] Sadly, these units have been no more resistant to corruption than the police; fifty members were suspended in 2014 after revelations that they had been involved in stealing $1.3 million in a drug-trafficking operation.[51] The high homicide rate remained constant through the electoral cycle. The security sector's performance does not improve during the election cycle aside from the month before the elections. Article 272 of the constitution calls for the entire military to come under the command of the TSE up to one month before the election, a transfer that takes place in a formal public ceremony in Tegucigalpa.[52] For its part, the police remains under its normal command but focuses on maintaining security around polling places to support the military's duties of transporting and protecting the electoral materials. This unusual arrangement brings a clear sense of mission to the military and the police and indeed seems to improve performance.

In five cities, citizens viewed security-sector engagement around the election as neutral to positive, acknowledging successfully safeguarded electoral material and increased security around polling places.

The immediate lead-up to the elections is an important bright spot in the performance of the security sector, but it is only one part of the picture. The electoral cycle begins with primary registration a full eighteen months before the general election. During this period, the most common form of violence was intimidation, individual violent attacks, and homicides, which generally occurred on a one-off basis and well before polling day. The security sector has the capacity to deter violence and maintain order on election day, but not to prevent targeted homicides or intimidation (fuzzy set score: 0.5).

Election Management and Administration

Honduras's Supreme Electoral Tribunal is considered politicized, and Hondurans of all political stripes—including TSE magistrates—are actively calling for a new electoral law.[53] Frequent criticisms of the TSE include that its composition does not accommodate the new multiparty reality, the complete lack of control over campaign finance, and massive fraud in the credentialing of poll workers. These criticisms are valid, and have unfortunately eclipsed some of the key TSE successes in the 2013 elections, including deft management of party registration, smooth logistics on election day, and creation of political party and journalist ethics pacts.

The TSE comprises three magistrates and one alternate, each of whom are elected by a two-thirds congressional vote. Although the electoral law stipulates that the magistrates cannot be elected from party leadership roles, this rule is routinely violated. Because three other parties were represented on the TSE during the 2013 electoral cycle, the newly formed LIBRE demanded a seat as well. TSE never accommodated the request, claiming that it was unconstitutional, a move that remains a source of consternation to LIBRE party members.

Campaign finance oversight and management are critical weaknesses for the TSE. Parties are required to track contributions and submit this data, but no mechanism to enforce this is in place and parties routinely fail to comply. The Center for Studies on Development in Honduras analyzed parties' media spending in comparison with known sources of licit funding for each party, including the allowance that comes from the state. The study found that more than 91.9 percent of funding is from unknown sources, and a mere 8.1 percent is traceable, licit funds.[54]

The TSE's electoral registry is another area where weak official data compromises the integrity of the elections, despite improvements in recent years. The National Democratic Institute's (NDI) 2012 audit of the electoral registry found that 36.1 percent of the registry is inaccurate, which compared favorably with recent studies in Nicaragua (49.4 percent) and Guatemala (45.1 percent).[55] Many inaccuracies result from changes of address within the country and from the extremely high rate of immigration. Deaths are another area of inaccuracy. The National Registry of Persons estimates that more than 30 percent of deaths go unreported, and the saying is common that "even dead people vote."[56] NDI's audit found that "55,863 citizens who appear on the electoral roll are actually dead."[57] In the months preceding the election, the National Registry of Persons and the TSE undertook a concerted effort to distribute backlogged voter registration cards, successfully delivering six hundred thousand of the just over eight hundred thousand waiting to be distributed.[58] The efforts to distribute ID cards resulted in a significant reduction in the backlog over previous years, which was widely acknowledged in national media and by the OAS observation mission.[59]

Perhaps the single most criticized aspect of the 2013 elections is the system of certifying poll workers. All poll workers are nominated through the political party system, which is not in accordance with international best practices. In 2013, the TSE created sixteen thousand *mesas electorales receptoras* (MERs), or polling reception panels, to administer 5,437 voting centers.[60] Each panel comprised two representatives of each of the nine registered parties, for a total of eighteen people. The implementation of this system was highly flawed in several regards. First, the public and poll workers came to view the critical work of administering the polls as an opportunity to exert partisan influence. Second, the abysmal logistics were basically an invitation to fraud. The smallest parties simply did not have enough members in certain areas of the country to fill the mandated two seats in each of the MERs. Furthermore, the TSE distributed blank ID cards to each party and instructed parties to select and certify poll workers. These two logistical errors combined to offer a perfect opportunity for party workers to buy and swap poll worker ID cards, which they did en masse.

Despite the failures, the TSE handled several aspects of the election commendably. The 2012 party registration season, when deposed President Zelaya's supporters first registered as the LIBRE party, had the potential to catalyze violence. TSE clearly and consistently promulgated information about the party registration process and met individually with interested groups to clarify the requirements. As the deadline approached and several smaller parties clamored that they did not have adequate time to register, TSE extended the deadline by two weeks. This extension allowed all interested parties that met the requirements to successfully register. Given the highly charged political climate, in which supporters of Zelaya and those who deposed him were both forming new parties, the decision was wise, effectively removing a potential justification for violence by ensuring that no one felt excluded from the process.

Election day administration was largely smooth and successful. The TSE distributed ballots and collected them from more than five thousand polling centers. The official results were announced on December 11 and closely matched the well-respected NDI/ Hagamos Democracia quick count.[61] The TSE promoted transparency by publishing each polling station's result form (submitted on election day by the panel of poll workers) alongside the official results.[62] The EU Observation Mission praised the transparency of the electronic vote tabulation, although a December 1 audit noted that three thousand of the forty-eight thousand results forms included mistakes.[63] Two final achievements of TSE were the certification of more than 1,800 observers and the August 2013 ethics pact between the political parties.

Although these achievements are significant, citizen perception of the TSE focused on its politicization. The Electoral Integrity Project's ratings mirror this dichotomy, the electoral laws category scoring fifty-one of a hundred and the electoral authorities category scoring seventy-one (overall fuzzy set score: 0.5).[64]

Preventive Diplomacy

International actors engaged in preventive diplomacy to encourage transparency and discourage violence in the elections. The United States and the OAS in particular had ample leverage because Honduras was still seeking to restore its standing in the hemisphere in the aftermath of the 2009 coup d'état. Preventive diplomacy took several forms, including interviews and outreach by the U.S. ambassador, statements by members of the U.S. Congress and the OAS observation mission.

In the aftermath of the 2009 coup, Honduras was suspended from the OAS and many member states individually severed diplomatic ties. After heated debate, the OAS reinstated Honduran membership in July 2011 despite the continued concerns of some member states about human rights violations against Zelaya supporters.[65] Most countries in the hemisphere had normalized relations with Honduras as the 2013 elections approached; Argentina, Bolivia, Brazil, Ecuador, and Venezuela did not.

Several subregional organizations and political blocs operate in Latin America, but the OAS is by far the most influential in the hemisphere. Through their membership in the OAS, Latin American countries participate in a variety of trade agreements as well as regional programs on peace, security, and development. The OAS also provides Latin American countries a structured forum for engaging with the United States, an important need in the past decade because U.S. foreign policy has turned increasingly toward Africa and the Middle East. Honduras thus had every reason to cooperate with the OAS electoral observation mission and work to ensure that the election received high marks.

The OAS began its engagement on the Honduran elections with October 2012 meetings with the TSE and other government authorities as they prepared for the November primary elections. OAS delegations of representatives from various member states then observed the November 2012 primaries and November 2013 general elections. The visits with high-level authorities and observation of the primary phase sent a clear signal to Honduran authorities that the OAS was closely watching the elections.

Both the U.S. Embassy in Honduras and the U.S. Congress exercised significant diplomatic pressure during the 2013 election season. Honduras and the United States have a complicated history; significant resentment lingers about outsized U.S. involvement in agribusiness in Honduras in the early twentieth century and mixed feelings about American use of Honduras as a base for Central American operations in the 1980s and early 1990s. Honduras depends heavily on foreign aid, though, and received $52 million in U.S. assistance in fiscal year 2013.[66]

In the months preceding the election, U.S. Ambassador Lisa Kubiske regularly appeared in the media to appeal to the public, political parties, and the TSE to uphold international election standards. Although she denounced the large quantities of dirty money underwriting political campaigns, her analysis of the TSE and of election day was generally favorable, to the extent that she was criticized in the media as being a "TSE spokeswoman."[67] Supplementing her efforts within the country, several members of the U.S. Congress exerted pressure from Washington. Senator Tim Kaine released a letter signed by twelve other members of Congress expressing "serious concerns over the Honduran government's ability to conduct free and fair elections." This was one of at least ten congressional letters on the Honduras election that included one from Representative Elliot Engel, senior Democratic member of the House Foreign Affairs Committee, directed to Secretary of State John Kerry.[68] In sum, international preventive efforts in Honduras were robust (fuzzy set score: 0.75).

Peace Messaging

Peace-messaging programs aim to elevate peaceful behavior as a universal value and persuade citizens to abstain from violence. Regular campaigns for broad societal peace in Honduras are often organized by churches. The peace-messaging campaigns in the 2013 election cycle, however, were limited in time and geography and also failed to strategically target those most likely to commit violence.

The Alliance for Peace and Justice (APJ), created in January 2012 as an umbrella organization promoting justice and rule of law, was a major player in prevention efforts. In December 2012, it issued a communiqué recommending that its members and personnel join efforts in a campaign called A Street for Peace.[69] This effort, envisaged by the sociologist and university professor José Osman Lopez, planned to use Honduran cultural symbols to promote peace. It did not come to fruition on any large scale, though some of APJ's member organizations carried out smaller-scale campaigns. In May 2013, the Honduran Catholic church issued a declaration of peace during the electoral cycle and followed this with an October 2013 statement encouraging voters to denounce any irregularities at the polls.[70] Messages by religious leaders are potentially powerful tools in a country where the church is the most respected institution. The Catholic and Evangelical churches have also been involved in monitoring the election.

Of peace-messaging efforts in the 2013 electoral cycle, the TSE undertook the most extensive campaign. Beginning in September 2012, it distributed posters, video, and audio content as part of the campaign named We All Win with Democratic Values. The three thirty-second video clips and two of the thirty-second audio messages used a soccer storyline to demonstrate democratic values and portray elections as a peaceful way to channel differences. Four additional audio clips were formatted as general public service announcements about democratic values.

The TSE and other institutions undertook thoughtful messaging campaigns to promote peace, but these did not ultimately have a wide reach. In dialogue sessions in three cities, participants failed to identify the existence of a campaign. In one city, participants mentioned it but noted that its reach was limited. Only in the more urbanized and developed San Pedro Sula did participants perceive the campaign as having a wide reach. Because peace-messaging campaigns must reach people to be effective, citizens' familiarity with them is an important criterion in defining their merit. Geographic reach of peace-messaging efforts were limited, however (fuzzy set score: 0.25).

Civic and Voter Education

Civic education efforts during the electoral cycle are aimed at reducing violence and frustration by empowering and educating voters. In Honduras, such efforts were undertaken by a variety of international and national actors. The efforts were limited in time and reached some but not all vulnerable electoral groups.

Immediately before the 2012 primary elections, the International Foundation for Electoral Systems (IFES) collaborated with the election commission to train 220 journalists on the electoral system and the role of journalists in reporting on the election. In 2013, IFES held a roundtable of civic leaders in San Pedro Sula in which the actors clarified their respective roles and responsibilities. Because the TSE focused on the challenges of administering the elections and guaranteeing security, its civic education efforts were limited. The TSE developed a series of flyers to educate voters on specific topics, including assistance to disabled voters, steps to cast one's vote, and the role of poll workers. These were distributed to each polling station for display on the day of the election. TSE also deployed sixteen mobile and forty stationary voter education brigades in early November 2013. Although voter education efforts reached a variety of vulnerable electoral groups, the European Union Observation Mission highlighted shortcomings in outreach to African descent and indigenous communities, which constitute a combined 5 to 10 percent of the population.[71]

Most identified the existence of a civic education campaign, but raised concerns that the nonpartisan civic education campaign was overshadowed by partisan messages conveyed through party trainings (fuzzy set score: 0.5).

Monitoring and Mapping

State and nonstate actors undertook robust monitoring during the 2013 election season. Despite the lack of a publicly shared effort to map conflict hotspots, election day monitoring covered all eighteen states, including many anticipated hotspots, and included highly credible delegations from the OAS and the European Union. The NDI/Hagamos Democracia quick count was another essential element, particularly in diffusing tensions in the weeks immediately after the elections.

The TSE certified more than fifteen thousand observers (741 of whom were international) and twenty-seven electoral observation missions.[72] The two largest delegations were sent by the EU (ninety-five) and the OAS (eighty-five). The TSE and Honduran media also highlighted the presence of the Carter Center delegation, which made three visits to meet with officials around the primaries and the general elections.

The more than fourteen thousand domestic observers came from a variety of nongovernmental organizations (NGOs) and social movements. TSE allowed the observation missions to select where they would deploy their observers. This certainly constitutes a missed opportunity to ensure nationwide coverage, but the sheer number of observers and the caliber of several of the observation missions resulted in wide coverage across the country. The EU observation mission discusses its monitoring efforts:

> The TSE's commitment to transparency was illustrated in its approach to election observation: the regulation issued on this element of the process fully complied with international declarations of principles for national and international observation, granting all accredited bodies full access to the relevant activities and locations, while committing observers to impartiality and non-interference.[73]

In addition to the domestic observers, the TSE also certified a *custodian* for each of the MERs. In 2013, the majority of the custodians were university students; in the past, the duty of naming custodians had alternated between the well-respected Catholic and Evangelical churches.

The NDI/Hagamos Democracia mission, which included representatives from several civil society organizations, is cited by the EU as being the most "technically adept" of the domestic observation missions. Its quick count mirrored the official TSE results within a percentage point. In sum, domestic and international monitoring were robust and the vote count quick and credible (fuzzy set score: 0.75).

Voter Consultations

Voter consultations in the months preceding elections are thought to improve citizen buy-in to the electoral process by sending the message that politicians are hearing their concerns. Although political parties did hold consultations in select areas, these were limited in substantive scope and geographic reach. Low trust in political parties and parties' systematic failure to craft policies that respond to citizen concerns further undermine the perceived integrity of voter consultations in Honduras.

The two long-standing political parties, the National Party and the Liberal Party, have historically been quite similar ideologically. Both parties represent the economic elite and there is thus very low appetite for promoting "substantive changes that will inevitably undermine the traditional hold on power of political and economic elites."[74] Politicians campaign on promises to provide goods or address issues at a highly local level, but often do not clarify the connection to a party ideology on a national level. The Latin America Public Opinion Project confirms the disconnect between Honduran people and their political parties; only 28.5 percent of those surveyed agreed with the statement "those who govern are interested in what people think."[75]

The emergence of the new LIBRE party and the new Anti-Corruption Party may represent a shift toward stronger party platforms. Considered radicals in the generally conservative political scene, LIBRE went a step further than most in defining a pro-poverty platform. The Anti-Corruption Party attracted a massive youth following with its promises to wipe out corruption and direct national resources to much-needed public improvements, including in the university system. Nonetheless, according to anonymous interviews, individuals close to the Honduran political scene continue to lament inconsistent and underdeveloped party platforms.

During citizen dialogues on electoral violence and its prevention, citizens in three cities acknowledged some voter consultation efforts. In two cities, participants did not know of any party efforts to meet with voters and listen to their concerns. Voter consultations were sporadic across the country (fuzzy set score: 0.25).

Youth Programming

Policy and programs to contain youth violence and criminality have been a major focus in all Central American states since the mid-2000s. Before the 2013 elections, some targeted efforts were undertaken to engage youth in the electoral process in order to reduce the likelihood of their participating in violence. These were far outnumbered, however, by the many ongoing youth programs to reduce gang involvement and youth violence more broadly. Given that lethal electoral violence in the country resembles lethal criminal violence, general efforts to reduce youth violence should spill over to electoral violence as well.

Youth involvement in gangs was estimated at thirty-six thousand in 2007.[76] Although gang involvement elevates risk for violent behavior, youth not affiliated with gangs commit violence as well. Hired killings are the second most prevalent type of violent death in the country, following only killings of an unknown origin.[77] Many of the election fatalities bore the hallmarks of contract killings (masked assassins on motorcycles or in cars surrounding the victim's vehicle or home at night or the early morning), which are frequently carried out by unemployed youth.[78] Youth gang and violence prevention programs plausibly contributed to reducing the targeted electoral violence across the country in 2012 and 2013.

The national government, civil society organizations, and the international community have made youth violence a priority in recent years. The U.S. Agency for International Development (USAID)'s multiyear Central American Regional Security Initiative (CARSI) spent $3.7 million on Honduras in fiscal years 2008 through 2011 and the program is ongoing. One of CARSI's four pillars is engaging youth in violence prevention. The German Ministry for Economic Development and Cooperation has a similarly large program in Central America running from 2009 through 2018 and focused solely on preventing youth violence. Smaller organizations are tackling this problem as well. Two noteworthy efforts are Cure Violence's health-based approach to homicide and Interpeace's work with Honduran municipalities in developing youth violence prevention strategies. Local and national Honduran organizations are also deeply involved in youth violence prevention efforts, in large part prevention of gang recruitment.

USAID's impact evaluation of the CARSI programs offer some of the most granular evidence available on results of youth violence prevention in Honduras. This extensive study included a survey of twenty-nine thousand respondents in treatment and control neighborhoods, 848 interviews, and forty-four focus group discussions. Compared with neighborhoods that had not received the community-based violence prevention program, those that did showed a 51 percent decline in reported murders and a 14 percent decline in reported youth gang involvement after receiving the programming.[79]

Although most youth programs in Honduras in 2012 and 2013 focused on criminal violence and not political violence, a few deliberately engaged youth in the electoral process. The Center for Democracy Studies organized and trained five hundred youth who visited twelve municipalities as election observers.[80] When asked, citizens generally identify the existence of one or more youth-focused electoral violence prevention efforts implemented by governmental, NGO, or party actors. In sum, then, youth programs in Honduras are robust and general efforts to prevent electoral violence among youth are relevant (fuzzy set score: 0.75).

Assessing Preventive Efforts

Election violence prevention measures were implemented to varying extents during Honduras's 2013 election season. Their adherence to international best practice was one factor in determining effectiveness, but impact was also influenced by the political context and the nature of the violence. In some cases, the preventive models were mutually reinforcing. The following analysis of the models' effectiveness is somewhat hindered by the lack of data on violence in previous elections and efforts to prevent it.

Security-sector engagement. Given that the security sector is known to be weak and ineffective, it is no surprise that it failed to prevent targeted homicides throughout the election season. If the everyday capacity of the security sector were higher, election-related intimidation and targeted homicides would likely diminish. Of course, this would also reduce the extraordinarily high rate of criminal homicides.

It is difficult to assess whether the one-month TSE command of the police is an innovation that meaningfully prevents mass violence. Since this policy was instituted in 2004, there have been no major election day disruptions, but the same is true of the several decades before the law was enacted. In theory, potentially violent actors may be deterred if they believe their actions will be stopped or punished by the security sector. Citizens' neutral to positive assessments of security-sector involvement on election day therefore point to the possibility that it was effective.

Election management and administration. Despite the lack of evidence that TSE acted with bias during the election season, TSE's overall reputation as politicized likely reduced citizens' trust in the electoral process and may have motivated violence by actors who viewed the electoral process as unfair. Moreover, the TSE's total failure to manage or document campaign finance effectively sanctioned illicit actors' political contributions. This in turn contributed to the general sense in Honduras that the playing field between parties was not level or fair, which may have also raised the risk of violence. Finally, the two electoral disputes in San Luis and San Francisco could have been prevented if the TSE had stronger dispute resolution mechanisms, and the intimidation of poll workers would have been far less likely if poll workers were not partisan. Aside from its success in administering the credentialing of voters and the election itself, the TSE was not particularly effective in preventing violence. If Honduras succeeds in passing a new electoral law that depoliticizes the TSE and the poll workers, this along with increased regulation of campaign finance could reduce violence.

Preventive diplomacy. Strong preventive diplomacy played an important role in strengthening the electoral process in Honduras. Media commentary and quiet visits with officials conveyed to the TSE that the international community cared deeply about the Honduran elections, which was likely one of the main motivating factors for the TSE's successes during the electoral cycle. International actors, many of whom are important donors, also reportedly placed significant pressure on key political actors to lead peacefully and discourage violence among their supporters. Moreover, the pressure to remain in good graces with the OAS and normalize relations within the hemisphere was a powerful motivator for the government to ensure peaceful elections. Although the campaign, particularly at the national level, was acrimonious, political leaders refrained from statements encouraging violence. Without this international pressure and leverage, events might have unfolded differently.

Peace messaging. In the absence of a robust peace-messaging campaign, it is not surprising that public energy and awareness about the importance of peacefully participating in the elections was limited. This may also be attributed to the historical absence of election day violence. Given the nature of election violence in the country, however, it is unlikely that a stronger peace-messaging campaign could have meaningfully reduced violence. Targeted homicide is generally carried out by hardened criminals or by people who are desperate for money (in the case of hired killings). Peace-messaging campaigns may deter low-level collective violence, but probably will not stop people from committing homicide.

Civic education. Civic education in Honduras was moderately strong and included thoughtful content that failed to reach certain populations. According to the theory of change behind civic education for electoral violence prevention, better-informed voters will be less likely to commit violence if they trust the system and understand how to participate. In Honduras, it remains doubtful that better or more civic and voter education would in fact have reduced violence. Lack of information about how to participate in elections can cause frustration that catalyzes election day violence, but it is rarely a motivation for targeted harassment and intimidation. Because Honduras's electoral violence primarily took these forms, civic and voter education are not the most promising programmatic strands for preventive programming.

Monitoring and mapping. The robust monitoring and mapping contributed significantly to preventing violence on election day and immediately afterward. Like preventive diplomacy, the important impact was felt at the elite leadership level. These missions sent a strong signal to national leaders that key constituencies and important international players were closely watching the election. The professionalism of the NDI/Hagamos Democracia quick count—and its close match to the official results—were also reportedly crucial in persuading defeated LIBRE candidate Xiomara Castro to concede the election and call off the LIBRE street protests. Without these efforts, it is possible that violence would have erupted in the days following the election.

Voter consultations. Voter consultations were weak to nonexistent during the electoral season. Had political parties engaged in substantive consultations with voters across the country, it might have increased the sense of "being heard" and reduced voter frustration. That said, meaningful voter consultations are a stretch of the imagination given the lack of sophistication of Honduran political parties. Citizens are keenly aware of their parties' lack of coherent platforms and inability to create policy. Thus, even if voter consultations were staged more systematically, Hondurans would likely still be skeptical that their concerns would actually be fed into policy. Political parties would have to evolve significantly for voter consultations to be a viable way to prevent electoral violence.

Youth programming. Youth violence is a robust area of programming, but whether it is successfully contributing to reducing electoral violence is not clear. Some programs sought to involve youth in leadership roles. The youth who participated in these programs are likely not those who might otherwise have committed violence. Youths committing electoral violence in Honduras do not do so in frustration about the lack of information about the election but instead for money. Violence prevention efforts that target youth should therefore address the high unemployment rate to make hire killings a less attractive path. Broader youth violence prevention efforts in Honduras, some of which are showing promising results, should take care to include employment components as well.

Interaction effects. Preventive diplomacy, monitoring and mapping, and electoral management mutually reinforced one another in the 2013 elections. The strong international interest in the elections motivated significant preventive diplomacy as well as international election missions. Observation missions depended on certification by the electoral management body, and the TSE was strengthened through these missions. The effective quick count provided the TSE with a strong tool to persuade defeated candidates to concede the election, and quiet diplomacy motivated key leaders to call for peace among their constituents. Without each other, these preventive models would have had less of an impact.

Conclusion

The 2013 elections in Honduras occurred without major disruptions and were recognized internationally, which was a significant step toward reconsolidating democracy in the country. Although the elections took place amid intimidation, threats, and targeted assassinations, these violations were insignificant in view of the overall crime rate, and fears of mass electoral violence were unrealized.

It is impossible to know whether electoral violence was lower than feared because the risk was exaggerated, the preventive models were effective, or some combination of the two. When Hondurans and the international community observed increased risk of violence, they acted quickly to deploy a variety of preventive models. In a highly polarized race that brought to the surface political rivalries from the 2009 coup, it was feared that the candidates themselves might deliberately incite violence. Because of this, the international community engaged diplomatically in the hope that political leaders would model peaceful behavior and encourage their constituents to behave peacefully.

Monitoring and mapping was another strong model of prevention primarily directed at influencing elite behavior. By deploying thousands of monitors and a rigorous quick count, the national government, the country's NGOs, and the international community made it difficult for the defeated candidates to convincingly argue that the results were inaccurate. Political elites therefore had little ground to stand on after the election when they briefly disputed the results. The TSE's efforts to create smooth and transparent party and candidate registration periods also aimed to ensure that political elites felt that they were treated fairly.

As Honduras adjusts to multiparty democracy, it can take certain clear steps to strengthen electoral politics. A revised electoral law should accommodate the newer parties into the TSE, establish clear dispute resolution mechanisms, and depoliticize the poll workers. Preventive diplomacy and monitoring and mapping, both of which had an impact in the recent elections, should be implemented in future elections as well, though international leverage may decrease as the coup recedes into the past. Other preventive models, including civic education, peace messaging, and voter consultations, are useful to improve citizen engagement in elections but are unlikely to mitigate electoral violence in their current form.

Electoral violence is far from the most pressing problem in Honduras. At the same time, it is impossible to fully separate it from criminal violence, particularly because the two often take similar forms. In her work on chronic violence, Tani Adams argues that chronic violence "perverts the practice of citizenship and undermines social support for democracy, provoking future violence."[81] This is indeed the case in Honduras, where citizens are inured to high levels of violence and widely disenchanted with democracy.

Electoral violence in Honduras will not diminish until criminal violence is addressed. This will require a multipronged approach that reduces the drivers of violence and improves the security sector's ability to deter and punish crimes. Even if it were possible to eliminate electoral violence before solving the broader societal problem of insecurity, doing so would not be a marked improvement to Hondurans whose daily existence is so seriously compromised by the high homicide rate. Addressing this problem is the most important step in allowing Honduran citizens a fuller and more meaningful experience with democracy.

Notes

1.   This chapter was researched in partnership with Victor Meza of the Centro de Docu-
     mentación de Honduras/CEDOH (Center of Documentation on Honduras) and Denis
     Gomez of the Federación de Organizaciones No Gubernamentales para el Desarrollo
     de Honduras/FOPRIDEH (Federation of Non-Governmental Organizations for the
     Development of Honduras). CEDOH and FOPRIDEH held one high-level political
     dialogue in Tegucigalpa and five regional dialogues on the topic of electoral violence
     in Honduras and its prevention. Additional data was gathered through key informant
     interviews and a review of existing literature.
2.   "Boletín Nacional: Edición 32" (Tegucigalpa: Observatorio Nacional de la Violencia, 2013);
     "Global Study on Homicide: 2013" (Vienna: United Nations Office on Drugs and Crime
     [UNODC], 2013).
3.   Blas Enrique Barahona, "Informe Final de la Conflictividad y Violencia Política Electoral"
     (Tegucigalpa: Institución Universitario en Democracia, 2014), www.redpartidos.org/files/
     informe_violencia_electoral_2.pdf.
4.   "Honduras: Final Report General Elections 2013" (Brussels: European Union Electoral Ob-
     servation Mission, 2013), www.eods.eu/library/EUEOM%20FR%20HONDURAS13.02.2014_
     en.pdf/.
5.   Dario A. Euraque, *Reinterpreting the Banana Republic: Region and State in Honduras,
     1870–1972* (Chapel Hill: University of North Carolina Press, 1996), p. 45.
6.   Ibid.
7.   For a discussion of the distinction between peaceful or successful elections and tense but
     calm elections, see Claire Elder, Susan Stigant, and Jonas Claes, "Elections and Violent
     Conflict in Kenya: Making Prevention Stick," Peaceworks no. 101 (Washington, DC: U.S.
     Institute of Peace Press, 2014), www.usip.org/sites/default/files/PW101-Elections-and-
     Violent-Conflict-in-Kenya-Making-Prevention-Stick.pdf. Honduras's elections have been
     generally been calm and without mass violence, but not entirely peaceful.
8.   James Dunkerley and Rachel Sieder, "The Military: The Challenge of Transition," in *Central
     American: Fragile Transition*, ed. Rachel Sieder (New York: St. Martin's Press, 1996), p. 71.
9.   Salvador Romero Ballivian, *Democracia, Elecciones, y Cuidadania en Honduras* (Washing-
     ton, DC: National Democratic Institute, 2014), p. 24.
10. Andrea DeGaetini, "Human Rights in Honduras" in *Review Digest: Human Rights in Latin
     America*, ed. Arianna Nowakowski (Denver, CO: Graduate School of International Studies,
     University of Denver, 2006), pp. 104–14.
11. Human Rights Watch, *Honduras: The Facts Speak for Themselves: The Preliminary Report of
     the National Commissioner for the Protection of Human Rights in Honduras* (Washington,
     DC: Human Rights Watch, 1994).
12. "Honduran Leader Forced into Exile," BBC, June 28, 2009, http://news.bbc.co.uk/2/hi/
     americas/8123126.stm.
13. "Bertelsmann Stiftung, "BTI 2012: Honduras Country Report" (Gütersloh: Bertelsmann
     Stiftung, 2012), www.bti-project.de/uploads/tx_itao_download/BTI_2012_Honduras.pdf.
14. Human Rights Watch, "After the Coup: Ongoing Violence, Intimidation, and Impunity in
     Honduras" (New York: Human Rights Watch, 2010), www.hrw.org/sites/default/files/
     reports/honduras1210webwcover_0.pdf.
15. Brazil and Ecuador were among the countries in the hemisphere that did not recognize
     Honduras's 2009 elections.
16. See "5 Journalists Killed in Honduras since 1992/Motive Confirmed," Committee to Protect
     Journalists, https://cpj.org/killed/americas/honduras/.
17. See "Freedom in the World 2013: Honduras," Freedom House, https://freedomhouse.org/
     report/freedom-world/2013/honduras#.VRC_w_nF98E; "World Press Freedom Index
     2013: Dashed Hopes Follow Spring" (Paris: Reporters Without Borders, 2013), p. 9, http://
     rsf.org/sites/default/IMG/pdf/classement_2013_gb-bd.pdf.

18. "There Are No Investigations Here: Impunity for Killings and Other Abuses in Bajo Aguan, Honduras" (New York: Human Rights Watch, 2014), p. 5, www.hrw.org/node/122980/section/5.

19. Council on Hemispheric Affairs, "Honduran Killing Fields: Repression Continues Against Campesinos in Bajo Aguan Valley," June 6, 2013, www.coha.org/honduran-killing-fields-repression-continues-against-campesinos-in-bajo-aguan-valley/; "There Are No Investigations Here," p. 2.

20. In Honduras, the phrase *Honduran style elections* has been used to refer to elections in which, fraud, bribery, and intimidation influenced the results. Salvador Romero Ballivian, interview, January 29, 2013. One possible explanation for this is Honduras's decision to implement residential voting in 1997, which was earlier than most Central American countries.

21. Comitè de Familiares de Detenidos Desaparecidos en Honduras, "Informe Situacion de Derechos Humanos en Honduras" (Tegucigalpa: COFADEH, 2010), www.cofadeh.org/html/documentos/tercer_informe_cofadeh.pdf.

22. Michelle M. Taylor-Robinson, "Honduras," in *Handbook of Central American Governance*, eds. Diego Sanchez Ancochea and Salvador Marti i Puig (New York: Routledge, 2014), p. 420.

23. Ballivian, *Democracia, Elecciones, y Cuidadania*, p. 29.

24. See National Democratic Institute for International Affairs, https://www.ndi.org/honduras.

25. "Democracy Index 2012: Democracy at a Standstill," Economist Intelligence Unit (EIU), www.eiu.com/public/topical_report.aspx?campaignid=DemocracyIndex12. Hybrid regimes are the second lowest of the four categories of full democracies, partial democracies, hybrid regimes, and authoritarian regimes.

26. "Democracy Index 2010: Democacy in Retreat," EIU, https://graphics.eiu.com/PDF/Democracy_Index_2010_web.pdf; "Democracy Index 2008," EIU, http://graphics.eiu.com/PDF/Democracy%20Index%202008.pdf.

27. Susan Berk-Seligson, Diana Orcès, Georgina Pizzolitto, Mitchell A. Seligson, and Carole J. Wilson, "Impact Evaluation of USAID's Community-Based Crime and Violence Prevention Approach in Central America" (Nashville, TN: Vanderbilt University, 2014), www.usaid.gov/sites/default/files/documents/1862/USAID-LAPOP%20Crime%20Prevention%20Impact%20Evaluation%20-%20Regional%20Report%20-%20Final%20-%202014-10-29.pdf.

28. Julia Schunemann, "Reform Without Ownership? Dilemmas in Supporting Security and Justice Reform in Honduras" (Madrid: FRIDE Initiative for Peacebuilding, 2010), http://fride.org/download/Reform_without_ownership.pdf.

29. Ballivian, *Democracia, Elecciones, y Cuidadania*, p. 57.

30. "Hondureños ven solución en presidente alternativo y elecciones, según sondeo," *Los Tiempos Internacional*, October 27, 2009, www.lostiempos.com/diario/actualidad/internacional/20091027/hondurenos-ven-solucion-en-presidente-alternativo-y-elecciones-segun_42683_72889.html.

31. New party registration is permitted under the Honduran constitution, but was infrequent before 2012. See Freedom House, *Countries at the Crossroads: A Survey of Democratic Governance* (Lanham, MD: Rowman & Littlefield, 2005), p. 273.

32. Carlos Melèndez, "Honduras Elecciones 2013: Compra de Votos y Democracia" (Tegucigalpa: CEDOH, 2013), www.clacso.org.ar/libreria_cm/archivos/pdf_214.pdf.

33. "Polemica por resultados de Cid/Gallup," *La Prensa*, September 26, 2013, www.laprensa.hn/honduras/apertura/390345-98/polémica-por-resultados-de-cidgallup.

34. The World Health Organization defines epidemic-level violence as higher than ten in one hundred thousand people. Eleven of the eighteen countries in Latin America meet this definition. See Khalid Malik, *Sostener el Progreso Humano:Reducir vulnerabilidades y construir resiliencia* (New York: Programa de las Naciones Unidas para el Desarrollo, 2014), www.undp.org/content/dam/undp/library/corporate/HDR/2014HDR/HDR-2014-Spanish.pdf.

35. Ibid., chapter 3.

36. See Washington Office on Latin America, "Pandillas juveniles en Centroamerica: Cuestiones relativas a los derechos humanos, la labor policial efectiva y la prevencion," *Un Informe·*

Especial de WOLA, October 2006, www.wola.org/sites/default/files/downloadable/
Citizen%20Security/past/gangs_report_spanish_final_nov_06.pdf.
37. Barahona, "Informe Final de la Conflictividad," p. 12.
38. See Supreme Tribunal of Elections of Honduras (TSE), http://siede.tse.hn/escrutinio/index.
php. The smaller parties' presidential candidates each won less than 1 percent of the vote.
39. Barahona, "Informe Final."
40. "Honduras: Final Report," p. 3.
41. Ibid, p. 7.
42. Jake Johnson, "Honduras' Flawed Election: the Case of El Paraíso," Center for Economic
and Policy Research (blog), December 6, 2013, www.cepr.net/index.php/blogs/the-ameri-
cas-blog/honduras-flawed-election-the-case-of-el-paraiso.
43. "Crisis Over San Luis Threatens Bigger Rift," EIU, May 6, 2014, http://country.eiu.com/
article.aspx?articleid=851786469&Country=Honduras&topic=Politics&subtopic=Fore-
cast&subsubtopic=Political+stability&u=1&pid=1632517947&oid=1632517947&uid=1.
44. "El liberal Leny Flores es el nuevo alcalde de San Luis de Comayagua," *El Heraldo*, July 14,
2014, www.elheraldo.hn/inicio/728486-331/inician-las-históricas-elecciones-municipales
-en-san-luis-comayagua.
45. "Honduras: Libre Party Activist Killed in Mayoral Dispute," *Argentina Independent,* May 27,
2014, www.argentinaindependent.com/currentaffairs/newsfromlatinamerica/honduras-li-
bre-party-activist-killed-in-mayoral-dispute/.
46. Schunemann, "Reform Without Ownership?" pp. 11–12.
47. Orlando J. Pérez and Elizabeth J. Zechmeister, *Cultura política de la democracia en Honduras y en las Americas, 2014* (Nashville, TN: Vanderbilt University Press, 2015), p. 131, www.
vanderbilt.edu/lapop/honduras/AB2014_Honduras_Country_Report_V3_W_010715.pdf.
48. United Nations Development Program, *Informe Regional de Desarrollo Humano: Seguridad
Cuidadana con Rostro Humano,* (New York: United Nations, 2013), pp. 111–34.
49. TIGRES is an acronym for the Intelligence and Special Response Security Group.
50. School of the Americas Watch, "U.S. Funded, Trained, and Vetted Special Forces Tigres
Unit in Honduras Mired in Corruption" (Washington, DC: SOA Watch, 2015), www.soaw.
org/about-us/equipo-sur/263-stories-from-honduras/4275-tigres.
51. Ibid.
52. "Fuerzas Armadas de Honduras Pasan a Disposicion de TSE," Radio Progreso y el ERIC,
October 24, 2013, http://radioprogresohn.net/index.php/comunicaciones/noticias/
item/340-fuerzas-armadas-de-honduras-pasan-a-disposición-del-tse.
53. This comment was heard frequently during a high-level political dialogue on electoral violence
in September 2014 and in key informant interviews in Tegucigalpa and Washington, DC.
54. Centro de Documentacion de Honduras, *Honduras 2013: Proceso Electoral, Financiamiento
y Transparencia* (Tegucigalpa: CEDOH, 2013), p. 81.
55. Neil Nevitte, Josè Cruz, Michelle Brown, and Salvador Romero Balliviàn, "Honduran Electoral Census Audit 2012" (Tegucigalpa: Hagamos Democracia Consortium, 2012), p. 20,
www.ndi.org/files/Honduras-voter-registry-2013-ENG.pdf.
56. Marilyn Mendez, "Censo electoral crece en 600,000 votantes: RNP," *La Prensa*, August 15,
2013, www.laprensa.hn/honduras/apertura/327807-98/censo-electoral-crece-en-600000-
votantes-rnp.
57. Nevitte et al., "Honduran Electoral Census Audit 2012."
58. "Honduras: Final Report," p. 18.
59. Organization of American States, "Preliminary Report of the Electoral Observation Mission
of the OAS in Honduras," December 19, 2013, www.oas.org/en/media_center/press_
release.asp?sCodigo=E-490/13.
60. Honduran Embassy to the United States of America, "Honduras: Las Elecciones Generales
del 2013," www.hondurasemb.org/HONDURAS%20%20Elecciones%20Generales%20
de%202013%20(21sept2013).pdf.

61.   Hagamos Democracia (Let's Do Democracy) is a consortium of Honduran civil society organizations.

62.   "Honduras: Final Report," p. 24.

63.   Ibid., p. 25.

64.   Pippa Norris, Ferran Martínez i Coma and Max Grömping, "The Year in Elections, 2014: The World's Flawed and Failed Contests," Electoral Integrity Project, February 2015, https://sites. google.com/site/electoralintegrityproject4/projects/expert-survey-2/the-year-in-elections-2014.

65.   Deborah Charles, "Honduras Readmitted to OAS After Coup," Reuters, June 1, 2011, www. reuters.com/article/2011/06/01/us-honduras-oas-idUSTRE75063P20110601.

66.   Zach Silberman, "Foreign Aid Is Part of the Solution to the Central American Crisis," U.S. Global Leadership Coalition, August 8, 2014, www.usglc.org/2014/08/08/foreign-aid-is-part-of-the-solution-to-the-central-american-border-crisis/.

67.   "Kubiske: Dinero ilicito de campañas arriesga proceso electoral," El Heraldo, www.elheraldo.hn/ pais/385045-364/kubiske-dinero-il%C3%ADcito-de-campañas-arriesga-proceso-electoral.

68.   Center for Economic and Policy Research, "U.S. Congress Continues to Slam Political Repression Ahead of Honduran Elections," November 15, 2013, www.cepr.net/ index.php/blogs/the-americas-blog/us-congress-continues-to-slam-political-repression-ahead-of-honduran-elections.

69.   Alliance for Peace and Justice, "Instalar 'Calle de Paz' recomienda a miembros de APJ," December 12, 2012, www.pazyjusticiahonduras.com/index.php/noticiasapj/item/91-instalar-calle-de-paz-recomienda-a-miembros-de-apj.html.

70.   Conferencia Episcopal de Honduras, "Message from the Episcopal Conference of Honduras," October 9, 2013, www.iglesiahn.org/images/download/MENSAJE%20DE%20LA%20 CONFERENCIA%20EPISCOPAL%20DE%20HONDURAS%20c.pdf.

71.   "Honduras: Final Report," p. 5.

72.   Supreme Tribunal of Elections (TSE), "Culmina proceso de acreditacion de observadores," November 12, 2013, www.tse.hn/web/sala_prensa/11132013_culmina_proceso_de_acreditacion_de_observadores.html.

73.   "Honduras: Final Report," p. 22.

74.   Freedom House, Countries at the Crossroads, p. 273.

75.   Pérez and Zechmeister, Cultura politica, p. 52.

76.   UNODC, Crime and Development in Central America (New York: United Nations, 2007).

77.   Ana Reyes Mendoza, "Piden una policia especial para combatir el sicaritio en Honduras," La Prensa, October 27, 2014, www.laprensa.hn/sucesos/762240-410/ piden-una-polic%C3%ADa-especial-para-combatir-el-sicariato-en-honduras.

78.   Barahona, "Informe Final," pp. 25–37.

79.   Berk-Seligson et al., "Impact Evaluation."

80.   "CESPAD firma convenio que involucra a jovenes como observatores electorales," Radio Progreso y El Eric, November 12, 2013, http://radioprogresohn.net/~rprog/index.php/ comunicaciones/noticias/item/380-cespad-firma-convenio-que-involucra-a-jóvenes-como-observadores-electorales.

81.   Tani Marilena Adams, "Chronic Violence and its Reproduction: Perverse Trends in Social Relations, Citizenship, and Democracy in Latin America" (Washington, DC: Woodrow Wilson International Center for Scholars, 2011), p. 9.

7

Findings and Conclusion

JONAS CLAES AND GEOFFREY MACDONALD

T he findings presented in this book advance our ability to evaluate efforts to prevent or halt election violence and broaden our knowledge of the most effective prevention measures. Evaluative research improves our work and expands the evidence basis of our practice. This volume presents compelling evidence that prevention works. The quality and scope of prevention efforts often correspond with lower levels of election violence. Similarly, the attitudes and behavior of political elites, voters, and perpetrators tend to shift in line with the theorized impact of prevention instruments. But all practices do not have equal impacts; a strategic selection of the appropriate instruments, driven by early and recurring assessments of the anticipated violence, is required for success. More prevention will not necessarily reduce violence levels. Success is highly contextual, so using the same approach in any election environment will lead to wasteful spending. The decision whether to invest in youth programs versus security-sector reform, or peace messaging, should be carefully considered.

Findings

- **Prevention works**. The comparative analysis and findings from the individual cases presented in this volume suggest that a strategically targeted increase in the level of prevention will reduce the intensity of election violence. Most of the prevention instruments selected for scrutiny correlate with reduced levels of election violence. In Thailand and Bangladesh, where prevention was minimal or absent, election violence was high. In Moldova and Malawi, violence was minimal but prevention activity was intense. In Honduras, violence and prevention activity were both in the middle range. The complementary case findings indicate both how prevention targeted the specific risk factors that characterized individual elections and the nature of the anticipated violence. The case studies also identify multiple instances where prevention realized the anticipated outcome in terms of behavioral or attitudinal change, affecting the incentive structure of perpetrators in line with its theory of change.

Dominik Tolksdorf makes a compelling argument that the repeat of the 2009 election violence in Moldova did not materialize because prevention was effective. Manuela Travaglianti similarly attributes the absent escalation of tension into violence in Malawi to the impact of dedicated peacebuilding measures taken in advance coupled with a favorable context for effective prevention. In Bangladesh, the historic comparison with previous elections furthers this argument because relatively weaker prevention instruments correlated with higher amounts of violence than in the past. Thailand saw few prevention measures and correspondingly widespread violence. However, the historic comparison does not fully mirror the trends observed in other cases: the unparalleled weakness or absence of prevention did produce unprecedented levels of intimidation and fear, but the levels of lethal violence were not extraordinary by Thai standards.

The case studies suggest that the relationship between election violence and preventive effort can run both ways. In the face of ongoing violence, internationally led prevention in particular often evaporates. Several countries experienced reduced levels of monitoring and mapping, in part because of both anticipated and ongoing violence. Even domestic approaches may not materialize in the face of imminently violent elections. In Bangladesh, the early turmoil ensured normal civic education efforts were reduced or could not be made. Diplomatic efforts are a clear exception because they consistently intensify in the face of escalating tensions and violence.

- **State actors are vital.** Our research identifies sound security-sector engagement and election management as the most promising and effective prevention tools. Strong implementation of these tools, both of which are at the heart of the state's electoral responsibilities, corresponds with low levels of violence. When security forces and election administrators are impartial across the election cycle, they reduce the incentives of potential perpetrators to foment violence. Long-term civic education—a responsibility shared by the government administration, the election management body, and civil society actors—also offers significant promise as an effective prevention instrument.

  Well-functioning election authorities help absorb the risk posed by tense elections—whether driven by conflict-prone electoral systems, centralized power structures, or uncertain election outcomes—and diminish the impact of triggering events. In contrast, the risk of violence often peaks when the security sector and election administration prioritize elite interests over their electoral responsibilities. The high levels of violence in Thailand and Bangladesh not only resulted from passivity by the election authorities and security services, but also followed from disproportionate or biased responses of the state apparatus.

Adequate domestic consideration of election security and the quality of the electoral process is necessary if grassroots or international prevention are to be effective. Even with the best of intentions or practices, domestic nongovernmental organization (NGO) and international efforts can only help realize the peaceful conduct of elections in the presence of minimal quality standards, effort, and buy-in from the national government organizing elections at risk. In Bangladesh and Thailand, even engaged international actors were unable to prevent election violence in the face of weak or ill-intended political institutions. The partisan character of the election commission and security sector is particularly harmful.

Finally, differentiating institutional structures and regulations from state agency, or the way laws and institutions are applied, is critical. Institutions and legal frameworks may appear strong on paper but prove dysfunctional when they are applied. In theory, the parliamentary democracy in Bangladesh is a suitable political system for an ethnically and religiously diverse country. The reality, with a culture of boycotts, is another matter, however. In Malawi, the Electoral Commission had clear guidelines or processes in place for voter and party registration and polling place monitoring, but voters remained dissatisfied with how these guidelines were implemented and enforced.

The centrality of state actors in resolving election violence reveals the paradox of prevention and the key to its complexity: state-led prevention is required to steer the perpetrators and enablers of violence away from violence; at the same time, political leaders are commonly responsible for the violence.

- **International engagement options**. The study reveals how election monitoring and preventive diplomacy are commonly applied in elections at risk. The relationships between these instruments—both available to international actors—and the intensity of election violence differ considerably. Comparative analysis reveals a strong correlation between systematic monitoring and reduced election violence. Malawi and Moldova welcomed strong monitoring campaigns and saw comparatively less violence than in Bangladesh and Thailand, where negligible monitoring and mapping efforts indirectly facilitated conflict. Honduras is an outlier in that it combines strong election monitoring with significant levels of violence. Given the resemblance between election violence in Honduras, characterized by isolated yet targeted attacks and intimidation before or after the elections, and overwhelming criminal violence, this anomalous relationship is not surprising. Although the study establishes the importance of monitoring as a preventive instrument, this practice is unlikely to mitigate the risk of violence without an election administration and security sector capable of ensuring the integrity of the voting process and acting on security risks as needed. Monitoring and mapping fulfills a vital checks-and-balances role for the state during an election by augmenting the traditional functions of the election commission and security forces and by pressuring them to perform well.

Preventive diplomacy does not have the same impact. The instrument is consistently used as a last resort when violence appears imminent or is already under way. Many diplomatic efforts end up being a crisis-management approach reacting to violence or fears. Investments in preventive diplomacy may in fact serve as an indicator of violence about to unfold, explaining the unique correlation between the prioritization of this instrument based on its scope and quality, on the one hand, and the intensity of election violence on the other. Malawi is certainly an outlier in this regard, combining strong diplomatic efforts with low violence levels; however, the strength of other prevention tools may have rendered diplomatic pressure or support less critical. Thailand and Bangladesh illustrate how, when used in isolation, preventive diplomacy is unable to halt large-scale election violence. In Thailand, the diplomatic efforts of the international community were unable to offset the technical deficiencies of the Election Commission and security provision that fostered a rise in election violence.

In addition to independent monitoring and mapping, the research findings support the case for international support to domestic state structures and regulations. Targeted police training early on in the election cycle offers a particularly commendable investment. The findings do not offer insight on the possible side effects of international support for domestic election processes and its impact on perceived state legitimacy and independence.

- **Civil society is less promising.** Despite the theoretically compelling logic, the measurable impact of citizen- or community-oriented instruments such as peace messaging, voter consultations, and even youth programming remains small or unclear. Implementation of this cluster of prevention activities is commonly dominated by local civil society in an effort to affect the attitudes and behavior of the broader electorate. The goal of long-term attitudinal or behavioral changes and a recalibrated incentive structure of potential perpetrators of violence appears overly ambitious. Long-term civic education is a notable exception. Its iterative and sustained character, in contrast with the ad hoc nature of the alternative approaches, likely explains its measurable impact.

Although peace messaging can have a positive effect under specific conditions, as illustrated in Malawi, the evidence suggests that it is not a vital prevention tool. The findings on youth programming are less conclusive, which seems counterintuitive given the common role of youth as the perpetrators of election violence; the potential impact of this instrument merits further research. Genuine buy-in from the national elite and continuous engagement across election cycles is indispensable for youth programming to function. Political engagement may reduce apathy and frustration, but also opens avenues for recruitment and mobilization in the hands of bad leadership. Voter consultations are not adequately implemented in any of the cases studied here. The underlying theory of change behind voter consultations appears flawed: the anticipated relationship between voters and political elite may be unrealistic within the context of weak democracies.

What Works?

Overall, this study indicates that prevention works. Individually, four instruments had significant impact: security-sector engagement, election management and administration, civic and voter education, and election monitoring and mapping (see table 7.1). Across cases, their correlation with low election violence was strong. When clustered into different combinations of prevention tools, state-led measures had a higher correspondence with low violence than civil society–led tools did, but both sets were statistically strong. These scores however, are preliminary and tenuous. Given that only five cases are reviewed, the correlation coefficients are highly responsive to change: small coding shifts in a single case would dramatically change the outcome.[1] Nevertheless, when coupled with in-depth case studies, these findings present a compelling argument for the power of prevention to alter the behavior

Table 7.1 Election Violence, PEV Strength, and Correlation Scores

	CORRELATION (R) WITH EV	MOLDOVA	MALAWI	HONDURAS	THAILAND	BANGLADESH
Election Violence (EV)	n/a	0	0.25	0.5	0.75	1.0
PREVENTION TOOLS						
Security-Sector Engagement	-0.9486	0.75	0.75	0.5	0.25	0.25
Election Management and Administration	-0.8660	0.5	0.0	0.5	0.25	0.25
Civic and Voter Education	-0.8488	0.75	0.75	0.5	0	0.25
Monitoring and Mapping	-0.8249	0.75	1.0	0.75	0.25	0.25
Voter Consultation	-0.3535	0.25	0.25	0.25	0	0.25
Peace Messaging	0	0	1.0	0.25	0.5	0.25
Youth Programming	0	0.25	0.25	0.75	0.25	0.25
Preventive Diplomacy	0.6454	0.25	1.0	0.75	0.75	1.0

Note: A correlation coefficient (*r*-value) measures the linear relationship between two variables. A negative *r*-value indicates an inverse linear relationship (as one variable increases the other decreases). A positive *r*-value indicates a positive linear relationship (as one variable increases the other increases). A 0 *r*-value indicates no linear relationship. There is no defined way to interpret *r*-values. The closer a score is to either 1 or -1 the stronger the linear relationship is. Scores in between are open to the differing analysis. Generally, *r* scores greater than (-) 0.8 are considered strongly linear.

Source: Author's calculations

of violent actors. This section outlines the correlation scores of individual PEV instruments and examines the correlation and effect of three PEV combinations—organized according to the implementing actor—on election violence.

Security-Sector Engagement

The intensity of security-sector engagement reveals the highest negative correlation score with the level of election violence across the five cases ($r = -0.9486$): the greater the engagement, according to best practice, the less violence observed. This finding demonstrates the vital role of a well-trained and equipped police and military force in preventing election violence, and the value of early security-sector reform or capacity-building as a prevention measure. Weak security sectors in Bangladesh and Thailand contributed to violence whereas effective security mitigated violence in Malawi and Moldova. Honduras, whose security sector was mediocre, saw a middle range of violence. This outcome is intuitive, but the case studies further demonstrate how the quality and scope of security-sector engagement affects the intensity of election violence.

Overall, Malawi's security sector performed well during the 2014 election cycle. Despite the perception that the police tended to favor the government, the security forces provided ample election support. This performance was a marked improvement over past elections. With international assistance, the recent government focus on domestic security enhanced police capacity well in advance of the elections. Mass protests and conflicts between party supporters were controlled with minimal violence despite logistical failures during election day. Like those in Malawi, important reforms in Moldova in the years before the election bolstered security-sector performance. The Moldovan government passed legislation that separated the General Police Inspectorate from its Ministry of Interior, boosting its political autonomy. Additionally, special paramilitary forces were trained in crowd control. The police and law enforcement agencies responded promptly to neutralize alleged security threats in the months before polling day. Critics claimed that these security measures were designed to intimidate government opponents, the sector in fact demonstrated capable and effective prevention.

The Honduran security sector generally functions poorly, but does feature an innovation that enhances its performance during elections. Although the military is generally trusted in society, the police are considered inept, corrupt, and poorly regulated. The constitution, though, mandates that the military comes under the command of the election commission during election cycles, putting a generally trusted and competent institution in charge of election security.

Thailand and Bangladesh faced similar challenges with their security sectors. The combination of perceived partisanship, weak oversight, inaction at some moments, and disproportionate action at others undermined election security. In Bangladesh, a similar narrative of egregious acts of omission and commission contributed to the instability. Before the election, protests were violently dispersed and opposition leaders killed by a security sector considered strongly pro-government. In Thailand, it was often the inactivity of the security forces rather than overaggressive suppression that fueled violence because pro- and antigovernment forces each had their own security guards recruited from hard-liner supporters. In both countries, the lack of a civilian-controlled army and effective police force created a deep-seated insecurity. The politicization of security actors is a common challenge in countries with centralized power structures that broader reform may help remediate.

Several conditions need to be in place for security-sector engagement to be effective as a prevention instrument. Given its ambitious objectives, sector reform and training needs to extend across electoral cycles to enable long-term institutional and culture change and to uncouple the popular association of elections with violence. Reactive and short-term engagements are unlikely to achieve the intended effect. Close integration is needed among training or capacity providers and security providers. Political buy-in at all levels and basic community trust are additional prerequisites. However, the security sector is also constrained as a preventive actor. Effective and visible security provision may intimidate voters and dissuade them from participating. Fear among international organizations or governments to become associated with potentially corrupt or abusive police presents another challenge.

Taken together, the five countries in this study demonstrate the vital importance of a well-trained, regulated, and nonpartisan security sector and—in particular—police. This does not mean that individual programs are inevitably successful. A World Bank experiment in Liberia, for example, found that security dialogues did not enhance the quality of electoral participation.[2] But this evaluation of practices implemented across different actors demonstrates the ability of a strong security sector to constrain perpetrators and prevent violence in the face of violence-inducing events or irregularities.

Election Management and Administration

Election management and administration was strongly negatively correlated with election violence (r = -0.8660). The correlation suggests an important violence-mitigating function, but evidence from the case studies is mixed. Both Honduras and Moldova had moderately strong election commissions, but Honduras had substantially more election violence. The Bangladeshi and Thai election commissions were blatantly partisan and presided over highly violent elections. The studies suggest that the negative effect of a weak election management body (EMB) is more consequential than the positive effect of a moderately strong one.

Despite some variation in election violence, election management bodies in Malawi, Moldova, and Honduras all performed in the middle range. The Malawi Electoral Commission has a strong institutional mandate, but nevertheless failed to fully carry out some of its duties. Specifically, the commission failed to distribute voting materials in time in certain regions and did not declare a winner until seven days after the elections, which amplified suspicion and frustration with an already tense process. It did, however, ensure transparency during the tallying process, openly communicated with the media, collaborated with all stakeholders during the electoral process, and handled electoral complaints in a satisfactory manner. The Honduran commission effectively managed election day logistics but failed to establish a transparent and nonpartisan system for identifying and certifying poll workers, which led to significant confusion and fraud in the nomination of poll workers. Moldova's Central Election Commission managed the 2014 election well but still displayed some limitations. Its inability to regulate party finances and the lack of full political independence exemplified important regulatory and structural shortcomings.

Thailand and Bangladesh illustrate the important negative effects of partisan election management bodies. Thailand's Election Commission has the legal and technical capacity to conduct free, fair, and peaceful elections. It was, however, against holding the 2014 election and continuously sought opportunities and pretexts to postpone the voting. On election day, many constituencies had too few polling station officials and only one security guard (even in high risk areas). Many polling stations were hastily closed in the face of protests as polling officials collaborated with protesters, making it impossible for many people to cast their votes. The Election Commission's deliberate mismanagement of the electoral process signaled clear political bias against the regime, inflamed protesters on both sides, and fueled violence.

Bangladesh's management body was pro-government but played a similarly detrimental role. The Election Commission of Bangladesh (ECB) is legally empowered with independence, funding, and a wide-ranging regulatory authority. It has nevertheless typically failed in its mandate. In 2014, the body was co-opted by the ruling party, which used the commission as a partisan tool to legitimize its push for elections despite opposition protest. Although the basic arrangements of the election process were successfully implemented, the overall process was deeply flawed. The ECB's partisanship provided the opposition an additional rationale to violently reject the election.

The evidence from the case studies suggests that even imperfect election management can have a positive effect on election violence. The moderately strong performance of these bodies in Malawi, Moldova, and Honduras was not reflected equally in the levels of violence. The three countries nevertheless saw less violence than the distinctly poorer performing election commissions in Thailand and Bangladesh, countries that prove the counterfactual: rather than deterring or mitigating conflict by administering election law, a defective EMB can trigger opposition protest or cause elite-mobilized conflict. In forthcoming research, Inken von Borzyskowski similarly demonstrates the potential of technical election assistance as an effective conflict management tool: it can improve the credibility of election commissions and increase the loser's consent to the election result. If the actual and perceived ability of the national election commission to organize a smooth and credible election process increases, losers will have fewer incentives to challenge the announced results.[3]

Civic and Voter Education

Civic and voter education had a strongly negative correlation with election violence ($r = -0.8488$) nearly identical to that of election management and administration. However, a close study of the cases suggests that the presence or absence of civic education during an election cycle does not determine violence levels. Education efforts had the greatest impact in countries with long-term programs across elections, such as Malawi and Moldova. In contrast, Bangladesh's weak civic education in 2014 was not itself the problem. Rather, it indicates a long-term deficiency in educating voters on election processes and democratic norms of nonviolent politics. Civic and voter education is important, but its positive impact is felt only over time.

Malawi's efforts in this field were widespread and multifaceted. The election commission along with several prominent civil society organizations extensively engaged the public on voting issues. Civil society organizations (CSOs) met with traditional leaders, educators, and religious groups to promote civic values around the country. Despite funding from the international community, these efforts did not reach some rural areas. Nevertheless, Malawi's civic and voter education programs seemed to increase awareness, boost voter turnout, and reduce the number of voided ballots. This preventive approach thus seems to have had a positive impact on its intended target over time.

Moldova's civic and voter education programming was mostly implemented by international actors, such as the United Nations Development Program (UNDP) and U.S. Agency for International Development (USAID), complementing local initiatives. These efforts reinforced existing societal knowledge on democratic norms and voting procedures. Despite limited government interest in civic and voter education, these efforts were widespread. Moldova's strong democratic culture was clearly illustrated in the decision of supporters of the banned Patria Party to support another party rather than commit violence. In Honduras, the election commission was actively involved in civic and voter education, created dozens of mobile and stationary voter education brigades before the election, and teamed with the International Foundation for Electoral Systems (IFES) to train journalists on election reporting.

Thailand and Bangladesh enacted the weakest civic and voter education programs and saw commensurately high levels of election violence. However, the tie between civic education and violence in Thailand's 2014 election is tenuous. In past elections, the election commission conducted extensive civic campaigns targeting voters. In 2014, with the election's legitimacy in question and the Election Commission itself opposed to the poll, interest in continuing previously strong education efforts was scant. In Bangladesh, already weak civic and voter education campaigns were largely disbanded. Although some civil society groups had carried out sophisticated voter-targeted programs in previous elections, many organizations withdrew training efforts either because of violence or to protest the electoral process.

Several conditions need to be in place for civic or voter education to realize its preventive ambitions. Campaigns are realistic only when the security environment is permissive and legitimate communication channels are in place. Sustained approaches are encouraged, and the approach seems better suited to prevent broad societal violence—driven by popular frustration—than election violence perpetrated by the state and its proxies, criminal organizations, or insurgents. The neutrality of the implementing actor is also critical. This requirement is also reflected in a World Bank study, which found that the credibility of the messenger and the social distance between the change agent and the subjects are each critical in determining the effectiveness of programming.[4] The study, conducted in Liberia, demonstrated how civic education workshops effectively improved electoral quality by boosting electoral participation, generating a shift away from parochi-al candidates, and increasing the willingness to report on manipulation.[5] A randomized control trial organized in Mozambique also observed that voter education campaigns can exert a negative effect on voter participation, given the free-riding effects related to costly participation. According to the research team, "the impact of voter education depends on the probability voters attribute to being pivotal."[6]

The five cases in this study demonstrate the impact of long-term civic and voter ed-ucation on the electorate's behavior. Although more robust short-term education pro-grams in high-violence countries would unlikely mitigate much conflict, the evidence suggests that sustained programming can over time diminish the public's propensity to violence. Although long-term civic education programming does not—as Thailand's example shows—guarantee a peaceful election, its effectiveness appears closely tied to the time frame of implementation.

Monitoring and Mapping

Monitoring and mapping was also strongly correlated with reduced election violence ($r = -0.8249$). Malawi, Moldova, and Honduras all had strong monitoring and mapping programs and comparatively less violence than Bangladesh and Thailand, where these efforts were significantly weaker. However, the levels of violence still varied under the presence of strong election monitoring, Honduras experiencing far more violence than Moldova despite comparable monitoring. Nevertheless, the evidence is compelling for the important impact of monitoring in particular on both elite-mobilized violence and citizen unrest.

Malawi's monitoring and mapping campaign fully met international best practices and confirmed that the election was fair. It included a myriad of international and local actors before, during, and after the election. The European Union (EU) and other inter-national actors deployed short-term and long-term observers across the country in the months before and after election day. Local monitors, including representatives from the election commission and prominent religious groups, dispatched monitors to nearly every polling station. This strong campaign was augmented by two features: electoral con-flicts were documented and reported to relevant authorities and stakeholders, and a civil society-run parallel vote tabulation (PVT) was conducted on election day to confirm the results. Malawi's strong monitoring and mapping campaign proved consequential. After poor logistical arrangements by the election commission, the PVT and other respected NGOs endorsing the process and outcome undermined any claims of malpractice. In addition, extensive mapping campaigns permitted timely identification of violent incidents and perpetrators, facilitating an effective security response.

Moldova and Honduras had minimally flawed but strong monitoring campaigns. In Moldova, a coalition of twelve NGOs conducted a long-term monitoring mission and prepared regular reports on election preparations. On election day, thousands of observers were stationed across the country to monitor violence and conduct a PVT. In addition, the Organization for Security and Cooperation in Europe sent a large observation mission, which monitored election processes before and during the election. Although these efforts lacked a concerted mapping component, they were nevertheless widespread, multifaceted, and effective. Honduras is anomalous in comparison with the other cases. Its monitoring effort was equivalent to Moldova and slightly worse than Malawi, but its violence levels far outpaced both countries. The election commission certified more than fifteen thousand observers from both international and local organizations. The missions did not cover the full country, however, and often toured polling stations rather than establish a sustained presence in potential hotspots. The nature of Honduras's election violence also limited the impact of monitoring. Targeted assassinations often take place away from polling stations at nonpolitical events, making observation missions less relevant for the type of election violence observed in Honduras.

Monitoring and mapping efforts were equally weak in Thailand and Bangladesh. Thailand has no tradition of international monitoring and is proud of its historical lack of foreign intervention. However, previous elections featured widespread monitoring by local NGOs. Given the controversy surrounding the election, these organizations held back on similar activities in 2014. In the end, only a small monitoring contingent was deployed, the international community having withdrawn its monitors to avoid seeming to legitimize the election. The Election Commission of Thailand neither assigned monitors nor distributed funding. Many of the NGOs were antigovernment so were not keen to monitor in the first place. In Bangladesh, monitoring efforts that had been strong in previous elections were largely abandoned in 2014. A few local NGOs did monitor violence during the election cycle, but only in few constituencies. As in Thailand, many international actors withdrew observers to protest the election. In neither case did rescinding monitors prevent the election. The move only ensured that violence went undocumented.

The case studies suggest that monitoring and mapping is an important feature of violence prevention. The most peaceful elections in Malawi and Moldova were accompanied by widespread monitoring carried out by local and international actors. They also included PVT programs, which had a tangible positive impact in Malawi. However, evidence from Honduras suggests strong monitoring itself cannot prevent all forms of election violence. Similarly, the high levels of violence seen during the elections in Bangladesh and Thailand would unlikely have been prevented by solely more monitors. Some of the existing evaluative research on election violence considered the impact of international monitoring, without reaching a firm consensus. This study echoes the work of scholars who argue that international monitors help keep the peace by bearing witness to the electoral process.[7]

Monitoring missions also highlight the potential competition between free and fair elections, on the one hand, and election violence prevention as a strategic objective, on the other. Although the legitimacy of elections generally corresponds with lower risk levels, peace and fairness do not necessarily reinforce one another. For example, most internationals emphasize the technical quality of the electoral process and will withdraw from an election if widespread fraud, repression, and violence are anticipated, out of fear that their monitoring is seen as legitimatizing illegitimate elections. The impact of these decisions on election violence is at times overlooked.

Voter Consultations

Voter consultations were weakly correlated with low levels of election violence ($r = -0.3535$) but their small positive impact seems to depend heavily on other factors. Across cases, voter consultations were a low-priority prevention tool. In its ideal form, this mechanism includes public forums in which voters express concerns to government officials to help shape party platforms. In Malawi and Moldova, the National Democratic Institute conducted such activities on a small scale. Local NGOs in Bangladesh and Honduras did the same. However, these consultations did not have the necessary formality, inclusivity, and geographic breadth to be influential. By all accounts, neither voters nor politicians took the programming seriously. Both Moldova and Bangladesh, the least and most violent cases respectively, had the same weak level of voter consultations.

The logic underlying the relationship between voter consultations and election violence could itself be flawed. Given the structure and role of political parties within partial or imperfect electoral democracies, voter consultations do not present a realistic mechanism to either reduce voter frustrations or enhance belief in electoral processes. The phased logic behind elite-voter consultations, the inclusion of community grievances in party programs, and the reduction in frustration, tensions, and violence rarely holds within societies that experience violent conflict. The five-case comparison suggests only a minimal importance of voter consultations in altering mass-level behavior. However, given poor implementation of the tool across the countries, the true impact of voter consultations remains unclear.

Peace Messaging

Across the five cases, peace messaging did not correlate with election violence ($r = 0$). Neither strong nor weak peace messaging consistently correlated with the expected change in behavior or attitude. Although peace messaging can have a positive effect under certain conditions, it does not appear to be a vital prevention tool.

Malawi's peace-messaging programs exceeded international best practices. Its multidimensional campaign featured local organizations with high social standing targeting a wide variety of election stakeholders. Leading this effort was a faith-based NGO—the Public Affairs Committee, known by its acronym, PAC—that had significant legitimacy among Malawi's highly religious populace. Given the unique legitimacy of Malawi's faith-based NGO community, peace messaging could go beyond normal efforts directed solely at voters to pressure political elites as well. Featuring the rare characteristics of moral authority and stakeholder inclusivity—combined with other strong prevention tools—Malawi's peace messaging was able to deter and mitigate elite mobilization during the election's most heated moments.

The other case studies indicate that peace messaging is minimally effective under less propitious conditions. Thailand's moderately strong messaging featured ad hoc groups and networks promoting peace online and in public. These actions, though, failed to impede violent opposition to the election. In Honduras, despite peace campaigns carried out by both the election commission and highly respected religious institutions, their limited scope failed to reach voters. In Bangladesh, NGO peace messaging was effectively nonexistent and state-led efforts were undermined by perceived illegitimacy. Alternatively, Moldova's peaceful election was without any peace messaging; clearly, other factors contributed to this outcome.

Similar to other instruments popular among civil society organizations, peace messaging generally aims to realize an overly ambitious outcome—changing popular and elite attitudes toward violence—within a short timeline. The campaigns often target the broader electorate yet fail to reach those violent groups or instigators primarily responsible for planning and executing violent attacks. This comparison does suggest that the independent mitigating effect of prominent peace messaging would be enhanced if conducted by highly legitimate actors that target groups or individuals predisposed to violence or demagoguery. Possibly more so than any other PEV tool, the implementer matters. In Bangladesh and Thailand, peace messaging was undermined by the alleged partisanship of state and ad hoc civil society groups. In Malawi, religious figures teamed with established NGOs to promote peace among party officials and the electorate. Engaging in violent behavior would not simply violate deeply rooted norms, but also challenge the guidance of respected religious authorities.

Youth Programming

Like peace messaging, youth programming did not correlate with election violence ($r = 0$). Honduras had the highest strongest youth programming, but still experienced mid-level violence. The remaining four countries gave youth programming equally low priority, but saw widely varying levels of violence. Given the prominent role youth play in election violence, good reason remains to believe that youth programming could be successful. The absent correlation could be explained by minimal implementation across the cases.

Since the mid-2000s, NGOs and the international community in Honduras have organized extensive youth programming directed at gang recruitment and violence rather than at election violence. Yet both problems are closely intertwined. The primary acts of violence during elections are contract killings by youth. Programs addressing youth violence therefore have the potentially secondary effect of reducing election-related violence. Before the election, one organization trained five hundred youth as election observers and deployed them in twelve municipalities. These efforts were minimal and largely misdirected, however. Long-term unemployment is a key driver of youth violence in Honduras and cannot be resolved through short-term election jobs.

In the other four cases, youth programming was given only cursory attention. In Thailand, monitoring organizations that normally employed students were less active in this election cycle, and appeared to include fewer students in the scant activities that did occur. Students were involved in some violent incidents, while middle-aged women dominated the crowd at mass demonstrations. In Moldova, international NGOs coordinated some youth-oriented programs, but youth interest and participation in politics remained minimal. In Malawi and Bangladesh, where youth are historically the primary perpetrators of

violence, programs were surprisingly scarce. Some programs for Malawian youth provided peer education, sport bonanzas, and business loans, but were still limited in scope. In
Bangladesh, small international and local NGOs carried out youth leadership training, but
their inclusivity and impact was extremely low in light of the challenge youth-perpetrated
violence presents.

Given the key role of young people in election violence, youth programs present the
potential to remove the primary perpetrators of election violence from the streets. Yet
most of the countries spent little effort on youth programming. Only Honduran youth
received significant attention, but this was not centered on election issues and correlated
with comparatively high levels of violence. Its minimal prioritization in four of the five
selected countries makes the potential influence of youth programs difficult to assess.

Preventive Diplomacy

Preventive diplomacy was the only PEV tool positively correlated with election violence
($r = 0.6454$): the greater the international diplomatic intervention, the higher the levels
of observed violence. This relationship indicates that the international community is
most likely to intervene in countries where election violence is imminent. The correspondence of preventive diplomacy with high violence levels likely results from its use as
a crisis-management tool. Confronted with competing policy priorities, senior officials
usually engage when violence is either threatening or ongoing based on intelligence or
news reports. Diplomacy is rarely applied in a truly preventive sense and fails to realize
a timely impact in its current application.

Second, the success of international mediation appears contingent on the existing prevention environment. When other PEV tools were strongly present, preventive diplomacy
enhanced election stability. Yet when other tools were weak, diplomatic efforts were futile.
Malawi and Bangladesh highlight the reliance of effective preventive diplomacy on the
strength of other prevention tools. In Malawi, several embassies actively monitored violence,
facilitated rapid response to conflict spots, and pressured parties not to use violence after
the contested election. However, the international community's determined engagement in
Malawi was complemented by nearly uniformly strong domestic prevention tools.

Bangladesh represents the opposite prevention environment. The international community was deeply involved in preelection diplomacy. The United Nations (UN) sent a
special envoy who met with party officials from competing sides. The United States, EU,
and others called for institutional reforms to precede the election. When these recommendations went unheeded, much of the international community withdrew monitors
and other forms of support to boycott the election, sending a strong signal by breaking
off communication channels. This pressure, however, did not prevent the vote or the
violence. With PEV tools consistently weak, parties opposed to the election had little
reason to trust the process. Violence consequently spiraled out of control despite the
diplomatic engagement of the world's most powerful countries and organizations.

The other selected countries further illuminate the theme of preventive diplomacy's
contingent effectiveness. In Thailand, the UN sent a representative to explore the possibility of UN mediation, but overall the international community efforts at conflict

prevention were uncoordinated and unable to overcome institutional and political conditions conducive to violence. In Moldova, peaceful elections occurred with only minimal and sporadic diplomatic intervention. When key prevention tools were strong, little preventive diplomacy was needed.

The positive correlation between preventive diplomacy and election violence does not refute its potential to change elite behavior. However, it underscores the dependence of international mediation on other prevention instruments.

PEV Combinations

Although individual policy instruments can have important consequences, their discrete functions are often closely tied to other prevention instruments. To investigate this possibility, the coding scores of various instruments were grouped in conceptually linked combinations, added, and correlated with election violence.[8] One conceptual combination is based on the lead implementing actor (table 7.2). One of three players typically takes the lead in prevention programming: the state, local NGOs, and international actors (including foreign governments, international organizations, and international NGOs). The state does so in strengthening and engaging its security sector and election management body. Local NGOs generally lead efforts at peace messaging, voter consultations, and youth programming. However, NGOs often share responsibility for civic and voter education with the state and for monitoring and mapping violence with international actors. The international community is uniquely empowered to target perpetrators or enablers through preventive diplomacy, and is therefore the lead actor for this tool.

When prevention tools are grouped by implementing actor, differences in effectiveness are clear (table 7.3). State-led tools are strongly correlated with low levels of violence, with security-sector engagement and election management scoring particularly well. Local NGO-led prevention has a weaker correlation with reduced violence levels, and much of this positive effect is buoyed by monitoring and mapping and civic and voter education. Internationally led efforts appear to have no effect on violence, but the relationship is more nuanced given the varied secondary roles the international community can play by funding or otherwise assisting local initiatives.

Table 7.2 Prevention Typology

LEAD IMPLEMENTING ACTOR	PREVENTION TOOL
State	Security-Sector Engagement, Election Management and Administration, Civic and Voter Education
Domestic NGOs	Peace Messaging, Voter Consultations, Youth Programming, Monitoring and Mapping, Civic and Voter Education
International	Preventive Diplomacy, Monitoring and Mapping

Source: Author's compilation

Table 7.3 Comparing PEV Combinations

PREVENTION TOOL	CORRELATION SCORE
Security-Sector Engagement	-0.9486
State-Led PEV	-0.9058
Election Management and Administration	-0.8660
Civic and Voter Education	-0.8448
Monitoring and Mapping	-0.8249
NGO-Led PEV	-0.6454
Voter Consultations	-0.3535
Peace Messaging	-0.1889
Internationally Led PEV	0
Youth Programming	0
Preventive Diplomacy	0.6454

Source: Author's compilation

State-Led

Individually and together, the state-led PEV tools of security-sector engagement (SSE), election management and administration (EMA), and civic and voter education have the highest correlation with low violence levels. When combined, their positive impact nearly equals the beneficial effect of a strong security sector alone ($r = -0.9058$).

SSE and EMA appear to have a strong impact on reducing violence levels. This powerful relationship is intuitive and empirically validated in these five case studies. An independent, competent, and empowered security sector and EMB will administer and secure the electoral process from start to finish. Malawi exemplifies the positive interactive relationship between these two approaches. The country's election commission performed reasonably well, but key logistical failures created frustration with the process. Amid protests and unrest, a well-trained, restrained, and professional police force controlled the situation and proved fully capable of quelling clashes among party activists during the campaign.

In contrast, Thailand and Bangladesh demonstrate the negative effect of combining weak SSE and EMA. Thailand's partisan election commission emboldened opposition forces, which battled pro-government activists in the streets in front of a disengaged army and inept police. Similarly, Bangladesh's overtly partisan election commission cemented the perception of a rigged electoral process, which drove the opposition to violently resist the election. In response, the pro-government security sector used disproportionate force that antagonized the opposition and escalated violence. In both cases, the weakness of one tool fed into the other, increasing violence. Of course, the beneficial impact of a security force and election administration is not entirely independent of other prevention tools. Their combined influence, however, has a higher correlation with low violence than almost any other PEV tool, individually or combined, save security-sector engagement.

The power of a strong security sector and EMB is their ability to engage, deter, or punish all potentially violent actors. The array of election-violence perpetrators, including the incumbent party, opposition parties, armed groups, youth wings, and individual voters, can be constrained by competent security forces and enforced election laws.

Combining strong state election institutions with strong civic and voter education broadens the scope of violence prevention. Effective SSE and EMA either punish violent perpetrators or present a clear regulatory framework. Over time, robust civic and voter education can change citizens' attitudes toward the legitimacy of violence, therefore diminishing the pool of potential violent actors. Together, state-led PEV instruments serve a vital short-term and long-term risk- and violence-mitigating function during elections.

NGO-Led

NGO-led prevention instruments work together, targeting various stakeholders to achieve the goal of a peaceful election. These tools—peace messaging, voter consultations, civic and voter education, youth programming, and monitoring and mapping—had dramatically different correlations with election violence. Combined, they had a strong correlation ($r = -0.6454$).

The combined effect of civic education and monitoring and mapping on election violence is illustrated in the case studies. In both Malawi and Moldova, voters were well informed about democratic procedures and norms through past and ongoing civic and voter education programs. In both cases, these campaigns spanned election cycles, creating a long-term inculcation process of civic virtues. It is unlikely that scaled-up civic education efforts would have a significant short-term impact on voters in high-violence societies, but they might nevertheless have a critical pacifying effect over time.

Despite the theoretically compelling logic of voter consultations, peace messaging, and youth programming, their tangible individual impact—and therefore their combined impact—was small or unclear. These three tools had the lowest correlation with election violence: their limited variation in strength across cases did not correspond to changing violence levels.

When examined holistically, NGO-led prevention had a moderately strong negative correlation with election violence across all five cases. However, the bulk of its negative correlation comes from civic and voter education and monitoring and mapping, which dramatically outperformed the collective and are both also led by other implementers. This suggests that NGO-led prevention, in total, works, but that some elements are more important than others. It appears desirable, for example, to have stronger civic education and monitoring efforts than peace messaging or youth programming (despite each tool's potentially positive effect under specific conditions).

Internationally Led

At first glance, international actors seem to have little influence over election violence. The sole international-only tool—preventive diplomacy—actually correlates with high levels of violence, which, when combined with monitoring and mapping, equals a weak correlation score for internationally led prevention efforts (r = -0.1889). However, the combined correlation score obscures more than it illuminates. Although preventive diplomacy seemed more prone to failure than success in the five countries, the international community can nevertheless make a difference by advocating for peaceful elections and intervening diplomatically amid crisis situations to pressure elites to halt an escalation to violence. The pacifying international influence during Malawi's election turbulence is representative. Given its current application as a crisis-management instrument, further consideration of diplomacy in a truly preventive sense—earlier in the election cycle—is merited to fully explore the potential of this instrument. Finally, international actors can also advance the full spectrum of prevention in a supportive role. For example, the British helped train police in Malawi and the UNDP aided the election commission in Bangladesh. These efforts were of course not always successful, but they exemplify the broad range of support and funding roles international actors can play in preventing election violence.

Contextual Vulnerabilities and Triggers

During the research for this volume, one senior U.S. embassy official said, "fiddling in the margins is the most internationals can achieve given the overwhelming root causes of political violence." Indeed, the deeply entrenched antagonisms and fears that often drive violence are a key challenge to determining the effectiveness of PEV tools. Election violence is a complex phenomenon that takes different forms depending on the social and historical context. Although the selected cases were for the most part equally prone to political violence, the nature of the risk differed widely. Six commonly cited contextual vulnerabilities are centralized power structures, horizontal inequality and social diversity, majoritarian electoral systems, uncertainty about the election outcome, unconsolidated democracy, and a history of election violence. The tense environment they generate precipitates violence. This section examines these potential causes as alternative hypotheses to the argument that the strength or weakness of prevention tools is key to explaining the level of violence. Evidence from the case studies challenges the probabilistic relationship between vulnerabilities and violence and clarifies the role prevention played or could have played.

Centralized Power Structures

One argument holds that a highly centralized power structure raises the stakes of national elections and induces violence. Competition over a single focal point of power as the entryway to self-enrichment, clientelism, or constituency services becomes fierce.

Thailand and Bangladesh exemplify the problem of limited decentralization. The Thai political order is highly centralized, both power and resources concentrated in the Bangkok elite. Although local governments are elected, they are also closely monitored by the central bureaucracy. Thailand's centralized power structure creates not only resentment at the local level, but also intense competition among the legislature, bureaucracy, police, army, and judiciary. Yet power centralization does not necessarily lead to election violence. Parties in Malawi have increasingly called for a shift to decentralization and federalism, but the country's unitary state was not a significant contributing factor in the minimal violence that occurred.

The constitutional structure of the state is beyond the purview of civil society and unrelated to election procedures, but evidence from these case studies does indicate the potential for PEV instruments to mitigate the fear and antagonism that centralization creates. Hyperpoliticized state institutions are a key feature of centralized states. The importance of effective and nonpartisan security and election management to ensuring minimal violence during elections increases the incentive to insulate each from politics. Ironically, Bangladesh's recently eliminated caretaker government system, in which a nonpartisan authority runs the election, is one possible solution. The Honduran law that places the military under the control of the election commission during the month before the election is another.

Horizontal Inequality and Societal Diversity

Under certain conditions, inequality and social diversity—together or separately—can be important drivers of election violence. Persistent economic inequality can leave groups antagonistic toward democratic institutions that fail to provide and distribute public goods. Additionally, if a power transfer from one ethnic group to another is possible, an election can become a life or death event. When inequality overlaps with ethnicity (or religion, caste, language, tribe, and so on), it could enhance the politicization of identity, encourage ethnic mobilization, and foster violent agitation against the state and electoral process.

The case studies present mixed evidence for the conventional generalizations about horizontal inequality, societal diversity, and election violence. In Bangladesh, election violence is primarily intra-Bengali and intra-Muslim, though it also saw attacks against Hindus. Malawi politics have ethnic overtones (particularly historically) and the 2014 election marked a transition of power with some regional implications. Yet violence was minimal.

Malawi indicates the importance of strong prevention instruments to legitimizing an election process in an ethnically diverse context. Regardless of relevant campaigning and power positions, adequate election management, disciplined security, and robust civil society programming are needed to mitigate social tension and undermine calls for violence.

Electoral Systems

The choice of electoral system design can be decisive in either generating or reducing conflict. A consensus among scholars is that first-past-the-post (FPTP) systems with single-member constituencies often cause conflict in newly democratic or conflict-prone countries.

These five case studies show that the potentially negative impact of FPTP depends on demographics and election legitimacy. Bangladesh is representative. Across elections, two ideologically polarized parties swap absolute control over the central government, leaving the opposition fully excluded and prone to violence. On the other hand, Malawi also inherited FPTP from its British colonialists, but the effect is markedly different than in

Bangladesh. Political parties mirror regional groups, none of which constitute a majority of the population. This triggers informal power-sharing coalitions between parties, which ensures partial inclusion from diverse political groupings. In Moldova, a brief move away from proportional representation drew criticism from opposition parties that feared exclusion. It was restored before the election, however, potentially averting election violence.

Prevention tools alone cannot resolve a situation that requires electoral reform. They can, though, potentially reduce tension that FPTP creates. Malawi's demographic structure reduces the potential strains of majoritarianism, but its successful PEV measures also validate and stabilize elections. In Bangladesh, violence is not driven solely by the electoral system. The acutely flawed election process increases the potency of fraud and injustice claims in a system that already denies power to opposition parties. Improving election administration and security as a preventive measure could reduce the pressure.

Outcome Uncertainty

The uncertain trajectory of an electoral race is perilous in a country beset by conflict. The incumbent party, hoping to hold onto power, might resort to violence to suppress the opposition's vote. The opposition party, sensing victory at hand, might use violence to prevent regime supporters from showing up at the polls.

Uncertain elections do not always translate into violence, though, as these case studies make clear. However, Bangladesh's 2014 election was prototypical. In the run-up to the election, the incumbent Awami League made a series of decisions that consolidated its hold on power. The opposition called a boycott, hoping to force institutional reforms that would reverse the trend. The League pushed the election process forward, using state forces to suppress opposition protesters in the streets. Many believe that the opposition might have won the election in a free and fair contest. Similarly, in Honduras, acrimony and tensions escalated as polls tightened. In both cases, small shifts in turnout could have had a significant impact on the outcome.[9]

Yet Moldova and Malawi show that strong PEV tools can alleviate anxiety in close elections. In Malawi, contradictory polls indicated victory for both the incumbent party and the opposition. The election outcome was highly uncertain and fears of rigging were rampant. In Moldova, the pro-EU bloc battled the pro-Russia bloc in a closely fought campaign that included fear of foreign meddling. Yet neither Moldova nor Malawi experienced significant violence during the election. In both cases, the security sector was mostly nonpartisan and effective, monitoring was strong, and the vote count was affirmed by official and unofficial sources. This suggests that the hypothesized tension resulting from uncertain election outcomes can be reduced if a legitimate election process is reinforced by strong PEV tools.

Consolidating Democracies

Edward Mansfield and Jack Snyder are among a group of scholars who argue that the period of democratization is vulnerable to violence. Generally applied to interstate war, the logic of democratizing instability can also be applied to internal conflict. Although consolidated democracies tend to have little election violence, the transition from autocracy to democracy can be turbulent. Weak institutions with little legitimacy are challenged to manage hotly contested elections, whose outcomes shape the distribution of power and potentially the safety of particular groups.

According to the most recent data from the Polity Project, of the selected cases only Bangladesh and Thailand are not considered full democracies. Instead, both countries just barely classify as an *anocracy*, or partial democracy.[10] Bangladesh and Thailand experienced the most election violence of the five cases, but it is unlikely that the minor coding difference between, for example, Bangladesh (5) and Malawi (6) accounts for the significant variation in election violence. All five cases have held successive free and fair elections with transitions of power, which is generally an indicator of institutionalized democracy, and have similar levels of institutional strength and effectiveness.[11]

History of Violence

Existing cross-national data, particularly from Africa, suggest that past election violence is a reliable predictor of future violence.[12] The exact triggers and perpetrators might change, but persistent election violence likely signifies unaddressed vulnerabilities and a political culture in which violent behavior is habitual and acceptable. Although every election cycle presents a new opportunity to break the pattern, few violence-prone states are able to significantly improve in the short term.

These case studies confirm this trend, but variation in the amount of violence suggests a more complicated dynamic than simple historical determinism. Moldova experienced large-scale rioting and violence in a previous election, but saw substantial reduction (to effectively none) in the most recent poll. In Malawi, low-level election violence in the form of intimidation, harassment, and property destruction has been relatively steady across elections. In Honduras, the generally high homicide rate dwarfs the number of threatened, attempted, or actual political assassinations. The little to no history of mass election day violence in Honduras may explain the minimal election day violence in 2013. The 2014 Thai election was as violent as previous ones had been. In Bangladesh, where a political culture of violence has grown since its independence, election deaths and destruction reached unprecedented highs.

Across the cases, a history of conflict is a good predictor of violence, but its intensity is not. A country's history of violence does not explain why violence occurs or why the situation changes for better or worse.

Controlling Triggers

Unlike contextual vulnerabilities, triggers are proximate causes of election violence. An assassination, blatant fraud, or inflammatory rhetoric can turn tension into large-scale conflict. Several cases had one or more actual or potential triggers for election violence. In Moldova, the opposition Patria Party was excluded from competing just days before the vote. In Bangladesh, the election commission's decision to hold the election without a caretaker system enraged the opposition. In Malawi, the election commission's logistical failures put the outcome under suspicion.

The variation in resulting violence across these cases signifies the important function prevention can have in diminishing the impact of triggering events. The professionalism of Moldova and Malawi's security sector was obviously vital to constraining violence, but both countries also used a parallel vote tabulation that verified the result. The PVT helped erode a narrative of fraud or error that could have threatened postelection stability. Moreover, Malawi's highly respected religious leaders acted as a peace-messaging rapid deployment force, intervening quickly amid mounting tension. In both Bangladesh and Thailand, the actions of a partisan election commission presented important trigger points. An independent election management body can mediate between competing parties, forcing all political competitors to abide by election law. Even the appearance of EMB bias, however, can trigger violence.

Theorizing Election Violence

In sum, evidence from Malawi, Moldova, Honduras, Bangladesh, and Thailand both confirms and refutes established hypotheses about contextual vulnerabilities and violence. No one factor proved to be a necessary or sufficient condition for election violence; contextual variables therefore do not provide a cogent alternative explanation of variation in election violence across cases. Similarly, short-term violence triggers come in many forms and do not always instigate conflict. Although each hypothesis provides some analytical power, they are all challenged in important ways by the case studies. A country's history of election conflict is the most compelling theory based on the evidence but cannot explain within-case variation in violence levels across elections. Nevertheless, the theory's strength is an important lesson for policymakers. If one violent election likely leads to another, peacebuilders have both forewarning and an extended time between elections to assess the causes of conflict and design long-term interventions.

The inability of contextual vulnerabilities and triggers to explain variation in election violence across cases bolsters our argument that the presence or absence of prevention can have an important independent effect. The case studies illuminate the critical role prevention can play as an intervening variable between contextual vulnerability, triggers, and violence. Where prevention was strongest—in Malawi and Moldova—underlying and proximate conflict drivers did not metastasize into widespread election violence. In contrast, in Bangladesh and Thailand, dangerous structural deficiencies bred distrust and animosity. The cases reveal that strong prevention efforts can tame the negative effects of contextual vulnerabilities and blunt violence triggers.

An examination of contextual vulnerabilities for violence compels a related question: what conditions enhance the effectiveness of prevention tools? It is difficult to disentangle positive conditions for prevention from positive conditions for peace generally. A strong, legitimate, and effective state, high economic growth, and social cohesion would certainly facilitate prevention efforts, but these conditions also reduce the need for dedicated prevention tools to begin with. The case studies illuminate the positive impact of a nonpartisan and respected civil society community, which enhances the legitimacy of prevention programming. Additionally, the type of election violence makes some tools more important than others. For example, conditions of dispersed and sporadic violence, such as the political assassinations in

Honduras, undermine the efficacy of monitoring efforts that focus on campaign events and polling stations and bolster the importance of security forces, which can provide widespread security. However, a focus on facilitating factors might be unhelpful because it could lead PEV practitioners to search for favorable conditions of implantation rather than to design innovative prevention approaches that work under the most difficult conditions.

Lessons for International Practice

For greater impact in preventing election violence, how should international practitioners prioritize or structure their efforts? New interventions are required that move beyond short-term crisis management. International practitioners should also advance their assessment and evaluative capacity and share this expertise with local actors. Their doing so will help ensure interventions match the anticipated violence and are subjected to more rigorous evaluations. This study also highlights the central role of state actors and the need for legitimacy in program implementation. Expectations about the impact of prevention, however, should remain realistic. Even after due diligence in assessing the local context, and strategic program design and implementation, prevention success is not guaranteed. This volume concludes with recommendations to render PEV practice more effective.

- **Close cycle of violence through conflict prevention.** The cases presented in this volume confirm the cyclical nature of election violence and the importance of historical precedent: political assassinations, violent protest and intimidation regularly stain the democratic process in the same countries, following a circular pattern. Most international interventions begin only when the election cycle is well under way or after violence has erupted. This is crisis management rather than effective prevention. To address the underlying causes of election violence and the frustrations, financial incentives, or fears of its perpetrators and enablers, sustained interventions across election cycles are needed. Long-term conflict prevention, with due consideration of deep-rooted conflict drivers, presents a more sustainable and evidence-based action agenda because election violence is typically driven by broader conflict dynamics.[13] Even though election violence occurs in the context of elections, the event itself is rarely the root of the problem.[14] An encapsulating conflict-prevention lens will help break the recurring cycles of election violence, combining both structural prevention and crisis-management tools.

  In Malawi and Moldova, voters were well informed about democratic procedures and norms through previous education programs. In both countries, these campaigns spanned election cycles, creating a long-term inculcation process of civic virtues. As a prevention tool oriented toward the broader electorate, civic education was distinctive in its impact; peace messaging and youth engagements did not adopt a conflict-prevention lens, however, and did not demonstrate impact.

A successful conflict-prevention approach to election violence rests on the assumption that long-term engagements are feasible and desirable. Effective crisis management that keeps the lid on volatile elections may be a justifiable niche tool. However, fiscally challenging times further the need for more strategic and cost-effective peacebuilding. Certain tools will not have impact across a single electoral cycle, even if fully prioritized on an ad hoc basis. Measures such as civic education, peace messaging, and youth engagement are unlikely to shape the attitude and behavior of the broader electorate within a single election.

- **Match anticipated problem.** As the range of national, international, regional, and local actors mandated to support peaceful elections continues to widen, the scant strategic vision behind the "patchwork of [PEV] interventions" becomes evident.[15] The decision to focus on youth rather than the election commission, or to stay three months rather than six months, for example, is primarily driven by the mandate and capacity of the implementing actors and its familiarity with a given preventive approach. Some organizations apply facilitated dialogue; others resort to popular culture. Commonly, a model of practice is repeated across countries without a solid evidence base, needs assessment, or rigorous evaluations indicating the likeliness of impact. Prevention can only work if the interventions match the nature of the anticipated violence in a given context. Improving the assessment and evaluative capacity of election practitioners will help fill this gap.

  Election violence takes different shapes and forms; each preventive approach targets different actors, affects a different motivation or incentive, and builds on a different theory of change. Tools should not be implemented as a habit, but in response to an identified need and a plausible anticipation of success. For example, the likely impact on violence of a technique targeting the general electorate, like civic education, is questionable in the event that well-organized insurgents are the sole perpetrators. Although strategically targeted prevention works, more prevention is not necessarily better. The creation of election assessment tools, such as USAID's Election Security Framework, is an important step forward. Too often, though, prevention strategies remain based on intuition and anecdotes rather than on empirical research and thorough assessments.

  The evaluation of PEV efforts has room for improvement as well. International donors commonly assess their election programs in a given country in isolation. The U.S. State Department's Bureau of Conflict and Stabilization Operations commissioned a frank evaluation of their efforts around the 2013 elections in Kenya. But smaller organizations lack the capacity to conduct any type of impact assessment. To evaluate the effectiveness of preventive programming, peacebuilders must look beyond the presence or absence of election violence in the aftermath. A more appropriate indicator is a measurable decline, immediately following the preventive intervention, in the structural risk identified as part of the assessment. Unless we improve the metrics for evaluating preventive success and address the underlying drivers of conflict, elections will remain a flashpoint for violence and tension, requiring the peacebuilding community to repeat its efforts each and every election cycle.

- **Prioritize state prevention and security.** International actors spend significant resources in support of civil society initiatives that engage voters and efforts to improve the technical quality of the election process. Our study highlights international support for state-led prevention efforts as an alternative with more potential for impact. A targeted focus on those institutions primarily responsible for election security and administration, that is, the security sector and the EMB, is merited. In the event that government actors are centrally involved in the violence as perpetrator or enabler, or are averse to training, capacity-building, and reform, international actors should try to ensure that a robust and independent monitoring and mapping effort is present to alleviate the scale of intimidation and killings, even if it risks legitimizing a botched election.

If strategic needs assessments highlight the need of civil society interventions, international donors can play an important funding or support role. However, the effectiveness of domestic NGO instruments depends on the legitimacy of the implementing actor. Civil society organizations have varying levels of social or moral standing, and this will determine their potential effectiveness.

International support for state-led prevention should not be limited to technical support for the democratic process. The aim of organizing free and fair elections may benefit the peaceful character of the electoral process. However, at times it also competes with and undermines election security as a strategic objective. To prevent election violence more effectively, international peacebuilders need to target the underlying frustrations, financial incentives, or fears of those behind the violence. The desire to pull out from or refrain from engaging in elections characterized by poor organization or anticipated fraud prioritizes quality over peace. The polls in Bangladesh were boycotted not only by opposition parties, but also by many international practitioners, who refused to legitimize a corrupt process by participating. Both in Thailand and Bangladesh, many international observers withdrew or remained absent to protest the election. In Bangladesh, the rescinding monitors did not prevent the election, and only ensured that the violence that did occur went undocumented.

Notes

1. The use of correlation coefficients is an attempt to build a unified and cumulative approach to studying prevention, toward which this project is a first step. As noted, the small case set limits the statistical significance of the scores. We make no claims based solely on the

correlation coefficients. They are used as suggestive evidence, which is matched against the case study evidence for each tool when making our argument.

2. As measured in terms of higher enthusiasm for voter participation, less receptivity to parochial appeals, and reduced voter manipulation. Eric Mvukiyehe and Cyrus Samii, "Promoting Democracy in Fragile States" (Washington, DC: World Bank Group, 2015), p. 31.

3. Inken von Borzyskowski, "Trust Us: Technical Election Assistance and Post-Election Violence," unpublished manuscript, August 24, 2015.

4. Mvukiyehe and Samii, "Promoting Democracy," p. 32.

5. Ibid., p. 35.

6. Marcel Fafchamps, Ana Vaz, and Pedro C. Vicente, "Voting and Peer Effects: Experimental Evidence from Mozambique," *NOVAFRICA* working paper no. 1303 (2013), p. 2, http://web.stanford.edu/group/SITE/archive/SITE_2012/2012_segment_1/2012_SITE_Segment_1_papers/fafchamps.pdf.

7. Barbara F. Walter, *Committing to Peace: The Successful Settlement of Civil Wars* (Princeton, NJ: Princeton University Press, 2002).

8. The same caveat applies to the correlation scores for PEV combinations as for the individual tools. With so few cases, the correlation scores alone are merely suggestive. However, for each combination's correlation score, a case study-based narrative is used to substantiate the accompanying conclusion.

9. In Bangladesh, the final result was not close, the incumbent party winning easily. Ironically, however, the opposition boycott likely cost it a victory. Even with rigging, the ruling party likely would have lost because of its deep unpopularity.

10. Edward Mansfield and Jack Snyder argue that the Polity Project's coding of "anocracy" is a useful approximation of partial democratization. Using Policy IV data, an anocracy is scored between -5 and +5. The scores are Malawi 6, Bangladesh 4, Thailand 7, Moldova 9, and Honduras 7. See "Turbulent Transitions: Why Emerging Democracies Go to War," in *Leashing the Dogs of War: Conflict Management in a Divided World*, eds. Chester Crocker, Fen Osler Hampson, and Pamela Aall (Washington, DC: U.S. Institute of Peace Press, 2007).

11. Each country is rated as partly free by Freedom House, which was part of our case selection criteria, and challenges Polity's coding that places the cases in different categories (democracy versus anocracy).

12. Dorina Bekoe, "Conclusion: Implications for Research and Policy," in *Voting in Fear: Electoral Violence in Sub-Saharan Africa*, ed. Dorina Bekoe (Washington, DC: United States Institute of Peace Press, 2012), 252.

13. Kristine Höglund, "Electoral Violence in Conflict-Ridden Societies: Concepts, Causes, and Consequences," *Terrorism and Political Violence* 21, no. 3 (2010): 413.

14. Andrea Iff, "Ballots or Bullets: Potentials and Limitations of Elections in Conflict Contexts" (Bern: Swisspeace, 2011), p. 5.

15. Bekoe, "Implications for Research and Policy."

Appendix

Table A1 Security-Sector Engagement

Score	
1.0	A clear regulatory framework for the provision of election security; integrated security-sector governance; and capable, nonpartisan, and professional security forces that are accountable to civil authorities.
0.75	The security sector is mostly but not entirely effective in achieving the ideal. Two of the criteria are fully met.
0.5	The security sector is partially effective in achieving the above ideal. One of the criteria are fully met.
0.25	The security sector is minimally effective in achieving the ideal.
0	The security sector has not at all achieved the ideal.

Source: OECD Guidelines for Security Sector Reform and Governance. www.oecd.org/development/incaf/31785288.pdf

Table A2 Election Management and Administration

Score	
1.0	The EMB independently establishes and enforces clear and fair election guidelines, including but not limited to: vote tabulation, voter and party registration, polling place monitoring, party code of conduct, party financing, results verification, and interparty dispute resolution. All important issues are clearly regulated and reforms are made as necessary.
0.75	The EMB fairly establishes and enforces guidelines for most election-related practices. Few issues are unregulated. Some reforms are made as necessary.
0.5	The EMB fairly establishes and enforces guidelines for some election-related practices. Significant issues are left unregulated. At times, some reforms are made as necessary.
0.25	The EMB establishes and enforces guidelines for few if any election-related issues. The body remains only partly independent, and almost all practices are left unregulated. Little, if any, necessary reform is made.
0	The EMB is nonexistent, nonfunctional, or entirely partisan. The election commission has no positive, independent effect on election management, or violence-mitigating reforms.

Table A3 Preventive Diplomacy

Score	
1.0	An international presence is on the ground, with access and leverage, engaged diplomatically through consistent pressure and support, over an extended period, targeting relevant national or local leaders.
0.75	Preventive diplomacy is broadly applied; three of the criteria are met.
0.5	The level of preventive diplomacy is significant, but only two of the criteria are met.
0.25	International diplomatic efforts are scant, one of the criteria is met.
0	There is no international preventive diplomacy.

Table A4 Peace-Messaging

Score	
1.0	Peace-Messaging campaigns with widespread societal and geographic reach, encourage vulnerable parts of the electorate to refrain from violence and practice tolerance, throughout the electoral cycle.
0.75	Peace messages are present in most but not all of the areas of the country most at risk for violence, or throughout most of the electoral cycle. Two of the criteria are fully met.
0.50	Peace messages are present in some of the areas of the country most at risk for violence, or only for a limited period. Only one of the criteria is fully met.
0.25	Peace messages are scant. None of the criteria is fully met.
0	Peace messages are absent.

Table A5 Civic and Voter Education

Score	
1.0	Civic and voter education efforts organized by state and nonstate actors; objectively inform citizens about their roles and responsibilities, election procedures, and outcomes; targeting broad segments of society including vulnerable communities; through various outreach mechanisms.
0.75	Although incomplete or imperfect, civic and voter education efforts inform a majority of the electorate about the electoral process. Three criteria are met.
0.50	The level of education efforts is significant, but only two of the criteria are met.
0.25	Education efforts are scant, and fail to reach a majority of the electorate. Ignorance or misinformation pervade the populace. Only one of the criteria is met.
0	Education programming is absent entirely. The populace remains ill- or misinformed about the electoral process. None of the criteria is fully met.

Table A6 Monitoring and Mapping

Score	
1.0	Credible and neutral state and nonstate actors systematically observe and evaluate the electoral proceedings (noting the source, location, type, perpetrator, and victims of election violence) throughout the country, and produce accurate, timely and actionable early warnings.
0.75	The monitoring and mapping of election violence has one of the following flaws: it is not fully credible; it is not systematically applied throughout the country or in identified hotspots; and there is no adequate early warning.
0.5	The monitoring and mapping of electoral violence has two of the flaws identified.
0.25	The monitoring and mapping of election violence is mostly flawed. It lacks credibility, reach, and adequate early warning.
0	There is no monitoring or mapping of electoral violence in any part of the country.

Source: USAID guidelines for electoral conflict monitoring and mapping

Table A7 Voter Consultations

Score	
1.0	A range of societal stakeholders is consulted by political parties and politicians. Voters are able to express their hopes, grievances and needs through a variety of participatory platforms.
0.75	The voter consultations suffer from one of the following flaws: they are not inclusive; they are not systematically applied throughout the country; or the voice of voters is not reflected or recognized in party programs or government policy.
0.5	The consultation of voters is significant, but suffers from two of the flaws identified.
0.25	Voter consultations are scant, and lack inclusiveness, reach, and voter recognition.
0	Voters are unable to express their hopes, grievances, and needs through formal or informal participatory platforms.

Table A8 Youth Programming

Score	
1.0	State and nonstate actors carry out youth programming across the country that includes targeted education; electoral mobilization; and employment opportunities.
0.75	State and nonstate actors carry out two of the programming types identified, across the country or in at-risk communities.
0.5	State and nonstate actors carry out one of the programming types identified, across the country or in at-risk communities.
0.25	State and nonstate actors carry out one or several of the programming types identified, but neither across the country nor in at-risk communities.
0	There is no youth programming.

Table A9 Dependent Variable-Intensity of Election Violence

Score	
1.0	Extremely violent campaign: repeated, widespread physical attacks leading to mass violence (more than one hundred deaths).
0.75	Highly violent campaign: repeated, widespread physical attacks leading to a substantial number of deaths over time (approximately twenty to one hundred deaths).
0.5	Violent repression: high level assassinations and targeted murder combined with long-term high-level arrests of party leaders, the consistent use of violent intimidation and harassment (approximately one to nineteen deaths).
0.25	Violent harassment: police or security forces breaking up rallies, party supporters brawling in the streets, confiscation of opposition newspapers, candidate disqualifications, and limited short-term arrests of political opponents (no or few deaths).
0	No reported electoral violence.

Acknowledgments

"Electing Peace" is deeply rooted in the mandate of the U.S. Institute of Peace. There are few institutions like USIP that invest the necessary time in addressing critical knowledge gaps in the peacebuilding field through applied research, while keeping a close eye on the final price: shaping practice towards greater effectiveness. The positive feedback following our briefings and presentations on this book indicates that our research team raised pertinent questions: what works to prevent election violence, what does not, and under which conditions?

The conceptual angle and analytical approach applied in this volume were carefully considered by a strong team of contributing authors. Geoffrey Macdonald was instrumental in shaping the comparative research design and managed the Bangladesh study brilliantly amidst challenging circumstances. Duncan McCargo confirmed his status as an authority on Thai politics; together with his co-author, Petra Desatova, Duncan applied an incredibly high standard in their analysis. Dominik Tolksdorf had already impressed USIP during his TAPIR Fellowship and demonstrated the quality and versatility of his academic work once again in his chapter on Moldova. Manuela Travaglianti infused our team with critical theoretical insight and designed a flawless data collection approach in Malawi. USIP is fortunate to have Elizabeth Murray on its team; her analytical talent and precision resulted in a strong chapter on Honduras.

Like many others working on election violence prevention, I have long been inspired by the work of Dorina Bekoe. I am humbled to build upon the excellent work she presented in "Voting in Fear" and other seminal publications she produced.

The coordination by USIP's Publications team was exemplary and demonstrated limitless patience when faced with my unrest. It was a pleasure to work with true professionals like Michelle Slavin, Molly Reid, Delsena Draper, Cecilia Stoute, and Erica Holsclaw. And thank you to USIP's graphic designer Peggy Archambault for my cover design. Thank you to Ian Proctor for the research support and critical reviews. Steve Heydemann and Lauren Van Metre served as the indispensable institutional champions for this work; Lauren's persuasion and energy continuously pushed us to go the extra mile. Helen Glenn Court offered constructive editorial guidance. Bob Cronan provided high-quality graphic illustrations. Thank you to the anonymous reviewers for taking the time to provide helpful feedback on early drafts of the manuscript.

Local partners were critical and ensured the quality of our data. Impressive contributions were made by IKI in Malawi, as well as FOPRIDEH and CEDOH in Honduras. Elizabeth and I are also indebted to Carlos Montoya for his perspective and generosity.

Personally, I am forever grateful to Lea Baeten, Edgard Claes, Roel Claes, Miek Verheyen, Hugo Blanco, and Luz Elena Cardona for their confidence and support. The book is dedicated to my precious Laura Blanco. Her encouragement, limitedness care, and love has been invaluable for the past decade. I thank you. The best is yet to come.

Jonas Claes
Senior Program Officer - Election Violence Prevention
U.S. Institute of Peace

About the Contributors

Editor

Jonas Claes is a senior program officer in the Center for Applied Conflict Transformation at the U.S. Institute of Peace (USIP), where he conducts research and analysis on the prevention of electoral violence and mass atrocities. In this capacity, Claes coordinates USIP prevention projects and consults with senior U.S. and UN officials in fine-tuning prevention practices.

Contributors

Geoffrey Macdonald is a lecturer of Political Science at The George Washington University. His research focuses on the intersection of political violence, conflict management, and democratic design.

Duncan McCargo is a professor of political science at the University of Leeds. His research deals mainly with the nature of power, and he is best known for his agenda-setting arguments about contemporary Thai politics.

Petra Desatová is a PhD student at the University of Leeds, where she was awarded a University of Leeds Anniversary Research Scholarship. She has earned degrees in Thai language and international relations.

Elizabeth Murray is a senior program officer on USIP's Africa Team, where she manages research and programming on Uganda and the Central African Republic. She also cochairs USIP's working group on national dialogues. Elizabeth has extensive experience on Latin-America, and first joined USIP to work on the Institute's grantmaking to Colombia.

Dominik Tolksdorf is director of the foreign and security policy program at the Heinrich-Böll-Stiftung North America in Washington, DC. He was a Transatlantic Fellow at USIP in 2014.

Manuela Travaglianti is a lecturer at the Peace and Conflict Studies (PACS) program at the University of California, Berkeley, which she joined after obtaining a PhD in Politics from New York University. Her research focuses on electoral violence, ethnic politics, and democratization in sub-Saharan Africa.

Index

United States Institute of Peace Press

Since its inception in 1991, the United States Institute of Peace Press has published hundreds of influential books, reports, and briefs on the prevention, management, and peaceful resolution of international conflicts. All our books and reports arise from research and fieldwork sponsored by the Institute's many programs, and the Press is committed to extending the reach of the Institute's work by continuing to publish significant and sustainable publications for practitioners, scholars, diplomats, and students. In keeping with the best traditions of scholarly publishing, each work undergoes thorough peer review by external subject experts to ensure that the research and conclusions are balanced, relevant, and sound.

About the Institute

The United States Institute of Peace is an independent, nonpartisan institution established and funded by Congress. Its goals are to help prevent and resolve violent conflicts, promote postconflict peacebuilding, and increase conflict-management tools, capacity, and intellectual capital worldwide. The Institute does this by empowering others with knowledge, skills, and resources, as well as by its direct involvement in conflict zones around the globe.